# Heidegger, History and the Holocaust

Available from the same author

*Heidegger and Authenticity,* Mahon O'Brien


Also available from Bloomsbury

*Heidegger and Aristotle,* Michael Bowler
*Heidegger and a Metaphysics of Feeling,* Sharin N. Elkholy
*Nature, History, State,* Martin Heidegger (translated and edited by Gregory Fried and Richard Polt)
*Heidegger and Happiness,* Matthew King
*Heidegger and Christianity,* John Macquarrie
*The Bloomsbury Companion to Heidegger,* edited by François Raffoul and Eric S. Nelson
*Heidegger and Nietzsche,* Louis P. Blond
*Foucault's Heidegger,* Timothy Rayner
*Heidegger and Logic,* Greg Shirley

# Heidegger, History and the Holocaust

Mahon O'Brien

Bloomsbury Academic
An imprint of Bloomsbury Publishing Plc

B L O O M S B U R Y
LONDON • OXFORD • NEW YORK • NEW DELHI • SYDNEY

**Bloomsbury Academic**
An imprint of Bloomsbury Publishing Plc

| 50 Bedford Square | 1385 Broadway |
| London | New York |
| WC1B 3DP | NY 10018 |
| UK | USA |

www.bloomsbury.com

**BLOOMSBURY and the Diana logo are trademarks of Bloomsbury Publishing Plc**

First published 2015
Published in paperback 2017

© Mahon O'Brien, 2015, 2017

Mahon O'Brien has asserted his right under the Copyright, Designs and Patents Act, 1988, to be identified as Author of this work.

All rights reserved. No part of this publication may be reproduced or transmitted in any form or by any means, electronic or mechanical, including photocopying, recording, or any information storage or retrieval system, without prior permission in writing from the publishers.

No responsibility for loss caused to any individual or organization acting on or refraining from action as a result of the material in this publication can be accepted by Bloomsbury or the author.

**British Library Cataloguing-in-Publication Data**
A catalogue record for this book is available from the British Library.

ISBN: HB: 9781472510198
PB: 9781350007925
ePDF: 9781472513328
ePub: 9781472509390

**Library of Congress Cataloging-in-Publication Data**
O'Brien, Mahon.
Heidegger, history, and the holocaust / by Mahon O'Brien.– 1 [edition].
pages cm
Includes bibliographical references and index.
ISBN 978-1-4725-1019-8 (hb)– ISBN 978-1-4725-0939-0 (epub)– ISBN 9781472513328 (epdf) 1. Heidegger, Martin, 1889-1976. 2. Holocaust, Jewish (1939-1945) 3. National socialism. I. Title.
B3279.H49O2725 2015
193–dc23
2015014515

Typeset by Fakenham Prepress Solutions, Fakenham, Norfolk NR21 8NN

*For Sophia, who asks questions.*

# Contents

| | | |
|---|---|---|
| Abbreviations | | ix |
| Acknowledgements | | x |
| Introduction | | 1 |
| 1 | Re-assessing the 'Affair' | 11 |
| | The 'Affair' and the rhetorical rules since the Second World War | 13 |
| | Heidegger's refusal to recant | 19 |
| | Heidegger's remarks on the Holocaust | 20 |
| 2 | The Essence of Technology and the Holocaust | 23 |
| | Heidegger's 'Agriculture Remark' as epigraph | 23 |
| | The Holocaust and the 'revealing' rhetoric of the Final Solution | 30 |
| | The Wannsee Conference Protocol | 32 |
| | Auschwitz: Factory of death | 34 |
| | But where have we strayed to? | 38 |
| 3 | Heidegger's 'Heritage': Philosophy, Anti-Modernism and Cultural Pessimism | 43 |
| | Adorno and the 'jargon' of German authenticity | 46 |
| | Bourdieu and Heidegger's ontological politics | 48 |
| | Zimmerman and the 'influence' of Spengler | 51 |
| | Oswald Spengler – *Man and Technics* | 54 |
| | Ernst Jünger | 65 |
| | Total mobilization | 66 |
| | *Bodenständigkeit*, *Gelassenheit* and the Memorial Address | 71 |
| 4 | The Authentic Dasein of a People | 77 |
| | Heidegger and the authentic Dasein of a people | 78 |
| | Freedom toward death | 90 |
| 5 | Heidegger and Antisemitism | 95 |
| | Nature, History, State | 98 |
| | The Origin of the Work of Art | 105 |
| | The Self Assertion of the German University | 114 |
| | The Nazi Rector | 117 |

| | |
|---|---|
| Conclusion | 125 |
| Notes | 133 |
| Bibliography of Works Cited | 163 |
| Index | 169 |

# Abbreviations

| | |
|---|---|
| BT | *Being and Time* |
| IM | *Introduction to Metaphysics* |
| GA | *Gesamtausgabe* |
| NHS | *Nature, History, State* |
| OWA | *'Origin of the Work of Art'* |
| QCT | *The Question Concerning Technology* |

# Acknowledgements

When I began work on this project at University College Dublin, I was fortunate enough to enjoy the co-operation of and at times critical feedback from numerous colleagues. In particular, I would like to thank Joseph Cohen who has been a great colleague and a dear friend since my earliest days at UCD. Professor Dermot Moran was my mentor when I first came to Dublin as an IRCHSS post-doctoral fellow and I learned an immense amount both philosophically and in terms of the practicalities and exigencies of academic life from him.

In 2013 I took up a lecturing post at the University of Sussex and I have been overwhelmed by the generosity and collegiality of everyone here. There is a real sense of community in the Philosophy Department which genuinely embraces a pluralist ethos. I would like to thank everyone in the department for their support and encouragement with this project; in particular I would like to thank Tanja Staehler, Paul Davies, Michael Morris, Sarah Sawyer, Gordon Finlayson and Corine Besson for supporting me in various ways. A special word of thanks is reserved for Anthony Booth, however, who has been a wonderful friend and an inspirational colleague to work with since I began lecturing here. I should also like to thank Christos Hadjioannou for many illuminating discussions on Heidegger as he finished his doctoral dissertation here at Sussex.

Tom Sheehan was kind enough to read the entire manuscript before it was submitted and I am immensely grateful for his feedback and support. Tom remains a genuine inspiration to all of us struggling to make our way through Heidegger's philosophical maze.

I have too many friends to thank individually – but I am grateful to you all. I have also had the good fortune to have moved to a part of the world where my cousin Tara lives with her husband Ciaran and I have been lucky enough to enjoy their hospitality and kindness more than I can hope to repay.

Finally, my family have, as ever, continued to overwhelm me with the love and support they extend to me. A few years ago I wrote words of thanks and acknowledgement for my first book in the house where I grew up in a valley in the West of Ireland. At the time, I expressed my gratitude for the world I had been thrown into all those years ago. Now, some three years later, for all the upheavals and obstacles that life has put in my way – the loss of loved ones, professional setbacks, financial struggles, the breakdown of relationships and all of the many hardships and realities that are the stuff of our existence, I see no reason to feel less thankful. As I look out once more over the valley of my childhood and the temporal horizon it reminds me of and the sense of history and belonging it brings with it, I am grateful for the gift of my throwness! I am all the more grateful when I consider all those who had that gift, the gift which is the source of all that is worthwhile and good in our world, stripped from them in the most inhuman ways.

# Introduction

> *Heidegger's postwar attempts to minimize the extent of his support for Nazism are no longer credible, and any interpretation that makes a simple distinction between his philosophy and his politics is no longer tenable – for in this seminar, Heidegger sketches a political philosophy, consistent with his views on the historicity of Dasein or human existence, that explicitly supports Hitlerian dictatorship and suggests justifications for German expansionism and persecution of the Jews.*[1]

Richard Wolin notes at the beginning of his own book on the Heidegger Controversy how he felt a certain redundancy in offering up another study on Heidegger given the proliferation of texts that continue to stream forth on the famous German philosopher.[2] And, in a way, given the volume of material that has been written on a rather jaded, repetitive debate, namely the one concerning Heidegger's political activities and writings, I fear that many academics will groan with resignation at the mere mention of another discussion of the Heidegger Controversy, confident that we have exhausted the whole sorry business to such an extent that there is nothing important left to say. Wolin's motivation for entering the 'fray', so to speak, issued from his belief that the topic had not been exhausted and though I cannot say that I am fully convinced that he has contributed quite as much to the debate as he might like to believe, we must at least concede that he forced a rather self-satisfied generation of English-speaking Heideggerians to sit a little less comfortably in their seats following the publication of volumes such as *The Heidegger Controversy: A Critical Reader*. More recently, we have seen from the reaction to Emmanuel Faye's sensational text on the political controversy surrounding Heidegger that this topic still excites a good deal of interest, not just in philosophy, but in intellectual circles more generally. And indeed given the furore already surrounding the recent publication of Heidegger's notebooks from the 1930s and 1940s which contain a handful of further disturbing remarks concerning the Jews and his own brand of antisemitism, it seems clear that this is an issue which doesn't appear to be anywhere close to being resolved. The reason that this particular controversy never seems to simply fade away or disappear completely comes down to one simple fact: the controversy continues to be prosecuted by two polarized groups who continue to miss the question that should exercise all of us; these camps either try to nullify Heidegger's Nazism and insist on his greatness as a philosopher as though the two are mutually exclusive or else they look to amplify his Nazism and diminish his stature as a philosopher – again – as though the notion of a great philosopher and a Nazi are mutually exclusive identities. This, of course, is a version of Lyotard's memorable assessment of the paradox at the heart of the Heidegger Controversy but it is an assessment that retains its significance.[3] The problem with these approaches, which orient the way the controversy continues to be thrashed out in various types of academic exchanges is that they miss the real problem that lurks beneath this somewhat jaded debate. The real problem, the problem that should vex us is the question as to how a great philosopher could, at any point, have pledged his allegiance to the Nazi Party and insist that the motivation lay in the essence of his philosophy and that is a question that has not been adequately addressed.[4] Moreover, since everyone who has tried to weigh in thus far has failed to adequately address *this* question, the controversy keeps returning with a vengeance in almost cyclical fashion. Indeed, ever since mention of Heidegger's infamous notebooks from the 1930s and 1940s was first made, we've seen the controversy and scandal revived and, alas, it is proceeding along familiar lines. Battle-hardened Heideggerians simply scoff at what they take to be another trivial ambush, a skirmish on the fringes of philosophy which will simply fade away with time. And those that are once again becoming embroiled in the debate are wheeling out the hackneyed old party lines regarding the relative merits and demerits of analytic or continental philosophy. The idea presumably being, for one camp, that if they can ultimately reject Heidegger and his philosophy, then they will have dealt the deathblow to continental philosophy while their adversaries are keen to rescue at all costs the image of Heidegger as a respectable and important thinker.

Now some might wish to counter that I am conveniently overlooking something in terms of the dichotomy that I am dismissing along the lines of Lyotard's characterization, namely, that it is precisely *because* Heidegger was a Nazi whose philosophy was influenced by his Nazism that he *cannot* be taken seriously as a philosopher and that this is a significant and substantive position. I would counter that the variants of this position have all ultimately been found wanting in terms of the way they have been defended in the Heidegger Controversy. Some critics simply state that Heidegger was clearly and undeniably a Nazi and that alone means that he can't have been a serious philosopher. I take it that that position is so obviously ridiculous as to not require a response. Another line of criticism suggests that because Heidegger's philosophy is *related* to his politics, it cannot be taken seriously. And, even though this is beginning to come closer to the problem, simply stating as much is not an argument. There are countless insights and observations in Heidegger's work that don't have any obvious political significance at all, so those critics tend to leave the door open to Heideggerians who can easily shoot that failure to offer a genuine argument down for what it is, in short, a failure to offer an argument in the first place. The real challenge, one that has yet to be met by critics of Heidegger and those who simply want to put another nail in the coffin of so-called continental philosophy, is to show exactly *how* Heidegger's philosophy intersects with his politics and that is something that we will attempt to undertake in this study. However, even when we manage to do as much, that will not be tantamount to the claim that Heidegger is therefore to be dismissed as a second-rate philosopher. Thus, for those who want to argue that I am trivializing one side of the debate, namely the side that wants to say that because Heidegger was a Nazi that he cannot have been a great philosopher – I say once again – that particular approach to the question has continued to run aground and has perpetuated a stalemate that stymies any chance of progress on this issue. If Heidegger's philosophy *is* related to his politics, that does not, automatically, mean that his philosophy must be rejected.

Heidegger's hermeneutics of facticity, his accounts of being-in-the-world, history of metaphysics, truth, the essence of technology and his readings of Western Philosophy are not suddenly rendered crass by that relationship. And, if that *was* in fact a viable argument, then the controversy was never a genuine *philosophical* controversy to begin with. Rather, a whole host of twentieth and twenty-first century philosophers were and remain quite stupid since we failed to see what our adversaries (many of whom never even had to read Heidegger to realize as much) have known all along, namely, that Heidegger is a charlatan. However, if that is the case, the controversy is very different to the one I wish to examine; if that *is* the case, then the controversy is simply one related to a sorry situation where about half of the academic profession in philosophy has been allowed to corrupt the academy with bad philosophy since about the middle of the twentieth century and all of this nonsense concerning hermeneutics, deconstruction, technology, temporality, historicity, truth, language and Heidegger's readings in the history of philosophy should be banned immediately.[5]

****

For those Heideggerians who bristle at the mere mention of the political controversy as though the whole sorry business is simply crude sensationalism, it bears recalling that is was Heidegger himself who insisted that his commitment to National Socialism was deeply indebted to and informed by the central concepts of his own thought, concepts that he developed most famously in *Being and Time*.[6] As we shall see, in the early 1930s Heidegger very deliberately tried to fuse his accounts of authenticity and the concomitant notion of historicity together with his political aspirations and, there is no point in sugar-coating it, Heidegger's political aspirations were and remain repugnant. However, that is not the end of the story and we cannot suddenly dismiss Heidegger once we realize what he was up to in section 74 of *Being and Time*! Why? Because Heidegger's attempts at a political philosophy based on his fundamental philosophical concepts *fail*; Heidegger's philosophy, in particular the relevant notions from *Being and Time*, *resists* what Heidegger attempts to do with those notions. That is not simply to say that we can separate Heidegger's philosophy from his politics (no matter how much we would like to do so) and, rather than Heideggerians spending so much time sniping at his critics concerning this interminable controversy, they would do well to remember that this controversy is one of Heidegger's *own* making. If we do want to find a way to continue to work on Heidegger in some kind of peace, then we are going to have to take responsibility for the mess that *he* left us with, a mess, moreover, which he did little to redress after the war.

It would be unfortunate then if Heidegger scholars dismissed this study as the noisy hysteria of another Faye or took me for an 'enemy' as part of some disastrously misguided and counter-productive siege mentality. I have learned more from Heidegger than any other philosopher and continue to learn from him. In Heidegger's work I discovered a philosophy that resonated with me as a person from a valley in the West of Ireland and suddenly all of the hitherto remote, abstruse metaphysical questions that I had never really been able to make a dent on suddenly began to open their doors. Clues and echoes and resonances of a profound wonder seemed to reverberate from the smells and sounds and traces of my past and present, from my home, and yes, from my native soil, from the distinctive smells of rain soaked earth and fomenting leaves that threw me back into my childhood and unlocked the fourth dimension of time that Heidegger had introduced in *Time and Being*. Suddenly a deep and profound universal humanism seemed to speak to me from Heidegger's work in a way which was particular to me and my locale and yet opened up a door to human beings in general. I still think this remains a fecund possibility within Heidegger's work; however, it is high time that we see the very dangerous ways he tried to manipulate those insights and the profoundly anti-human ways he looked to exploit the central concepts of his own thought in the service of a noxious political vision.

This study, while not for one moment pretending to be the definitive study on this topic, nevertheless looks to make a decisive contribution by articulating a position from outside of the traditional camps; I want to argue that Heidegger is indeed a great philosopher but that he is also very much a Nazi. Not only that, I believe that Heidegger was a committed National Socialist and not just a token Nazi for a few months for the purposes of academic expediency. I also want to say, and here I suppose I am perhaps signing my own death warrant as far as legions of card carrying members of the Heideggerian Faithful are concerned, that I believe that there are very serious questions to be faced concerning the relationship between Heidegger's philosophy and his politics. Moreover, the idea that one can scoff at suggestions to the effect that Heidegger's philosophical and political views are deeply intertwined strikes me as somewhat bizarre to begin with since it is Heidegger's own repeated asseverations as to the inter-relationship between his philosophy and his Nazism which one must reconcile with such a strategy of interpretive evasiveness. In saying as much, I believe that we are subsequently faced with far more serious and worrisome questions than those that issue from Victor Farias' tendentious book or Wolin's repeated efforts to make a dent on fortress Heidegger or indeed Emmanuel Faye's sensational polemic penned a little less than a decade ago. Heidegger's philosophy has had a profound influence and impact on generations of philosophers ever since about the middle of the twentieth century. He has had decisive influences on many of the greatest thinkers of the twentieth century and beyond – not least some of the great French philosophers of the last sixty years. His influence has spread to fields as diverse as psychology/psychiatry and architecture and even those working in the digital humanities. Phenomenology, Existentialism, Postmodernism, Poststructuralism, Hermeneutics, Deconstruction and Feminism are all indelibly marked by his thought and are often heavily indebted to his work. However, what most intellectuals associated with these movements have not fully acknowledged is the danger lurking in Heidegger's powerful challenge to Modernity, a challenge which they have all found to be a liberating and insightful confrontation, a confrontation which paved the way for much of their own work.

****

It is important to stress the fact that this study does not pretend to be an exhaustive examination of absolutely everything that is relevant in Heidegger's burgeoning

*Gesamtausgabe* with a view to having the last word on the Heidegger Affair – rather I see this as an attempt to begin a new controversy. In the first place, I don't know why we need to keep burrowing away looking for further proof of Heidegger's Nazism in some hidden trove of previously unpublished writings or correspondence as though that settles things once and for all. Indeed, I expect that whatever else turns up concerning Heidegger's hugely problematic political views will very much echo more of what we already know: Heidegger was willing to use terms such as '*Verjudung*' (Jewification); Heidegger wrote and said things which were nakedly and distressingly Nazi in tone as the zealous Nazi Rector of Freiburg University; Heidegger was adamant that there was a dangerous international alliance of Jews and openly professed as much to his then close friend, Karl Jaspers, fully aware of the affront it was to Jaspers, whose wife was Jewish. We can continue to add to the chronicle of biographical details which will copper-fasten what we already know, namely that Heidegger wrote, said and did things which any of us would find and certainly many of his Jewish friends and colleagues found deeply offensive. That is not to say that Heidegger was one of Goldhagen's willing executioners but that is hardly a commendation for a man who many believe to be one of the most gifted philosophical minds of the twentieth century. Furthermore, rather than wait patiently for any and every scrap of philosophical writing he ever penned to be made public before we begin to draw any conclusions on this or any other matter concerning Heidegger, what if we can establish that some of our greatest fears are in fact confirmed by reading some of Heidegger's most 'sacred' and revered texts? It is Heidegger himself who professes a deep affinity between some of his most important concepts in *Being and Time* and his political views and actions in the 1930s. What if Heidegger's notion of historicity and related discussions in *Being and Time* are indeed relevant to his politics but in ways which point to a massive shortcoming in his own thought? What if we can show that Heidegger deliberately tried to use notions which first emerge in *Being and Time* as a justification for a type of ethnic chauvinism? If *Being and Time* itself is 'implicated' in certain ways, then what does it matter if we find thousands of further problematic texts concerning Heidegger's political views? If *Being and Time* is in 'trouble', then we already have all the controversy we need since few would continue to deny the importance of Heidegger's magnum opus to twentieth and twenty-first century philosophy.

This work is, in many ways, an invitation to those that read Heidegger to begin to approach the texts that are discussed and many others as offering us portals into some deeply troubling ideas that are central to Heidegger's attack on Modernity. I have no doubt that there will be critics who are quick to point to relevant or crucial texts and sources which *should* have been discussed but in doing as much they will have missed the intention and the spirit of the book. I do not wish to offer an exhaustive chronicle or deal with absolutely everything that has been said in anger or despair on the question of Heidegger's political affiliations. Rather I hope to show how a revisitation of some of Heidegger's least controversial texts along with some of the more controversial ones, many of which have been in circulation for as long as this affair has existed, already contain most of the gravest problems and issues that need to be treated.

****

In the chapters that follow, we tackle a range of questions including the intellectual and cultural background against which Heidegger's commitment to National Socialism must be understood, the question of his antisemitism,[7] the role that victor's morality has played in the way the Heidegger affair has been pursued in the intellectual world and the question as to whether Heidegger is philosophically 'silent' with respect to the Holocaust or whether in fact his examination of the essence of technology is an attempt to respond philosophically to the Holocaust. In the first two chapters then, the second in particular, we shall, among other things, look to offer a sustained analysis of how Heidegger's meditation on technology, in particular its essence – *Gestell*, can be understood as a philosophical confrontation with the Holocaust.[8] Read in such a way, Heidegger's philosophy offers the possibility of a searching examination and indictment of the way we understand and reveal the world around us which makes such an event not just the very antithesis of a singularity or an anomaly in Western history but rather an ongoing possibility. And while countless commentators, journalists, film-makers, popular moralists, demagogues and artists continue to bay loudly about the importance of historical remembrance, thoughtlessly invoking Santayana's famous epigram to that effect, far too few of them successfully identify what needs to be remembered; too few of them manage to really address the lesson that history continues, unsuccessfully, to try and teach us. Our 'failure' in this regard is attested to by the numerous acts of genocide and ethnic cleansing which have marred our political landscape since the end of the Second World War. Far from having grasped what history *should* have taught us, our wilful self-deception has ensured the recurrence of the same problems right to the present day. As Christopher Browning notes.

> From the Nazi 'war of destruction' in eastern Europe and the 'war against the Jews' to the 'war without mercy' in the Pacific and most recently Vietnam, soldiers have all too often tortured and slaughtered unarmed civilians and helpless prisoners, and committed numerous other atrocities. Dower's account of entire American units in the Pacific openly boasting of a 'take no prisoners' policy and routinely collecting body parts of Japanese soldiers as battlefield souvenirs is chilling reading for anyone who smugly assumes that war atrocities were a monopoly of the Nazi regime.[9]

'Anti-Heideggerians' (and no doubt custodians of the Holocaust's historically 'singular' character) will protest that this is an exculpatory strategy, yet another in a long line of misbegotten exercises in Heideggerian apologetics.[10] But I am no apologist and, as an intellectual who has spent the majority of his intellectual life trying to come to grips with Heidegger's thought, I, as much as anyone, am *appalled* at some of the things Heidegger said, did and wrote during his years as a Nazi and, in particular, during his tenure as Rector of Freiburg University. Nevertheless, I still insist on my right as a liberal and as a democrat to abstain from the victor's moralizing which dogmatically maintains that any opponents of its narrative be tarred 'with the brush of Auschwitz'.[11] I will argue moreover, that far from making apology or excuses for what happened during the Second World War, some of Heidegger's postwar philosophy implicitly undermines an erroneous show trial that has taken place; I argue further that what we must face up to is the shocking possibility that *we are, all of us,* at some level complicit

– that ultimately what needs changing is the way we are revealed and the way the world in turn is revealed *through us*. We share a collective 'guilt' which needs to be 'confessed' before we can hope to make any progress. The defeat of Nazi Germany did not signal the end of the problems we face as a species and we have witnessed nothing less than the steady accumulation of countless horrors associated with the rampant dominion of the technological mindset.

Lest our intentions be misconstrued at the outset, we must make one thing clear: reading *some* of Heidegger's work as a profound commentary and reflection on the Holocaust is *not* to suggest that Heidegger's philosophy 'succeeds' or that it is equal to the enormity of the task at hand. However, if, as is generally conceded now (apart perhaps from the most blinkered adherents to one side of a phony war between the analytic and continental traditions) Heidegger *is* in fact one of the most important philosophers of the twentieth century, then what that philosopher has to say about the greatest ever crime against humanity merits serious attention. And given Heidegger's own Nazi allegiances, his philosophical 'response' is doubly important. Heidegger has been consistently maligned for his moral bankruptcy, not least as a result of his 'silence' concerning the Holocaust following the end of the Second World War. I have argued that Heidegger's silence, in many respects, spoke volumes. That is, in refusing to acquiesce in the Western auto-da-fés that have continued since the middle of the twentieth century, Heidegger was already in some respects 'saying' something.[12] What is more, if we are in fact justified in taking the infelicitously named 'agriculture remark' as an epigraph and thereby a 'key' to 'The Question Concerning Technology', then Heidegger had quite a lot to say, philosophically at least, about the Holocaust. That is certainly *not* to say that it is 'sufficient' or that it is not ultimately bankrupt both morally and philosophically, but we have to first see how Heidegger's thoughts concerning technology *might* be relevant to our reflections on the Holocaust before we make such claims! And, I would submit, though it won't satisfy the entirely reasonable demand to produce an outright condemnation on purely ethical grounds, it may offer us some important insights which will allow us to reflect on the Holocaust and indeed other acts of genocide in ways that might be of some benefit.

Heidegger's silence is also consistent, of course, with his antipathy towards Modernity and his belief that Western Liberalism and Democracy were simply the logical outcomes of a Modernity which itself belonged within the history of Western Metaphysics. And while we may well end up crediting Heidegger with a certain intellectual honesty here, we also find ourselves at the precipice of the gravest difficulties that beset Heidegger's thought: Heidegger cannot consistently resist Universalism in all of its forms in the way that he wishes to in such a way as to protect his own thought from inconsistency. Moreover, his desires to do so (for a period of time) seem to very obviously spring from a kind of 'spiritual' ethnic chauvinism which is simply inconsistent with the aspects of his thought (in particular certain key sections of *Being and Time*) which he looks to found an authentic provincialism on. So, while we can compare Heidegger's anti-modernism with the work of various relevant contemporaries and we can identify his willingness to use the *Blut und Boden* rhetoric of his day, we must also bear in mind that Heidegger is trying to find a way to put these ideas on a philosophical footing which does not reduce to the work of his contemporaries. Seeing this clearly allows us to avoid the pitfall of assuming that Heidegger's philosophy is simply derivative which is a recurring mistake. Rather what we should see is that Heidegger looked to inaugurate his own brand of National Socialism through what proves to be an unhappy and unsuccessful attempt to meld his own philosophy with elements of National Socialism which he thought he could develop in rather idiosyncratic ways.

We will, of course, spend some time discussing the lay of the land in terms of the authors that loomed large in Germany at the time who are typically associated with Heidegger's own politically loaded philosophical self-understanding in the early 1930s. I compare and contrast then the work of some of Heidegger's contemporaries with Heidegger's own work with a view to on the one hand identifying overlapping themes and tropes and at the same time showing the fundamentally incomparable nature of Heidegger's philosophy and how incompatible it is with the work, for example, of Spengler and Jünger. This has further necessitated a response to the work of certain commentators who have examined Heidegger's political views and indeed his philosophy in the light of his contemporaries. Some effort is devoted then to responding to the work of Adorno, Zimmerman and Bourdieu all of whom look to reduce Heidegger's philosophy, in one way or another, to a variant of his cultural, political and historical heritage and situation. And while I can go a certain way with these views since they dovetail with some of Heidegger's own views concerning one's hermeneutical position, I cannot agree that Heidegger's philosophy reduces to nothing more than a reproduction of his contemporaries' views. Quite simply, I am convinced that Heidegger's philosophy is more interesting than that and certainly more interesting than what was on offer from contemporaries such as Jünger and Spengler. Hence, while I can appreciate the importance of comparing Heidegger's views on technology with Spengler's views in *Man and Technics*, for example, I simply cannot see how one could suppose that the texts reduce to each other in anything more than superficial respects. To my eyes and ears the affinities are very much surface affinities and the same can be said of Jünger. It should come as no surprise to learn then that Heidegger himself was quite critical of both thinkers.

\*\*\*\*

There is no denying then that there *are* issues concerning the level and extent of Heidegger's Nazi involvement which are deeply disturbing. Hugo Ott's findings at times stand as rather incriminating reminders, though Ott manages to avoid the sensationalism of Victor Farias' efforts.[13] More recently Emmanuel Faye has offered a most sensational polemic; however, Faye's book is such an intellectual scandal and outrage that it doesn't seem possible to engage the author's work in any meaningful or potentially constructive way.[14] The accounts of Heidegger's behaviour towards once close friends and colleagues such as Jaspers and Löwith are upsetting to say the least. However, robust claims insisting that Heidegger was a rabid, foaming antisemite, summarily dismissing anyone with any trace of Jewish ancestry that happened to be at Freiburg University during his tenure as rector are grossly excessive. If Heidegger did indeed share his wife's allegedly extreme antisemitism, surely his onetime lover and lifelong confidante, Hannah Arendt, would have found it next to impossible to continue a relationship with him, never mind champion his work subsequent to the war. Jaspers, who had a Jewish wife and was himself outraged by some of Heidegger's behaviour, never took Heidegger for a biological racist. Much has been made of Heidegger's relationship with Husserl which had deteriorated badly before the latter's death. Husserl was highly critical of Heidegger's work, not least *Being and Time*, and chose a public platform to emphatically distance himself from his former protégé. As one studies the development of Heidegger's thinking it is clear that they were bound to drift intellectually.[15] Nevertheless, Husserl did famously complain to a friend about Heidegger's increasing antisemitism. As for the claim that Heidegger, as rector, revoked Husserl's right of access to the library, that has been rejected as a slander. What about the removal of the dedication of *Being and Time*? Perhaps it was a deliberate slight on Heidegger's part! Even so, since he did retain the dedication in a footnote, it seems plausible to suppose that he was, as he claimed, acting on appeals for prudence from his publishers. Dedicating a book to a well-known Jewish[16] intellectual in that particular climate may well have been less than judicious. Furthermore, subsequent to that edition Heidegger continued to include the dedication as it was in the original. There is an element of 'straw grasping' with respect to a good deal of this, on *both* sides. That Heidegger was not outraged by the virulently antisemitic vein that coursed through National Socialism or by his own wife's alleged antisemitism is surely indictment enough. Whether Heidegger was sympathetic to the more moderate antisemitism which was to prove so disastrously instrumental in making Europe itself complicit up until or after it was already far too late, that is yet another unsettling question. We know of letters Heidegger wrote criticizing those who were not properly politically aligned, we know of his comments concerning a dangerous international alliance of Jews; it is also clear from Heidegger's recently published private notebooks that he subscribed to some form of antisemitism. We are shocked by the fact that Heidegger would don the swastika and yet sit down to a meal prepared by Jaspers' Jewish wife while a guest in their home as we are outraged at Heidegger's callous, cavalier attitude to the distress Jasper's wife suffered at what was happening in Germany (when Jaspers reported to Heidegger that his wife was overwrought with grief, Heidegger remarked glibly that at times it is therapeutic to have a weep). Moreover, as we shall see below, in his recently published notebooks and in some of his seminars from the early 1930s, Heidegger looks to justify his antisemitism philosophically. It is impossible to defend Heidegger on *any* of these issues, but the matter is not resolved by supposing that he was a fully fledged Nazi replete with the standard racial biological outlook.[17] It seems clear that that was not the case, and while his own 'official story' has been largely discredited, the question remains: what exactly *was* National Socialism for Heidegger and where does it intersect with his philosophical vision? And if Heidegger was not in fact the typical antisemite we associate with Nazism, did he nevertheless support a kind of ethnic chauvinism which is in itself hugely problematic?

Pierre Bourdieu's attempt to 'contextualize' Heidegger's thought would appear to recommend itself as eminently useful here.[18] Bourdieu, for one, looks to avoid the rash tendencies to convict or acquit Heidegger either on the basis of his Nazi involvement or the aspects of his thought which seem to resonate with National Socialist ideology. The frenzied, triumphalist delirium with which certain commentators lift segments of Heidegger's writings and lectures and amplify within them resonances with features of Nazi ideology is horrifically irresponsible. Bourdieu, however, looks to demonstrate that instead of characterizing Heidegger's work as that of a Nazi ideologue, we should rather see evidence of the cultural revolutionary context from which he emerged. There is no question that this 'contextualizing' of Heidegger's thought is crucial, and Zimmerman himself expands on this question in *Heidegger's Confrontation with Modernity*. Aspects of Heidegger's thought then that are inflated into full-blown Nazi, biologically racist tendencies need rather to be pursued 'backwards' into the context Heidegger shared with a whole host of German 'mandarins' in the Weimar and post-Weimar era. That National Socialism arrogated some of those notions as part of their dreadful ideological rhetoric is not to expose all of these German intellectuals to blame for biological racism or antisemitism. However, even though aspects of Heidegger's writings and thought, both political and non-political, share certain trace elements with a class of German intellectuals, that is not to say that Heidegger's thought in its entirety simply reduces to German conservative nationalist rhetoric either. And, it is precisely for this reason that Bourdieu's proposed 'approach' to Heidegger's work in the light of his political activities ultimately fails. While Bourdieu avoids the excessive tendencies of the apologists and the accusers, locked as they are in their own mutually sustained stand-off, he precipitously characterizes Heidegger's philosophy as a series of conservative revolutionary views hiding behind an abstruse idiolect. Even as one reads his interview some years later when his avowed approach in *The Political Ontology of Martin Heidegger seemed* rather prophetic, insofar as it identified accurately the manner in which the debate would polarize into two camps, one still finds Bourdieu refusing to acknowledge Heidegger's importance as a philosophical thinker. One hears him instead damn Heidegger's thought with such faint praise as being 'highly professional', Heidegger himself as having 'an extraordinary capacity to maintain forms ... an incredible sense of the game of philosophy' but he refuses to acknowledge that Heidegger is a serious philosopher.[19] He essentially identifies Heidegger's thought as negligible along with his Nazism which circumvents the problem – if Heidegger is not a great thinker, the question of whether or not he was a Nazi and the extent to which he was ideologically committed to National Socialism becomes considerably less important. Thus, with little left with which to navigate our way through this minefield, we find ourselves stranded amidst the volleys of accusation and counter accusation from the acolytes and the accusers. Unfortunately, on a battlefield teeming with agendas, everything tends to get lumped together and put upon the hazard. And it is as a result of this sorry state of affairs and with the perhaps naïve hope of ameliorating this situation that this project has been undertaken. If we can begin to even sketch the outlines of the discussions that those interested in Heidegger and this particular affair *should* be having – then that will suffice for the time being.

# 1

# Re-assessing the 'Affair'

*Nazism was not born in the desert. We all know this, but it has to be constantly recalled. And even if, far from the desert, it had grown like a mushroom in the silence of a European forest, it would have done so in the shadow of big trees, in the shelter of their silence or their indifference but in the same soil. I will not list these trees which in Europe people an immense black forest, I will not count the species... In their bushy taxonomy, they would bear the names of religions, philosophies, political regimes, economic structures, religious or academic institutions. In short, what is just as confusedly called culture, or the world of spirit.*[1]

*somewhat hysterical phrases are deployed by critics who, recognizing Heidegger's rejection of biologism, none the less wish to tar him with the brush of Auschwitz.*[2]

It has proved next to impossible for most commentators to discuss Heidegger's 'politics' without eventually becoming mired in polemics or apologetics.[3] All too often, a binary code obtains such that one is 'required' to declare allegiance to either the acolytes or the witch-hunters before one is lent an ear. In this chapter, we will look to situate the Heidegger controversy within the context of a prevailing 'agenda' and concomitant set of attitudes that have come to monopolize this debate. Indeed, we have seen the same problems that have stymied any progress in previous incarnations of this controversy emerge most recently as soon as there was the mere mention of possibly further incriminating evidence concerning Heidegger's Nazism and his antisemitism in his notebooks from the 1930s and 1940s. The irony is that the most vigorous clashes in this particular version of the Heidegger controversy had already blown themselves out before the notebooks had even been published. And even then, one almost wished to remind those involved that we hardly needed any further evidence of Heidegger's Nazism or his antisemitism. Having said as much, when one considers the lengths that some Heideggerians have gone to in order to brush his antisemitism under the carpet or indeed to explain it away as though it were a trifling matter, the recent discovery of further disturbing passages from Heidegger's notebooks and some of his seminars from the early 1930s helps to delegitimize any such efforts as hopelessly delusional. Moreover, what we also begin to see in the recent publications is incontrovertible evidence that Heidegger was trying to make connections between not only his philosophy and his political views but with his antisemitic prejudices as well.

Our aim in this chapter is to demonstrate that the way this controversy has unfolded reflects a kind of victor's morality and a collective strategy of self-deception concerning the Second World War and the Holocaust. The controversy itself, I believe, needs to be set against the backdrop of a series of sedimented attitudes concerning the Holocaust and National Socialism. The victor's morality which motivates and distorts the perspective of certain commentators who have looked to pass final judgment on Heidegger's work for scholars and readers outside of philosophy betrays a set of inveterate prejudices which seem to point to a worrisome trend concerning the terms of reference that have been settled on when it comes to the Second World War. Historians such as Victor Farias, intellectual historians such as Richard Wolin, not to mention the more sensational example of Emmanuel Faye, are prime exponents of the kind of commentary which is symptomatic of precisely the critical sclerosis which has set into our Western attitudes concerning the Second World War and Nazi Germany. As Lewis Coser writes in his preface to the English edition of Jünger's *The Peace* (under the pseudonym of Louis Clair):

> Modern man has a fatal propensity for attempting to free himself from his own feelings of guilt, his own anxieties and terrors, by projecting them onto some scapegoat, some incarnation of absolute evil, which he burdens with all the sins, all the shortcomings that he cannot face within himself. The Jews were made to assume this burden for the Nazis; for the addicts to the Stalin myth, the 'trotskyites' are the scapegoat; and for many an otherwise liberal and 'normal' American, this role has of late been assigned to 'the German' – a sort of corporate entity, an amalgamation of all that is hateful and despicable.[4]

\*\*\*\*

In the latter stages of this chapter, we shall gloss a 'possible' intersection between Heidegger's account of technology and the Holocaust in terms of a 'philosophical response' – a possibility, moreover, which has been routinely rubbished or precluded hitherto and this in turn shall pave the way for a detailed analysis of this possibility in Chapter 2. In pointing to the tenability of such a project, we are again resisting the agenda of those commentators who insist that no such dialogue with Heidegger's later philosophy on technology, for example, is possible. This blinkered intransigence when it comes to what I contend is a latent possibility in Heidegger's thought again reinforces the suspicion that many critics are so completely yoked to a continually reinforced referential framework concerning the Second World War and the Holocaust that they distort and derail debates such as this one with melodramatic appeals to the gallery. Or, equally unhelpful, they look to 'shape' things in order to fit pre-arranged schemes and maintain the unquestioned ascendancy of the status quo.

## The 'Affair' and the rhetorical rules since the Second World War

Heidegger possessed a willingness to question the supposedly indisputable which John Caputo correctly locates at the epicentre of his thinking; yet Caputo sees this as *exclusively* Heideggerian, and exclusively so to its unequivocal detriment since it involves a thinking that *is* willing to question the putatively *indubitable*, putting our much revered Western, democratic, liberal, and, in that sense, somewhat *localized* sensibilities to radical question.[5] A recurring theme in this controversy and one which has stymied promising studies is the tendency to take it as a given that, as a result of the Second World War, democracy and liberalism are indubitable. There is a kind of futility then in spending so much time debunking Heidegger's 'anti-democratic' sentiment as is the case in such influential studies, heavily relied on by non-philosophers, as Richard Wolin's various contributions.[6] Heidegger was avowedly sceptical concerning democracy throughout his life, but to locate such anti-democratic sympathies within his work is not sufficient reason to dismiss the same work as so much fascist ideology.[7] That is not to say that there are not serious problems with just how far Heidegger wants to take his challenge to modernity. But it simply is not sufficient to conflate Heidegger's anti-modernism with Nazism and, in one clean sweep, to dismiss everything he wrote. Heidegger's philosophy is far more sophisticated than that and the problems that mire his project run far deeper. In effect, what precipitous critics of Heidegger have done is allowed Heideggerians to hide behind 'Fortress Heidegger', easily rebuffing such rash and poorly conceived objections!

\*\*\*\*

Since the end of the Second World War, or perhaps nowadays one should say since the Holocaust, it is, perhaps, not alone the fact of Heidegger's 'silence' which should scandalize us but the ensuing heteronomy which has oppressively framed the discursive rules when it comes to discussing the Heidegger 'affair'. The discursive currency restrictions we have been levied with are suffocating and have little purchase philosophically.[8] The Salem-like mentality so often in evidence functions as a telling indictment of our mindset when it comes to the Heidegger controversy. For many commentators the only acceptable response is condemnation and boycott; we are to send anyone who does not conform to 'a moral Coventry'! The repugnancy of Nazism is, I believe, beyond dispute, but the subsequent vilification of everyone and everything associated with that period in Europe's past is not a move which I endorse so readily.[9] Nor am I convinced that everyone who fought against the Germans were faultless paragons of virtue – public and private;[10] indeed as soon as the war was over, so the 'West' would have us believe, the Russians became the villains. One is reminded here of Alastair Cooke's both eloquent and salutary warning concerning the perils of romanticizing history in his address before the House of Representatives in 1974 to commemorate the Bi-centennial of the First Continental Congress in Philadelphia:

> I wish only to suggest the dangers that lie ahead, and that have lain in the past, in our tendency, especially in the movies and in television, and in too many school books, to sentimentalize our history or to teach it as a continual clash between the good guys and bad guys.[11]

It is this prevailing tendency, I would submit, which has led many to denounce Heidegger unequivocally or to engage in apologist, exculpatory tactics which are equally misleading and unhelpful. The attempt to find the seeds of a fully conceived, robust Nationalist Socialist programme in Heidegger's most famous work is as wrong-headed an enterprise as the attempt to purge his work of *all* such allegiances. As Carroll summarizes in his foreword to Lyotard's *Heidegger and 'the jews'*:

> Even though Lyotard claims that the deduction of Heidegger's 'Nazism' from *Being and Time* is impossible, the claim that the work is 'apolitical' is equally absurd, given the project associated with *Dasein*.[12]

To say that there are political ramifications, at some indirect, tenuous level is not to say that the seeds of brutish Nazi policy are latent in *Being and Time* – one of the most important philosophical texts of the twentieth century. The insistence on partisanship to either side of opposed poles is an impediment to any genuine attempt to examine Heidegger's 'politics' and how it might relate to his philosophical thinking. The inference drawn is 'if a great thinker, then not a Nazi; if a Nazi, then not a great thinker – the implication being: either negligible Nazism or negligible thought'.[13] The irony here lies in the fact that, though this is the essential stand-off which has characterized each recurrence of the Heidegger Controversy, there would in fact be no controversy if either side proved correct. That is, if Heidegger is not really a Nazi, then there is nothing for anyone to be alarmed by. If he is not a great philosopher, then the question of his political affiliations instantly disappears as a problem. The controversy instantly dissolves in any of the previous debates since there was nothing to worry anyone in either position; the real problem is the issue of how a great philosopher could also be a Nazi and, not just that, but supposedly *on the basis* of that same philosophy and that is what should trouble us most. Of course, some might want to counter that the claim of critics of Heidegger is that since his philosophy is *clearly* implicated in his Nazism, that it cannot, for that reason be thought to be the work of a great thinker. There are at least two problems with this. First, it is not at all clear that simply because one thinks dangerous or disturbing philosophical thoughts that one is therefore, *de facto*, not a great philosopher. There would appear to be far too many counter examples to that position. Second, those that want to maintain that we can draw a straight line from Heidegger's philosophy to his politics rarely manage to do so, it is usually simply thrown into the debate as a claim in some breezy review where the real agenda is a rather sinister one in its own right: to use this opportunity to finally put the nail in the coffin of a philosophy which they have never taken the time to read or engage with seriously to begin with. The question of Heidegger's Nazism is often just an opportunity which the same critics pounce on as part of a long-standing ideological feud between analytic and continental philosophers. Consequently, when these same critics and their supporters claim that it is because Heidegger's philosophy is obviously Nazi to the core that they insist that it must be dismissed, they are engaged in a rather obvious subterfuge since the same critics have typically refused to read or take seriously the same work, even when the question of Heidegger's political misdeeds were not a concern for those same critics.

It is next to impossible and yet crucial to try and maintain a position on this issue and yet resist 'the numerous variants expressed in favour of one or the other thesis'.[14] The confusion, misnomers and misinterpretations involved are evident most acutely perhaps in the way this controversy has continued to rear its ugly head within French intellectual circles and, alas, we have seen similar patterns emerge in the wake of more recent scandals. So desperate are some to condemn and others to preserve Heidegger's work that precipitous claims to have discovered a Nazi ideology as the theoretical foundation for all of Heidegger's thought abound almost as often as erroneous moves to 'localize' the Nazi rot with a containment strategy whereby the 'tainted' texts are amputated and the later or earlier work preserved! Both approaches, oriented by the cultural and political terms of reference handed down concerning the Second World War and the Holocaust serve to obfuscate and distort more than they clarify or explain. Even the approaches of such noteworthy commentators on Heidegger as Derrida and Lacoue-Labarthe succumbed, in the end, to what Gregory Fried refers to as 'exculpatory contortions'.[15] Derrida and Lacoue-Labarthe together represented a 'respectable' front for French-Heideggerian apologetics when it came to the controversy. Their positions, moreover, are afforded a modicum of respect by even the most ardent opponents since they do not simply scoff at the revelations which rocked the French intellectual scene to the core and since each offers a thoughtful defence for the elements of Heidegger's thinking which they wish to preserve. The ingenuity of their strategies however, is matched by an alarming impetuosity when it comes to their dim estimation of either *Being and Time* or Heidegger's earlier thinking in general as the corrupted residuum of an inveterate metaphysical humanism. They are both overly inclined to suddenly find in Heidegger's 'early' thought a subjectivist, humanist tumour which was directly responsible for the myopic totalitarianism he succumbed to in the 1930s.

The main battle-lines were drawn in France, of course, and the situation reached critical mass with the translation of Farias' controversial text. Both Derrida and Lacoue-Labarthe, however, presented complex, philosophical perspectives on Heidegger's Nazism which amounted to both philosophers conceding that Heidegger's thought had a thread of metaphysical humanism woven into the fabric of the early parts of the tapestry, a humanistic thread which was no longer in evidence in parts of the cloth woven later. Granted, their positions do not reduce immediately to one another, even if something of the general thrust reprised above obtains in both accounts.

In *Of Spirit: Heidegger and the Question*, Derrida argues that Heidegger's political speeches, not least the Rectoral Address, involve an extraordinary 'departure' which goes beyond anything to be found in either *Being and Time* or the later work. To be sure, Derrida insists, elements of a metaphysical humanism are to be found in *Being and Time* which remained mired in subjectivism despite Heidegger's best efforts. But this existentially qualified subjectivism was not nearly the launching-pad required for the magnitude of the political leap Heidegger made in the 1930s. In the early 1930s,

Heidegger commits to a voluntarism that demands more than either the existential framework or the concept of resoluteness in *Being and Time* can support:

> How are we to explain this sudden inflammation and inflation of Geist? *Sein und Zeit* was all tortuous prudence, the severe economy of a writing holding back the declaration within a discipline of severely observed markers. So how does Heidegger get from this to the eloquent fervor and the sometimes righteous proclamation dedicated to the self-affirmation of the German university? What is the leap from the one to the other?[16]

Subsequently, Heidegger recoiled from this 'monstrous', voluntaristic willfulness and moved toward a position even closer to the deconstrucionist attitude favoured by Derrida if not fully divested of traces of Western humanism/metaphysics. So while *Being and Time* is 'glued' together with a hidden humanism, it is not of the same 'consistency' as the humanistic, voluntarist posture of Heidegger's political thought in the 1930s. Heidegger's thought then, though contaminated with an ever-present, if ever diminishing, metaphysical humanism, which may in turn have facilitated the move to the far more radical 'humanism' of the 1930s, at no point either side of his fateful political misadventure simply reduces straightforwardly to Nazi ideology.

In *Heidegger, Politics and Art: The Fiction of the Political*, Lacoue-Labarthe echoes some of Derrida's sentiments concerning Heidegger's early humanism.[17] However, Lacoue-Labarthe finds the seeds of Heidegger's humanist, voluntarist rhetoric in the 1930s in a dangerous humanism which goes to the very foundations of *Being and Time*. Again, Lacoue-Labarthe seems eager to preserve the integrity of the later work, in his case, at the expense of *Being and Time*, riddled as it is with this alleged surfeit of metaphysical humanism which paved the way for Heidegger's commitment to National Socialism. Lacoue-Labarthe then, sees Heidegger's political writings and views from his Nazi years as entirely consistent with *Being and Time*'s erroneous and dangerous humanism which Heidegger disavowed in his work from the Nietzsche lectures onwards. In many ways, Derrida and Lacoue-Labarthe can be seen as victims of a cultural and political atmosphere which ordained that anything that bore the least relationship to National Socialism or *conservative nationalism* had to be expunged or rejected from work they were favourably disposed to or indeed artificially transplanted into areas of Heidegger's work that they were willing to sacrifice for the greater good of their interpretative schemes.

For other critics and commentators, it seems preferable to scapegoat Heidegger in the intellectual kangaroo courts so prevalent since the publication of Farias' massively controversial *Heidegger and Nazism*;[18] it would certainly seem less troublesome than the casuistry and apologetics often engaged in. The condemnation of Heidegger's activities before, during and after the war mirrors the manner in which we have collectively perpetuated a comfortable myth concerning the Second World War (the 'good' allies against the 'evil' Nazis). These 'approaches', once the clamour subsides and the dust settles, tell us as much about ourselves as they do about thinkers such as Heidegger who enthusiastically supported his own rather idiosyncratic vision of National Socialism. George Santayana famously warned that those who did not remember the past were condemned to repeat it.[19] I would submit that what we currently accept as 'remembering', whereby everything and everyone associated with National Socialism is seen as an aberration – grotesque elements of a demonic singularity, as is so prevalent in much of what we see and read – is not to *remember* the past at all but to concoct a myth thereby leaving us blind to the very real possibility of further shocking episodes of man's capacity for inhumanity.[20] In this 'orgy of self-righteousness' we are not only engaged in an act of wilful *forgetfulness*, we further run the very real risk of doing an 'enormous disservice to the young'.[21] Perhaps to *remember* the Holocaust ultimately will be to *remember* that it is not the legacy of a handful of evil Germans brokering a final solution in the 1940s, rather it is the legacy of *we good Europeans*. It is a complex, horrific, and *not just German*, but ultimately *human* story; the true evil, the true horror of it, as Hannah Arendt so vividly portrays is the *banality* of it.[22] To believe that the possibility of 'similar' future events ended with the lives of those who were the immediate perpetrators misses the very important lesson to be learned! Zimmerman, for example, argues that: 'Heidegger glided over the fact that the Holocaust was a *German* phenomenon involving the slaughter of millions of *Jews*. Instead, he chose to view the Holocaust as a *typical* episode in the technological era afflicting the entire West.'[23] Zimmerman agrees with Lacoue-Labarthe that Heidegger's great failing was his refusal to see Auschwitz or the Holocaust as a 'caesura'. For Zimmerman then, the challenge is to treat the Holocaust as entirely singular, a dreadful and *specifically* German anomaly. It seems clear that even if Heidegger had been keen to explicitly discuss the Holocaust at length philosophically and to indeed repent publicly for his own Nazi allegiances or express profound grief for what had happened, which would have more than satisfied many of his most ardent critics, he would yet eschew this parsing of the narrative concerning the Holocaust as missing its deepest essence. This was clearly *part* of the point he wished to make in his correspondence with Marcuse as well as in his infamous 'agriculture remark'. Marcuse dismisses the question as to whether or not it is possible to make comparisons between the Holocaust and other 'horrors' of the Second World War. Instead Marcuse wants a 'word', that is, a public confession from Heidegger concerning his personal feelings on the Holocaust that would indicate clearly to everyone his revulsion at what took place. And, more than that, he wants Heidegger to reinforce the discursive rules that had already been sanctioned concerning the Second World War. When Heidegger responds with a suggestion to the effect that it is a mistake to look on the Nazi regime in the singular way demanded by the 'Allies', Marcuse accuses him essentially of a *tu quoque* fallacy,[24] a criticism levelled against this alleged 'strategy' of Heidegger's by subsequent critics also (that is, of trivializing through comparison).[25] And yet, Zimmerman seems at least *partially* sensitive to what Heidegger was trying to draw attention to when he quickly qualifies his own criticism as mentioned above:

> in speaking of the Holocaust in the same breath with the hydrogen bomb, Heidegger was making an important point. Mass extermination in the Nazi camps was possible only because of developments within industrial technology. Moreover, the Nazis spoke of the Jews as if they were little more than industrial 'waste' to be disposed of as efficiently as possible. Officials in charge of planning strategic use of nuclear weapons must be trained to conceive of the enemy

populace in wholly abstract terms. Heidegger argued in several places that the hydrogen bomb – an instrument of mass extermination – was not the real problem facing us. Instead, the problem is the perversion and constriction of humanity's understanding of being itself in the technological era. Extermination camps and hydrogen bombs, from Heidegger's viewpoint, were both symptoms of humanity's conception of itself and everything else as resources to be produced and consumed, created and destroyed, at will.[26]

It is interesting to note that, when Zimmerman offers this *less* critical reading of Heidegger's 'agriculture remark', he draws the comparisons between the deployment of nuclear weaponry and death camps. This is noteworthy since, Zimmerman himself, along with the majority of commentators, usually overlooks the rather interesting parallels that can be drawn from these developments in the Second World War and inveighs instead about Heidegger's attempt to measure the suffering at Auschwitz against the industrial harvesting of crops. Indeed, the more obvious comparison with the slaughter houses which have since become conveyor belts for death on factory farms is also typically omitted in order to scandalize things further. The very fact that the whole statement is referred to as the 'agriculture remark' as opposed to the 'Atomic Bomb Remark' is indicative in its own right.[27]

Many commentators, in their capacity as human beings, want Heidegger to show some smidgen of humanity and to publicly condemn the heinous crimes that took place in camps such as Auschwitz. That he chose not to for the most part is something that gives us all pause. But that we should somehow demand of his philosophy that it offer us the basis for such a condemnation, when it was never designed or intended for such ends, is wrongheaded. Heidegger consistently steered clear from all forms of ethics or moral anthropology. He believed his questions were more preliminary or preparatory. He insisted that this was the case in *Being and Time* and he maintained this stance throughout his career. If one wanted an ethical response, one should have discontinued reading Heidegger half way through *Being and Time*. Heidegger did argue, however, that there were essential features of the Holocaust, the use of nuclear weapons, the blockading of countries and indeed the assembly line production of meat for consumption which were symptomatic of the peculiar *Gestalt* of the technological age. They were all symptoms of the holding sway of *Gestell* and tackling the question of human freedom in the face of this 'danger' is where Heidegger invested his energies. That he chose not to make moral distinctions between the horror of the Holocaust and the horrors of a factory farm – that is, perhaps, a human failing. Nonetheless, the possibility of a very penetrating insight into the philosophical backdrop to the Holocaust *is* available in Heidegger's extraordinary confrontation with technology.

Heidegger is asking why it is that things reveal themselves to us in the ways that they do. He eventually concludes that since the early part of the twentieth century, everything is more or less revealed through a technological lens and Heidegger looks at the levelling gaze at work in some of the worst abominations of technology witnessed in the twentieth century: nuclear weapons and the razing of Nagasaki and Hiroshima, the Holocaust – gas chambers and the crematoria, the ability to systematically blockade a country to the point of starvation and indeed the application of techniques for mass production to the rearing and slaughtering of livestock on factory farms. Regardless of the ethical or ontic distinctions one might want to make between these various events, Heidegger's concern is not with *why* people choose to wage war, act on xenophobic impulses or eat meat – these have ever been human 'shortcomings'. Rather, for Heidegger, the question is how we came to prosecute those ends in the shocking ways in which we have done in the twentieth century and Heidegger wants to suggest that this relates to the peculiar way in which we reveal the world which in turn is revealed to us in the technological age under the stamp of *Gestell*. The real challenge is perhaps to try and see how we begin to think events like the Holocaust from *this* perspective and, as we shall see in the next chapter, there is some potential in Heidegger's 'later' work for such an engagement. Objections to the effect that Heidegger is guilty of a category mistake are completely wrongheaded; Heidegger is not comparing agriculture with atomic energy and genocide – Heidegger is suggesting that the manner in which agriculture, military conflict and genocide have been undertaken in the twentieth century have been very heavily influenced by a technological type of understanding.

## Heidegger's refusal to recant

Perhaps the *least* contested 'issue' in all of this concerns Heidegger's 'silence'. Heidegger's supporters no less than his critics find it difficult to countenance his refusal to offer any public apology for his actions under Nazi rule.[28] The sporadic remarks he did make have been widely disparaged for what is seen as an appalling, utterly indefensible lack of humanity or compassion. Yet Heidegger's 'silence' and the cryptic remarks he made *can* be taken to indicate that he was wary of the way that our discourse concerning this blackest night in Europe's turbulent history was already predetermined according to certain schemes. One reason, I believe, Heidegger remained silent was because anything short of a public spectacle of self-flagellation was 'out-of-joint'. It *might not* simply be the case that Heidegger lacked the ability to apologize publicly (though I am quite sure that that had something to do with it[29]). He may also have been loath to simply join the procession of reformed Nazi flagellants in a way that would only expedite the spread of the plague of myth that was sweeping through the West.[30] It was something of a 'lose-lose' situation for Heidegger. One of the most important thinkers of his generation who, in some ways due to his insights into the real essence of technology, was supremely well equipped to 'situate' the Holocaust could not possibly do as much explicitly since what was demanded was a reinforcing of the discursive rules. People wanted an *auto da fé* (in the original sense of that term) or they wanted a public, medieval spectacle of harsh corrective punishment for unrecanted heresy. To be true to his conscience publicly would have been the end for him, to placate the mob would have destroyed whatever intellectual integrity he had left, and so in a rather 'pregnant' silence, punctured only sporadically with a smattering of ambiguous remarks, he managed to secure a grudgingly afforded exile.[31] Indeed there's a curious irony to the fact that what is demanded of one of the twentieth century's most important intellectual luminaries by those outraged by a regime that encouraged numerous *auto da fés* (in the later sense of that term) is his own submission to a spectacle of public confession and the sacrifice of his thought and texts to a very public 'burning'.

## Heidegger's remarks on the Holocaust

Few efforts are made to think carefully about Heidegger's 'silence' on the Holocaust or the context of when and where he made his most explicit remarks concerning the essence of the Holocaust. Instead, commentators are quick to point to the disgrace of comparing the mechanized harvesting of crops, for example, with the efficient production of corpses in the concentration camps. Again, it is noteworthy that commentators generally tend to suggest that Heidegger wants to compare the mechanized harvesting of crops with the Holocaust as opposed to the mass production of meat on factory farms. Furthermore, within the same tirades, there is often little mention of the dropping of the bombs in Nagasaki and Hiroshima, or the blockading of countries since the aim is to scandalize as much as possible. We are typically reminded of the irreducibly 'singular' nature of the Holocaust. To compare it, to refer to it outside of the discursive parameters permitted, is 'sacrilegious' and it is taken as further evidence of Heidegger's fundamental lack of humanity, his hamstrung philosophical outlook, his deeply entrenched commitment to Nazi ideals and an unmistakable identification with the basest kind of antisemitic sympathies. But any variant on this kind of conclusion is grossly inadequate and misses the opportunity for a dialogue between Heidegger's thinking on technology and our understanding of the Holocaust.

Let us turn, then, to the question as to whether there is a silent entreaty from Heidegger himself to think through his 'silence' and his clipped yet massively provocative remarks concerning the Holocaust on the basis of his philosophy, albeit in ways which he had not seen before the Second World War. And this is not to exonerate Heidegger the philosopher *or* the man. It might indeed be the case that Heidegger is, after all, hamstrung irreparably when it comes to questions of a political nature. It might further be the case that there are dangerous tendencies in some of Heidegger's work. Not least, we might decide, if we haven't already, that as a human being, his shortcomings are lamentable in the extreme, all the more lamentable for the suffering they caused many of his friends and colleagues. Nevertheless, is there not still a duty to at least *try* and think of the 'silence' as though it spoke to us on the basis of the 'hints' and the vast amounts of words that leave the Holocaust and the Third Reich 'unsaid', though perhaps not 'untouched'?

The fact that his only explicit remarks concerning the Holocaust were made in the context of his lectures on technology at the Bremen Club: does that offer us a clue? Is it possible that Heidegger's extraordinary meditation on the essence of technology (*Gestell*) with the concomitant reduction of the entire planet to a coherence of forces and the tendency to look on everything as resource or as standing reserve is simultaneously his attempt to think through the Holocaust, even if he cannot say as much explicitly, especially given the fact that he maintained an almost deafening silence concerning the Holocaust apart from these remarks? Might we go further and say then that 'The Question Concerning Technology' is at a very immediate level, perhaps, a discussion of the philosophical roots of a mindset that can look on entire peoples as resources or objects to be used and disposed of as 'industrial waste'.[32] Is it perhaps a *not*-so-veiled 'comment' on the *essence* of the Holocaust?

The occasion for Heidegger's infamous remark was at a series of lectures given at the Bremen Club in 1949 where he discussed many of the themes found in 'The Question Concerning Technology'. In this context, during one of the lectures, Heidegger makes a massively controversial remark. The comment has provoked extreme outrage. The common denominator running through the responses is that Heidegger's remark is shockingly inadequate and insensitive, that he grossly diminishes the horror of the Holocaust and the gas chambers by comparing them to agricultural practices. The general thrust of these objections, then, stems from a belief that Heidegger has trivialized the most significant atrocity of the documented history of human peoples. Now, in part, this is a response which already moves within the framework of a discursive currency which treats the Holocaust as a singularity, in *essence*, a singularity beyond compare. To compare the Holocaust with *any* other event is, in a sense, to blaspheme! It is treated as beyond human comprehension insofar as it was *not*, we are required to believe, carried out by ordinary people who might or would do something similar in the future. In this 'remembering', however, we are engaging in a kind of collective denial! Moreover, even those that *do* see in Heidegger's treatment of the essence of technology a very real opportunity to comment on National Socialism, *from that very* vantage point, are outraged that he didn't make more specific reference within the body of his work. After all, there were plenty of references to Nazi Germany in his lectures and seminars in the 1930s before he had to acknowledge the dreadful aberration that was historical National Socialism! This I suppose is understandable, however, it does not mean that we cannot persevere ourselves, and perhaps that was what Heidegger hoped for, perhaps not, but again, philosophically we have bigger fish to fry here.

## 2

# The Essence of Technology and the Holocaust

### Heidegger's 'Agriculture Remark' as epigraph

Heidegger's 'Agriculture Remark' has continued, then, to provoke impassioned denunciations from all sides in *L'Affaire* Heidegger and is, I would submit, a source of continuing confusion and misdirected indignation. As we suggested toward the end of the previous chapter, Heidegger's 'remark' can fruitfully be read as a kind of epigraph to his seminal meditation on the question concerning technology's essence. After all, why make such a bold statement early on in a public lecture on the essence of technology if it is not directly relevant to the theme of that lecture? And, given that the published essay is based directly on the lectures he gave at the Bremen Club, it seems plausible to infer that Heidegger is thereby intimating that his published philosophical confrontation with the technological age is simultaneously his confrontation with the worst example of technology's deep-seated hold on our understanding of the world around us and the people within it, namely, the Holocaust. Further credence is lent to this admittedly controversial view when we find that Heidegger reprises a somewhat sanitized version of the same remark in the middle of the published lecture:[1]

> But meanwhile even the cultivation of the field has come under the grip of another kind of setting-in-order, which *sets* upon [*stellt*] nature. It sets upon in the sense of challenging it. Agriculture is now the mechanized food industry. Air is now set to yield nitrogen, the earth to yield ore, ore to yield uranium, for example; uranium is set upon to yield atomic energy, which can be released either for destruction or for peaceful use. (QCT: 15)

Of course, if Heidegger's work on technology *can*, in fact, be interpreted as a robust confrontation with the Holocaust, we are faced with the unenviable task of showing how that is in fact the case as well as then assessing its adequacy. That is not to suggest that Heidegger's work in 'The Question Concerning Technology' reduces to a moral commentary; neither does Heidegger wish to suggest that the Holocaust is comparable in moral terms to other atrocities. What concerns Heidegger involves what *is* comparable, and that is something that, for Heidegger, goes beyond the question of morality.

****

Let's consider first the remark itself and the occasion on which Heidegger made it; Heidegger issued this remark near the beginning of a lecture he gave (as part of a series of lectures) at the Bremen Club in 1949. The lectures focused on many of the issues and themes which we now associate with his famous essay 'The Question Concerning Technology'. The notorious statement reads as follows:

> Agriculture is now a mechanized food industry, in essence the same as the production of corpses in the gas chambers and extermination camps, the same as the blockading and starving of countries, the same as the production of hydrogen bombs.[2]

The word 'essence' in the passage above is *crucial*. Heidegger does *not* say that the Holocaust is identical to modern agriculture, that there are no differences,[3] nor does he say that it is the same as the use of atomic weaponry or the issuing of punitive sanctions. What he says is that they share the same 'essence'. And the essence that Heidegger has in mind here is the essence of technology, *Gestell* (Enframing).[4] That is, Heidegger believes that what holds sway as common within each of these events, despite their many differences (not least moral), is the holding sway of technology's essence. So Heidegger is not suggesting that the manufacture of corpses in gas chambers is straightforwardly identical to the harvesting of grain. Indeed, it is disingenuous, obtuse and irresponsible in the extreme that commentators so tendentiously scandalize Heidegger's comment when the obvious comparison to be drawn is with the industrial approach to animals and the precursors to factory farms which were already in evidence.[5] Even then Heidegger would never suggest that there are *no* differences between the conveyor belts of death that secure our meat and the Nazi death camps, rather what he wants to examine is the *way* people's understanding of the world around them led them to proceed with various objectives *as they did*. It is not so much factory farming that Heidegger wants to compare with Auschwitz. Rather, I would submit, Heidegger is interested in how what is operative here is indicative of a manner of understanding and revealing the world, animals and indeed other human beings which we do *not* in fact control but rather are controlled by. Heidegger confirms this view in 1966 in a way which accords with our reading of his infamous remark almost twenty years previous:

> I would characterize them as half truths because I do not see behind them a genuine confrontation with the technological world, because behind them there is in my view a notion that technology is in its essence something over which man has control. In my opinion, that is not possible. Technology is *in its essence something which man cannot master by himself.*[6]

We can think of Heidegger's work on technology as an attempt to demonstrate the way in which everything tends to be revealed in the technological age, for example, as resources to be used. This claim, in particular, affords us an insight into the connection between the Holocaust and factory farming, for example, since Heidegger is not looking to compare them from some kind of moral framework, but rather in terms of how they both involve a particular way of 'revealing' – human beings in one instance and animals in the other. This way of revealing is what Heidegger refers to as the essence of technology and it is technology's essence which, despite their more or less unfathomable differences in other respects, Heidegger believes is shared by factory farming, nuclear bombs, blockades and the Holocaust. But, how do we arrive at such conclusions? How can we interpret Heidegger's views on technology as intimating as much? In order to answer these questions, we will have to consider his most extensive treatment of technology's essence which is found in 'The Question Concerning Technology'.[7]

\*\*\*\*

That Heidegger's concern is with the 'essence' of technology, in particular, is made clear from the very beginning of the essay. Typically, when we want to identify or locate the essence of something, we ask what it is, that is, we ask 'What is x?' And, by and large, the answer to that question is what we identify as the essence of 'x'. If we apply the same principle to technology, Heidegger suggests that the question 'What is technology?' will afford us both an anthropological and instrumental definition. On the one hand, we will define technology in terms of human activity (anthropological) and that activity will be described as a means to securing various ends (instrumental). And, while these kinds of definitions may well be correct, they are not, Heidegger claims, the 'truth' of the matter, as it were. They do not capture the 'essence' of technology.

Heidegger unsettles any conventional interpretative tendencies we might have with respect to technology arguing that the 'current conception of technology, according to which it is a means and a human activity ... the instrumental and anthropological definition of technology' (QCT: 5) is entirely insufficient. It is insufficient insofar as it does not yet reach technology's essence, which is nothing technological. The instrumental then involves the connection between means and ends while the anthropological definition is based on the fact that using means to secure ends is, obviously, a type of human activity. This leads Heidegger to consider where the notions of means and ends are most readily discovered and, of course, the answer is in the notion of causality. Heidegger spends a good deal of time tracing the notion of causality to its origins in Greek thought and unpacks Aristotle's famous doctrine of the four causes (material, formal, efficient, final). In what has been a progressively narrowing trajectory, the history of our understanding of causality eventually arrived at a point where causality was understood in purely efficient terms. In other words, we were interested in the cause and effect relationship; when we looked at events in the world or at various 'consequents' we looked at the grounds or causes of those same events or consequences and that in turn limited the scope of our understanding of causality. The original Greek understanding of causality, however, was at quite a remove from the mere notion of 'effecting' in that sense. Heidegger looks to return then to the original four causal elements to see if he can identify or uncover what was fundamentally at work within the older notion of causality which cohered between these four types of cause. The four causes can be understood as being 'responsible' for the production/creation of something or other; they start something on its way and issue its arrival into presence. Heidegger famously uses the example of the conceiving and manufacturing of a silver chalice and suggests that what is significant about the chalice, fashioned by the silversmith, is that it is lying there ready for our use *as something*, in this instance, *as* a sacrificial vessel. In other words, the four types of cause, which culminated in the appearance of this chalice *as* a chalice for us, are what allow it to now lie there, to belong to a place and to be interpreted by us *as* something within that context. The chalice lies there before us ready for our use and the four causes, or ways of being responsible bring the chalice into appearance: 'They let it come forth into presencing [*An-wesen*]. They set it free to that place and so start it on its way, namely into its complete arrival' (QCT: 9). It is, if you like, 'occasioned', for us by the four causes, that is, it is something which we can take in specific ways and contexts *as* something determinate. So Heidegger is interested in these four modes of being responsible/occasioning and their unifying feature and he concludes that they

> bring something into appearance. They let it come forth into presencing [*An-wesen*]. They set it free to that place and so start it on its way, namely, into its complete arrival. The principal characteristic of being responsible is this starting something on its way into arrival. It is in the sense of such a starting something on its way into arrival that being responsible is an occasioning or an inducing to go forward [*Ver-an-lassen*]. (QCT: 9)

Occasioning, in *this* sense, is 'the name for the essence of causality thought as the Greeks thought it' (QCT: 10). These four ways of occasioning then 'let what is not yet present arrive into presencing', they are 'unifiedly ruled over by a bringing that brings what presences into appearance' (QCT: 10). This in turn leads to a discussion of the Greek term *poiesis*, since, Heidegger argues, this is the word that Plato uses to describe this type of 'bringing'. In particular, Heidegger zeroes in on a passage from Plato's *Symposium* where Diotima discusses the causal nature of poetry – poetry itself understood here as a kind of 'production'.[8] Heidegger argues then that *poiesis* meant a certain *kind* of production or bringing-forth[9] and that it is this general sense of production/bringing-forth which Diotima has in mind in her discussion with Socrates. This kind of production, moreover, involves producing something 'new', turning one thing into another, much as a craftsman might have turned the block of timber into a piece of furniture. Heidegger even discerns this type of revealing within nature itself arguing that the highest form of *poiesis* is *physis*:

> For what presences by means of *physis* has the bursting open belonging to bringing-forth, e.g., the bursting of a blossom into bloom, in itself (*en heautoi*). In contrast, what is brought forth by the artisan or the artist, e.g., the silver chalice, has the bursting open belonging to bringing-forth not in itself, but in another (*en alloi*), in the craftsman or artist. (QCT: 10–11)

What is crucial in all of these cases, for Heidegger, is that they involve the bringing-forth of something that was concealed into unconcealment. We might say then that Heidegger is offering yet another variation on an old theme (which is something of a red thread throughout his work), namely, the interplay of presence and absence.

Heidegger has begun to speak more and more in terms of occasioning and bringing-forth/*poiesis* as part of his investigation into the underlying unity of causality, and, since 'bringing-forth' is a type of revealing, Heidegger is now in a position to conclude that 'If we inquire, step by step, into what technology, represented as means, actually is, then we shall arrive at revealing. The possibility of all productive manufacturing lies in revealing' (QCT: 12). And it is this particular insight which cements the inner coherence of the essay and in turn allows us to get some purchase on the question as to how/why Heidegger compares the Holocaust, factory farming and atomic bombs from the standpoint of their shared 'essence'. They indicate something about the unique way we are thrown into the world and interpret it and project according to a filtering apparatus which is designated in advance, *Gestell*.

We can chart the essay's course as follows then: Heidegger determines that the conventional definition of technology reduces to an instrumental one. He further insists that the instrumental definition of technology is insufficient insofar as it doesn't yet capture the essence of technology. He concedes that the instrumental definition is correct, but not yet 'true' and proposes to analyse further the notion of instrumentality itself. In delving deeper into the notion of instrumentality, Heidegger reminds us that the notion is derived from the idea of causality. However, it is a long-standing convention that we tend to think of causality in purely efficient terms, that is, we think of causality in terms of effects or consequences and the ground or cause of those same effects/consequences. Heidegger is quick to note however that the notion of causality initially involved four 'ways' in which objects or things were thought to be 'caused' or 'produced'. That is, causality was more holistically conceived; the Greeks had a fourfold understanding of causality as an activity that resulted in various objects, works of art, manufactured items and so on. The Greeks further conceived of this fourfold responsibility for the production of something as a kind of 'occasioning' and any such occasioning as, if you like, a way of allowing something to come to presence, to be revealed.[10] Even nature (*physis*) involves this kind of bringing-forth or revealing:

> The modes of occasioning, the four causes, are at play, then, within bringing-forth. Through bringing-forth, the growing things of nature as well as whatever is completed through the crafts and the arts come at any given time to their appearance.
>
> But how does bringing-forth happen, be it in nature or in handwork and art? What is the bringing-forth in which the fourfold way of occasioning plays? Occasioning has to do with the presencing [*Anwesen*] of that which at any time comes to appearance in bringing-forth. Bringing-forth brings hither out of concealment forth into unconcealment. Bringing forth comes to pass only insofar as something concealed comes into unconcealment. This coming rests and moves freely within what we call revealing [*das Entbergen*]. The Greeks have the word *aletheia* for revealing. The Romans translate this with *veritas*. We say 'truth' and usually understand it as the correctness of an idea. (QCT: 11–12)

Heidegger argues then that the essence of technology belongs to the realm of truth, that is, that the essence of technology is a kind of revelation or unconcealment:

> Every bringing-forth is grounded in revealing. Bringing-forth, indeed, gathers within itself the four modes of occasioning – causality – and rules them

throughout. Within its domain belong end and means, belongs instrumentality. Instrumentality is considered to be the fundamental characteristic of technology. If we inquire, step by step, into what technology, represented as means, actually is, then we shall arrive at revealing. The possibility of all productive manufacturing lies in revealing.

Technology is therefore no mere means. Technology is a way of revealing (QCT: 12).

By way of copperfastening his analysis, Heidegger looks at the etymology of the term technology itself; the word comes from the Greek term *Technikon* and that in turn is a word used to describe anything which 'belongs to *techne*'. *Techne* itself 'is the name not only for the activities and skills of the craftsman, but also for the arts of the mind and the fine arts. *Techne* belongs to bringing-forth, to *poiesis*; it is something poietic' (QCT, 13). Heidegger goes on to unpack the Greeks' understanding of the term *techne* on the basis of a discussion of the term in Aristotle's *Nicomachean Ethics* which supposedly corroborates Heidegger's claim that the term denotes a kind of revealing:

*Techne* is a mode of *aletheuein*. It reveals whatever does not bring itself forth and does not yet lie here before us, whatever can look and turn out now one way and now another. Whoever builds a house or a ship or forges a sacrificial chalice reveals what is to be brought forth, according to the perspectives of the four modes of occasioning. This revealing gathers together in advance the aspect and the matter of ship or house, with a view to the finished thing envisioned as completed, and from this gathering determines the manner of its construction. Thus what is decisive in *techne* does not lie at all in making and manipulating nor in the using of means, but rather in the aforementioned revealing. It is as revealing, and not as manufacturing, that *techne* is a bringing-forth ... Technology is a mode of revealing. Technology comes to presence [*West*] in the realm where revealing and unconcealment takes place, where *aletheia*, truth, happens. (QCT: 13)

Heidegger has now satisfied himself that the essence of technology lies in revealing, that it has always involved a way of revealing; he now wishes to examine the difference, as he sees it, between the current way in which technology reveals (which isn't *poietic*) and the previous *poietic* revealing of older forms of technology.

What is so unique or different then about the modern technological filtration system which calibrates our interpretative gaze? Why is this particular revealing so different? Heidegger's answer is that the revealing we are dealing with here is a 'challenging revealing'. Everything is ordered to 'stand-by'; we look on everything as standing-reserve (QCT: 17). Heidegger suggests that everything is captured and made to stand as part of this standing-reserve by this 'challenging revealing'. The world and nature are revealed for us in precisely this way. More distressing still is the fact that no one seems to be responsible for this development, no person or collective has ordained that things should be as such. And yet, this situation has come about as a result of 'us'; it is human beings that are 'responsible' for the situation we find ourselves in. But to say that we are responsible is to say that we have responded to a situation we find ourselves thrown into. We are reacting and projecting in ways which do not reflect independence or autonomy of thought. Freedom in the Heideggerian sense is not to be confused with unfettered arbitrariness of thought or action. We are not in control of technology any more than we govern the direction of either the world's destiny or our own. The way things become revealed to us and the way we in turn project and determine on the basis of that ordinance of revealing is not something that comes under our control. This is an abiding notion in Heidegger's work, from the undercutting of traditional accounts of subjectivity in *Being and Time* onwards. Heidegger is invoking a notion then familiar to readers of *Being and Time*. In terms of the impact of technology, we are not the pilots of its progress; rather we are 'thrown' in such a way that we ourselves and the world around us are revealed technologically and it is not a result of us having chosen to reveal the world in these ways. Rather it is a situation within which we find ourselves, or indeed, for the most part, do *not* find ourselves:

> Modern technology as an ordering revealing is, then, no merely human doing. Therefore we must take that challenging that sets upon man to order the real as standing-reserve in accordance with the way in which it shows itself. That challenging gathers man into ordering. This gathering concentrates man upon ordering the real as standing-reserve. (QCT: 19)

The way we interpret the world and others then, is not a neutral exercise; it involves a very specific kind of calibration of our interpretative apparatus. We are directed, in ways that we are seemingly unaware of, to reveal the world quite specifically, in our case, through the lens of *Gestell*/Enframing. Our viewing the world as a stockpile of resources, as standing-reserve, is neither necessary nor inevitable, in the sense of moving us closer and closer to the way things *really* are. It is a 'way' that has been ordained in advance; we did not always look on the world in this way and part of the reason that we think the world must be looked at in this way is due to the eliminative character of Enframing. It renders other types of interpretations and ways of revealing obsolete; it endures at the expense of every other mode of interpretation and revealing. This, in part, is what Heidegger means when he says in his posthumously published interview with *Der Spiegel*:

> Everything is functioning. This is exactly what is so uncanny, that everything is functioning and that the functioning drives us more and more to even further functioning, and that technology tears men loose from the earth and uproots them. I do not know whether you were frightened, but I at any rate was when I saw pictures coming from the moon to the earth. We don't need any atom bomb. The uprooting of man has already taken place. The only thing we have left is purely technological relationships. This is no longer the earth on which man lives. As you know, I recently had a long conversation with René Char of the Provence, the poet and resistance fighter. Rocket bases are being built in the Provence and the country is being devastated in an incredible way. This poet, who certainly cannot be suspected of sentimentality and of the glorification of the idyllic, tells me that the uprooting of man which is taking place there will be the end, if poetry and thought do not once more succeed to a position of might without force.[11]

The limitless functionality of the technological age is, I imagine, something that most of us have to come to be dismayed by at some point or other. There seems to be no end to the intrusive nature of technology; every facet of our lives seems to come under the insidious sway of the technical. It is as though we have relinquished our capacity to look on the world in any way other than through this technological 'lens'. The way we are currently thrown such that we reveal the real in the ways we do seems insurmountable. Perhaps what Heidegger is suggesting then is that the mindset of those involved at various levels in the implementation of the Final Solution, for example, was partly determined by a technological revealing which they themselves exercised no control over. This challenging revealing was something that, at least in part, contributed to the way whole peoples were rendered as mere logistical problems to be solved. In the same way that cities were revealed as military targets to be eliminated, despite the horrific 'collateral damage' that entailed, hundreds of thousands of people at a time were reduced to simply a surfeit of physical waste to be disposed of as efficiently as possible; and not just Jews, rather every group that found themselves on the wrong side of the Nazi world-view.[12] Granted the revealing that Heidegger characterizes as the essence of technology did not make anyone antisemitic; to that extent Daniel Goldhagen's[13] objections to the functionalist's arguments cannot be completely ignored. However, it must also be recognized that people were (and remain) eminently amenable to the idea of reducing people to mere stock, resource and waste; the process whereby people are dehumanized and indeed treated as commodities is long standing and this prevailing tendency certainly did play a part in the Final Solution.

## The Holocaust and the 'revealing' rhetoric of the Final Solution

Can we think of Heidegger's analyses then as shedding light on how/why the xenophobic aspirations of the Third Reich were realized in the way that they were? What do we make of the fact that significant numbers of Russian POWs were murdered using the same industrial means as those used to exterminate millions of Jewish people as part of the Final Solution? Yet the extermination of Russian POWs was part of a different set of objectives to those associated with the fervent antisemitism which yoked itself onto the other military and political objectives of the Third Reich. Should we not say, in that case, that it was not so much that antisemitism led to the methods of extermination, rather the way the world (and many people within it) was revealed 'technologically' prompted antisemitic aspirations to be realized through such methods, just as that same ordinance of revealing allowed the German military to envision the industrial slaughter and disposal of Russian POWs.[14] Our brief analysis of Heidegger's essay concerning technology may yet seem at something of a remove from the monstrous industrial brutality of the Final Solution and the factories of death. And yet, if we consider Heidegger's claim that what is at work in the essence of modern technology is a type of 'revealing', in other words, that everything is revealed for us as through a 'frame', and is in that sense *En*framed, we might begin to make some inroads.[15] What we must do then is look at the 'revealing' at work in the Final Solution and the factories of death before comparing that type of revealing to the other types of revealing Heidegger alludes to in his notorious remark on the Holocaust. Can we understand the Final Solution, ultimately, as an extreme expression of Enframing?

****

Let's consider firstly the phrase itself: 'Final Solution'. We might assume that to describe what came to be known as the Holocaust with that horrifying euphemism is straight-forwardly, self-evidently reprehensible. And yet, the very fact that so much ambiguity and controversy has benighted our understanding of Heidegger's misleadingly dubbed 'Agriculture Remark' indicates that we have not sufficiently thought through the question of what makes the phrase 'Final Solution' so repugnant! In many ways, it is Heidegger's own work which offers us the deepest insights into what is so utterly disturbing about even this particular phrase.

The phrase itself (Final Solution) is infamous of course, but not much time has been devoted to considering the specific words used.[16] Again, it may seem unnecessary to wonder as to what is so dreadfully offensive about the phrase. Some might even go so far as to suggest that pursuing such a line of questioning represents a level of obtuseness which is unbecoming even in a philosopher. But, in this instance, what may be deemed obtuse in the court of public opinion or the conventional moralizing of the Agora, seems like healthy inquisitiveness to me. The word 'final', on its own, is a relatively inoffensive, innocuous word. The same can be said of the word 'solution'. Indeed the conjunction of the two words seems relatively innocent. So there is nothing obviously ugly or nefarious about either word, or their conjunction. What makes the phrase 'Final Solution' so horrifying then? I imagine that most of us would venture that the wickedness of the phrase relates to the *context* – the fact that this rather sterile, seemingly innocuous phrase denotes the efficient, industrially organized dispatching of millions of Jews as rubber stamped at a meeting near Berlin on 20 January 1942. All of this may appear obvious. Clearly, using such a banal phrase to refer to something so remote from any kind of banality offends our moral sensibilities; at least one would hope that that is the case. However, not enough time has been spent wondering about the specific words used. Where did they come from? Why were they chosen in this context? Does this way of dehumanizing and sanitizing things resemble the way we have reduced the significance and importance of other people, creatures, things or places? Is it in fact, a common enough occurrence? Not the Holocaust itself, of course, but the language which was used to conceive of and set in motion this horror, *is* it the language of singularity and anomaly?

This infamous phrase originated as one of Hitler's stated aspirations: 'The Final Solution to the Jewish Question'. Already then, we need to make a distinction between: 1. Hitler's notorious statement and 2. the equally notorious conference in Berlin in 1942 when the terms of the Final Solution were brokered and finalized. While there can be no denying the viciousness of Hitler's statements and objectives, what is most deserving of our attention here, I would suggest, is the conference at

Wannsee and the way this 'problem' was approached both in the conference itself and in the events which paved the way for how that meeting would proceed. After all, one hardly needs to be reminded that the expression of extreme xenophobia is not exclusive to Hitler or indeed to German Nazis; would that that were the case! Xenophobia is very much an ongoing issue and the concomitant problems of genocide and 'ethnic cleansing' have not, as it happens, remained historical anomalies belonging only to the accounts of the Nazi regime in our history books. Xenophobia and genocide have continued to ravage countries and communities right to the present day. What makes the Holocaust interesting for our purposes is the manner in which xenophobia and its genocidal aspirations were realized during the Third Reich and that leaves the door open for some startling comparisons which suggests, perhaps for the first time, where our most urgent interpretative energies should in fact be directed![17]

## The Wannsee Conference Protocol

The minutes of this notorious conference, where plans for the Final Solution were apparently finalized, report that Heydrich opened the meeting with an avowal that he had been appointed 'delegate for final solution of the Jewish question in Europe'.[18] Heydrich goes on to note that the meeting had been convened to clarify 'fundamental questions'. Other delegates confirmed that they too had been charged with finding a solution to the Jewish problem 'without regard to geographic borders'. This would seem to suggest that the Nazis looked on the Jewish question as, at the very least, a European-wide 'problem', one that they were bent on 'resolving'. The problem to date had been approached on the basis of two fundamental aspirations: 1. 'the expulsion of the Jews from every sphere of life of the German people' and 2. 'the expulsion of the Jews from the living space of the German people'. These objectives were initially achieved through mass deportations of the Jews from German territory; this was seen as the only feasible solution at that time and every effort had been made to that point to maximize the efficiency of that process. However, the process of enforced emigration had begun to place a considerable strain on resources; already over-extended officers, administrators and supervisors were levied with even more work and demands were issued from the newly occupied countries for financial aid in order to deal with the influx of Jewish 'guests'! Notwithstanding the various difficulties encountered, from the time of the Nazi seizure of power until 31 October 1941, the Nazis had managed to deport 537,000 Jews from German territories. The minutes then describe a new approach which had been employed in recent times involving

> the evacuation of the Jews to the East, *provided that the Führer gives the appropriate approval in advance*. These actions are, however, only to be considered provisional, but practical experience is already being collected which is of the greatest importance in relation to the future final solution of the Jewish question.[19]

What exactly does this important 'practical experience' refer to? What kinds of practical experience had been acquired or indeed perfected from the evacuation of Jews to the East during Hitler's invasion of Russia? We know now that the levels of summary atrocity had reached staggering extremes of barbarity on the Eastern front and incidences of mass murder and extermination had taken place using a variety of means; could this be what the delegates were referring to as invaluable 'practical experience' concerning the Final Solution to the Jewish problem?[20]

We then come to one of the most remarkable parts of the meeting, as summarized in the minutes. It is noted that '11 million Jews will be involved in the Final Solution of the European Jewish question' and a breakdown of the number of Jews living in each individual country is provided. Some of these countries were as yet unoccupied, hence, we know that the Nazis saw the Jewish question as one they were determined to solve for the entire continent of Europe. Following some cursory considerations of Jewish numbers in the Soviet Union and a breakdown according to occupation, the meeting determined that the appropriate course of action would mean that

> the Jews are to be allocated for appropriate labor in the East. Able-bodied Jews, separated according to sex, will be taken in large work columns to these areas for work on roads, in the course of which action doubtless a large portion will be eliminated by natural causes. The possible final remnant will, since it will undoubtedly consist of the most resistant portion, have to be treated accordingly, because it is the product of natural selection and would, if released, act as the seed of a new Jewish revival (see the experience of history). In the course of the practical execution of the final solution, Europe will be combed through from west to east. Germany proper, including the Protectorate of Bohemia and Moravia, will have to be handled first due to the housing problem and additional social and political necessities.[21]

Some of the characterizations and descriptions of the Jews are in terms of an infestation, a problem with pests or rodents; they are referred to as epidemic carriers, clearly evoking the image of rats carrying the bubonic plague which ravaged Europe in the 1300s. It is perhaps somewhat less than surprising to learn then that one of the great 'breakthroughs' in terms of successfully implementing the directives of the Final Solution involved an impromptu 'experiment' with a common pesticide by Rudolf Höss's second in command at Auschwitz, Karl Fritzsch; Fritzsch conducted an experiment which clearly shows how he looked on the inmates in the camp (in this instance Russian POWs) as pests to be exterminated. That is, the inmates at the camp were *revealed* to him as practical, logistical problems that could be approached as one would approach an infestation of rodents or vermin within a factory.[22] And yet, we should note that it was Russian POWs on this occasion that were revealed to Fritzsch as vermin, not Jews! In other words, the mere fact of being inmates at the camps seems to have been sufficient for Höss's second in command to reduce the same people to rodents to be removed from industrial premises using these kinds of means.

## Auschwitz: Factory of death

If we consider briefly the expansion and development of Auschwitz during the 1940s, we begin to get yet another insight into the emergence of mass extermination as a real 'possibility'. The evidence would seem to suggest that Auschwitz was initially acquired and intended for rather less horrifying purposes. When Rudolf Höss first assumed command of the former Polish army barracks it was to serve as a detention camp for approximately 10,000 Polish political dissidents per year. Twenty-three thousand Poles were rounded up and in a 20-month period about half of that number perished. The camp was designed to function as a deterrent to would-be political dissidents in Poland and was noted for its appalling living conditions and extreme brutality.

The first major plans for 'developing' Auschwitz were conceived as a result of its location. Scientists at IG Farben had spent years conducting research and experiments on how to manufacture synthetic rubber and fuel. They identified water, coal and lime as the crucial components and since Auschwitz was very close to sources of fresh water and lime along with some of the richest coal seams in Europe, it was quickly earmarked as an ideal location for IG Farben's synthetic rubber (buna) factory. Himmler visited Auschwitz and decided that a 30,000-person slave camp, the biggest of its kind, would be constructed at Auschwitz where a somewhat Arcadian German municipality was simultaneously to be developed for pure-bred Germans.[23] Himmler himself was to have an apartment in the town and the elaborate and lavish plans, down to the very décor, were drawn up by an architect charged with working on the project. So Auschwitz, as we can see, was initially shaped according to political and subsequently industrial objectives which had little to do with the implementation of the Final Solution. Hitler's rather more spectacular plans, which involved the invasion and conquering of Russia, were to outstrip the slightly less ambitious aspirations of Himmler and would ultimately lead to the transformation of Auschwitz from a political concentration camp for Polish political dissidents to one of the first (and certainly the most infamous) factories of death in the history of humankind. But again, we have to understand that this was not the simple realization of the diabolical designs of an evil, Jew-hating demagogue; Auschwitz was the result of a series of visions, measures and ideas which had emerged from above and below within the political and military hierarchy of the Third Reich. The evolution of the camp is indicative of the revelatory ordinances which came from the Nazis and yet from beyond them. Auschwitz and its original function predated the plans for the Final Solution and the way the infamous death camp was revealed to the Nazis was something that was determined according to circumstance. Initially it functioned as a detention camp for political dissidents, then as a work camp for the manufacture of synthetic rubber. Subsequently these requirements were usurped by the need to find a location for the swelling population of Russian POWs before the Nazis finally decided that the best solution to the Jewish problem in Europe was in fact the 'dissolution' of the Jewish race which led to Auschwitz revealing itself to them as an exterminationist installation which could be used to dispose of all of the human 'waste' which was generated during their expansion through the East.

As Hitler's expansionist programme for the East materialized as war on a second front (Operation Barbarossa), new strains began to burden the concentration camps in the East. Initially, Himmler's *Einsatzgruppen* combed through the villages and towns left in the wake of the Blitzkrieg advancing toward Moscow in an almost ad hoc implementation of the Nazi policy of extermination. Soon however, large numbers of Russian POWs were in need of accommodation. Suddenly, Auschwitz was 'revealed'/envisioned as a site which would have to accommodate up to 100,000 Russian POWs. While the mortality rate was already quite high due to the appalling conditions and the ravages of disease in such a festering cesspit, a more reliably systematic mortal intervention was required. At the same time, plans were already taking shape to begin the extermination of Jews from all German territories, which in effect meant all of Europe since Germany's expansionist plans seemed to account for the entire continent, with estimations of the number of Jews in all European countries to be covered by the terms of the Final Solution already made available for the Wannsee Conference in 1942.

Camp Commander Fritzsch, acting on a hunch, decided one day to experiment with the pesticide Zyklon B (which the camps had in copious supply for the purposes of delousing and fumigating premises) in an attempt to efficiently dispose of a number of Russian POWs:[24]

> While I [Höss] was on an official trip, my second in command, Camp Commander Fritzsch, experimented with gas for these killings. He used a gas called Cyclon B, prussic acid, which was often used as an insecticide in the camp to exterminate lice and vermin. There was always a supply on hand. When I returned Fritzsch reported to me about how he had used the gas. We used it again to kill the next transport. The gassing was carried out in the basement of Block 11. I viewed the killings wearing a gas mask for protection. Death occurred in the crammed-full cells immediately after the gas was thrown in. Only a brief choking outcry and it was all over. The first gassing of people did not really sink into my mind. Perhaps I was much too impressed by the whole procedure … At the time I really didn't waste any thoughts about the killing of the Russian POWs. It was ordered; I had to carry it out. But I must admit openly that the gassings had a calming effect on me, since in the near future the mass annihilation of the Jews was to begin. Up to that point it was not clear to me, nor to Eichmann, how the killing of the expected masses was to be done. Perhaps by gas? But how, and what kind of gas? Now we had discovered the gas and the procedure.[25]

After a period of time, in a sealed chamber, and with sufficient tinkering with the amount of Zyklon B needed, Fritzsch determined that they could successfully kill a whole roomful of people more or less 'effortlessly'. These prisoners were 'revealed', even to this relative nobody within the regime, in such a way that they were 'vermin' to be disposed of – no differently to pests or vermin at a factory complex; they were revealed to him as a 'problem' which he and others needed to 'solve'. Why else would it even occur to this military man to experiment with the canisters of powder (which had an entirely different function) in such a way? Of course, one might rejoin, and they would be justified to an extent, that this accounts only for the *how* of the killing; what is not as clear is why these people would have appeared to Fritzsch as non-people.

Having said as much, it seems clear that, in the age of Enframing, people seem more and more amenable to the possibility of looking on other people as nothing more than resources to be used or waste to be disposed of. What's more, we can see again from this 'discovery', as recounted by Höss, that the primary considerations were efficiency and productivity which were to be maximized; they wished to make the process as 'straightforward' and stress-free as possible for both the executioner and those 'marked' by the Nazi regime for death:

> Now I was at ease. We were all saved from these bloodbaths, and the victims would be spared until the last moment. This is what I worried about the most when I thought of Eichmann's accounts of the mowing down of the Jews with machine guns and pistols by the Einsatzgruppe. Horrible scenes were supposed to have occurred: people running away even after being shot, the killing of those who were only wounded, especially the women and children. Another thing on my mind was the many suicides among the ranks of the SS Special Action Squads who could no longer mentally endure wading in the bloodbath. Some of them went mad. Most of the members of the Special Action Squads drank a great deal to help get through this horrible work.[26]

The other major consideration was of course the disposal of the corpses which would now tax the camp's resources more than ever before. Due to the high mortality rates at many of these installations, a number of systems were already in place for the disposal of bodies including mass graves, open pit burnings and crematoria. Eventually, when the Final Solution was at full tilt, so to speak, it became clear that the burning of the bodies in furnaces reducing them to ash was the obvious solution. To this end, Topf & Sons and other manufacturing firms vigorously lobbied for lucrative contracts for the numerous furnaces with nauseating rapacity. Indeed as one reads some of the correspondence between Topf & Sons' chief engineer, Kurt Prüfer, and Nazi officials such as Karl Bischoff, one cannot help but be astounded by the sheer scale of their objectives – as they blithely discuss the need for greater productivity to be achieved by larger ovens with increased capacity. And, as one scans the figures, one realizes that once the genocidal juggernaut was in top gear, the only real considerations for these people revolved around efficiency and productivity:

> On 22nd October Prüfer met the new head of the Bauleitung ('Construction Management') at Auschwitz, SS Captain Karl Bischoff. The SS wanted to build another crematorium in the camp, considering that Krematorium I, even with 6 muffles, would soon reach saturation point. Bischoff was well-placed to know this because he had been posted to Auschwitz to build a POW camp [KGL] (for Russian prisoners) to hold 125,000 men. The site chosen was Birkenau, flat land, but marshy and therefore requiring drainage. The working conditions and then living conditions were terrible and were to remain so. The result was an extremely high mortality rate, which required a modern and efficient crematorium. Bischoff was not yet sure where the new crematorium would be located, but in his conversation with Prüfer it was to be in the main camp. On 30th October, it was included in the estimates for the POW camp, at Birkenau. Wherever the location was to

be, Prüfer could hardly believe his ears, for Bischoff was thinking big, very big. And Prüfer, encouraging him in this direction, was reflecting and calculating. The result of this conversation was agreement on a project for a crematorium with five three-muffle furnaces, fed by two big underground morgues. In addition there was to be a single-muffle waste incinerator. The cremation capacity envisaged was 60 corpses per hour, or a throughput of 1,440 in 24 hours. The expected cost of the entire building was 650.000 RM and the minimum Topf could expect would be 5 three-muffle furnaces at 12,000 RM each, making 60.000 RM, to say nothing of the waste incinerator worth about 5,800 RM and the sundry other supplies [in fact Topf received a total of 110,000 RM for their installations in Krematorium II as the 'new Krematorium' came to be designated]. It is quite likely that at this date Prüfer had not even designed the three-muffle furnace yet. But he set to work the moment he got back to Erfurt.[27]

Höss himself outlines the 'productivity' of the camps and their optimum efficiency in the most alarmingly detached manner:

> The two smaller crematories [IV and V] were capable of burning about 1,500 bodies in twenty-four hours, according to the calculations made by the construction company called Topf of Erfurt. Because of the wartime shortage of materials, the builders were forced to economize during the construction of Crematories [IV and V]. They were built above ground and the ovens were not as solidly constructed. It soon became apparent however, that the poor construction of these two ovens, each with four retorts, did not meet the requirements ... [Gas Chamber] II [the white farmhouse], later designated Bunker V, was used up until the last and was also kept as a standby when breakdowns occurred in Crematories [II or III]. When larger numbers of transports were received, the gassing was carried out by day in Crematory V, while Crematories I to IV were used for the transports that arrived during the night. There was no limit to the number of bodies that could be burned at [the white farmhouse] as long as the cremations could be carried out both day and night. Because of the enemy air raids, no further cremations were allowed during the night after 1944. The highest total figure of people gassed and cremated in twenty-four hours was slightly more than nine thousand. This figure was reached in the summer of 1944, during the action in Hungary, using all the installations except Crematory [IV]. On that day five trains arrived because of delays on the rail lines, instead of three, as was expected, and in addition the railroad cars were more crowded than usual.[28]

The more we read and hear about the concentration camps and the Final Solution, the more we begin to appreciate the aptness of the characterization 'factories of death'. These houses of horror functioned with industrial efficiency. There was a highly organized, mechanized approach; the objectives were achieved with a mechanical level of precision. In the same way that factories began to organize the various stages of manufacture such that each component was built and assembled quickly and discretely at one station before being conveyed along to the next station for the subsequent stage in a manufacturing process, so these people were conveyed along through a 'process' which involved, but did not culminate, in terms of the 'process', in their death (not unlike the 'processing' of animals on factory farms today). From first being designated as one among a number on a page for 'relocation', to being herded onto cattle-cars, sent by train to the ramps at Auschwitz, corralled into an undressing area, all the while being calmed and reassured by a carefully choreographed routine acted out by the *Sonderkommando* and guards – they were finally ushered into gas chambers before being poisoned to death. But that did not signal the end of the 'process'; once the chambers were opened, heads were shaved and hair collected, mouths were checked for gold fillings and false teeth which were duly removed – much of the gold eventually finding its way back to bank vaults in Berlin after being melted down. Clothing was gathered up and sent to 'Canada' where it was searched for valuables and cash.[29] It was quite the bounty, by all accounts, and corruption and theft were rife, regardless of the stiff punitive measures in place for such transgressions. The now lifeless vessels that had been transported from all corners of the continent for this singular purpose finally reached their terminus – stacked before the oven doors, then loaded onto retractable trays which fed the ovens designed and built by Topf & Sons. These ovens were specially designed to meet the new consumptive demands of the Final Solution by Topf & Sons' chief engineer, Prüfer; the corpses of the recently murdered innocents were reduced to ash at an average rate of 60 corpses per hour!

## But where have we strayed to?

In part, Heidegger's unusual remark, which we choose to read as an epigraph to his meditation on the essence of technology, illuminates the manner in which we interpret or reveal the world. Heidegger's account of technology's essence does not so much show that there are no differences between factory farms and gas chambers. Of course there are differences! But with that we cannot scream 'blasphemy' at anyone who suggests that there are discomfiting similarities as well. What Heidegger's account suggests, I would submit, is that part of what made factory farms, atomic bombs and extermination camps possible is a particularly and oppressively dominant interpretative gaze which reduces everything to the level of atom, stock, resource. What makes the term 'Final Solution' most worrisome, then, is the fact that it is *not* the exclusive language of a roomful of diabolical architects of evil, but rather that it betokens a tendency to 'reveal' the world and people through the lens of Enframing as resource, stock, number, cog, commodity and, indeed, in terms of a 'problem' to be 'solved', as, finally, 'waste'.

Of course, that is not at all to suggest that Heidegger's analysis of modern technology's essence is 'sufficient'! We are not suddenly divested of our need to deal with this appalling episode in our shared European history. The Holocaust is a trauma and a crime which needs to be commemorated, discussed and understood; but that is not to say that imbuing the event with an air of rarified religiosity or singularizing it is the way to proceed. We must be able to compare this event and treat it historically. Notwithstanding, as we consider how people began to conceive of the world (and people in it) in technological ways and how the world was revealed to them as such, we cannot suddenly abandon the question as to *why* people would actively pursue a policy of genocide. Understanding the revealing at work in the technological world tells us a lot about the 'how' but less about the 'why'! And while I cannot agree with the strategy and foundational premises of Goldhagen's hugely controversial book, he is right about one thing: we cannot simply explain away the complicity of hundreds of thousands of men and women. Inveterate antisemitism clearly did exist in Germany and it played an undeniable role in facilitating the plans for and indeed the implementation of the Final Solution. That being said, xenophobia remains a problem in many countries around the world and it has been a prevailing issue that litters the pages of our history books and yet not all of these problems lead to genocide and certainly none have ever led to the level of mass extermination which took place under Nazi rule. Xenophobia on its own then, doesn't really account for the Holocaust! Neither, however, will an account of the revelatory ordinances of the essence of technology do the trick; that account doesn't tell us *why* one group of people came to look on another group of people as no-longer-people. Coming to grips with the problem of discrimination and the concomitant failure in terms of empathy and recognition, remains a problem, even if we do begin to get some sense of how we tend to reduce everything in the world to problems to be solved through technological means. The question of how we come to look on other people as vermin, after all, is not answered by Heidegger's discussion of technology's essence; rather it sheds some light on *how* people have disposed of the same 'problems' in the technological 'age'.

So, we must dispel the myth that Heidegger is saying that there is no difference between the mass production of crops or meat and the systematic extermination of millions of people! He insists that they are the same thing 'in essence'. Heidegger suggests that the essence of technology is nothing technological. He is critical of the traditional concept of essence. For Heidegger, the essence of something is what holds sway within it such that it appears *as* what it is. Heidegger believes that the mechanized food industry, the Holocaust, the splitting of the atom, nuclear bombs, have as their common feature a technological backdrop. That is, regardless of the moral status of what happens or is done, they involve a *technological way of revealing* the world, or people or energy or animals. That is not to say that Heidegger is morally equating the consumption of animals with genocide.[30] What he is saying, I would submit, is that the essence of technology, *Gestell*, holds sway as what is common in their approach to situations which we would *never* have conceived of in that way before. They indicate a mode of revealing the world or people or animals hitherto unimaginable. The fact that we were able to 'reveal' a *people*, in this instance 'the Jews', in such a way, might well be more morally repugnant than any of the other examples mentioned. But there is also something terribly sinister in looking for solutions to military problems through the unleashing of nature's stored up and harnessed power and thereby eradicating entire cities. The mass production of meat itself represents a change in the way we look at animals and their habitats. The point is that all of them have at their core a way of revealing the world which Heidegger is trying to call attention to. It is not a moral judgment to the effect that there are no qualitative differences. He is drawing attention to the fact that each of them involves a very specific and disturbing way of *revealing*.

Moreover, *failure* to reflect on how they each share this manner or way of challenging revealing may itself condemn us to a fate that *does* indeed 'compel'. By the time of his posthumously published interview with *Der Spiegel*, one can almost get the sense that Heidegger believes that while there is always hope, it is diminishing all the time; we are enveloped by the extreme danger since we cannot seem to extricate ourselves from this inadvertent and automatic reductive ordering and levelling of everything in the world to calculable resource or waste to be used or disposed of. Heidegger is not so much looking to diminish the undeniable inhumanity of simply erasing from existence vast numbers of people with staggering efficiency, nor is he comparing the moral weight of that atrocity with what happens in an abattoir, or the events at Hiroshima or Nagasaki. Rather what he is drawing attention to is the way that we take a levelling gaze to all of these situations which points to something extremely disturbing. We reduce them down to problems to be solved; we treat everything as calculable resource or obstacles to be efficiently dealt with. Helping us to see that this very way of *revealing* the world and others around us stands as a very immediate underlying problem is, for Heidegger, one of the most pressing tasks. After all, many people will continue to eat meat, ethnic conflict will continue to emerge as will conflicts between nations. For Heidegger, there is an important question as to how we approach these situations, which in turn requires that we reflect on how we have come to view the world around us along with those in it. 'War', 'conflict', 'bombing raids', 'xenophobia', 'genocide' ... these words are hardly archaic – they are common enough in our daily news. More recently the euphemized language of military conflict (with casualties calculated to within acceptable limits and the frequently employed, yet no less dreadful, phrase 'collateral damage') should strike us as impossibly sinister. 'Calculated' and 'acceptable' losses – such rhetoric begins to smack of a certain ruthlessly mercantile idiom – for example, how many items in a given batch will typically perish before reaching the shelves; what kind of losses and bad debts can be brooked as part of a larger business plan? The parallels proliferate more and more since the lens with which we routinely filter the world and people around us is quite close to that described by Heidegger. When it comes to the Holocaust we are all shocked by the cold, desensitized industrial-speak employed by those who either conceived of or ran the factories of death where people were treated much as animals are on factory farms today, or perhaps as little more than industrial waste, as either resources to be used or waste to be disposed of. That human beings could even begin to conceive of an entire race of fellow creatures in those kinds of terms required that they look through an interpretative lens which Heidegger believed was fast becoming the dominant one throughout the world. If we want to progress past the mythical characterizations of the Nazi regime and the Holocaust and to begin to reduce the risk of history 'repeating' itself, then we need to come to terms with how it is that human beings can reveal themselves, the world and others in the ways that we have done since the early part of the twentieth century. The Holocaust should be understood as the zenith of Enframing's holding sway, not as a singularity beyond compare that was perpetrated by those who were not 'like' us!

Of course, as Lacoue-Labarthe has remarked on a few occasions, there is a scandal! It 'leaps out at you',[31] so to speak. The scandal concerns the 'refusal', the refusal to simply break down at the absolute *in*humanity of what happened as a result of a hideous, nightmarish vision of a people. A vision that, almost as an expression of the 'danger' Heidegger warns against, can actually look on a people as a 'problem', the Jewish problem, and come up with a 'solution', the Final Solution. This devastating 'solution' may well articulate the *Gestell* that holds sway as the most extreme danger of the essence of technology. But why not shed a tear at it all? Why not show the world that he was, after all, not just a thinker but an emotively engaged human being, moved like the rest of us? These are difficult and uncomfortable questions, and yet, *philosophically*, they don't really do a whole lot!

Heidegger's brief remarks concerning the Holocaust itself, in the context of his comprehensive meditation on the essence of technology, *can* however serve as cautions against what has happened, against the historical palliative we have swallowed. His remarks are not intended, in my view, to diminish the horror of the Holocaust but more to show that *part* of the horror is something that transcends the boundary fences at Auschwitz, something that lingers on in our atmosphere long after the languorous legions of liquidated lives rising from the chimney stacks of the crematoria have dissipated. And the danger, the very real danger, is that if we do not see how such intolerable cruelty *can* happen again, if we treat the Holocaust and Nazi rule as the kind of singular aberration which emerges from out of nowhere human, then we are indeed condemned to repeat such 'pasts' until such time as we 'confess' their origin in the way we have looked and do look on the world and each other. Might we not argue then, admittedly with Heidegger to an extent, that the Holocaust, far from being different in *kind*, far from having a different, singular 'essence', was to the most extreme degree imaginable, the very quintessence of how we had begun to 'reveal' large numbers of people, entire races, as 'problems' that admitted of 'solution', in this instance, a solution through dissolution? Can we not say that the Holocaust was in fact the purest and, in that sense, the most grotesquely vivid expression of the extreme danger of *Gestell*? That is not, however, to look to exculpate Heidegger and his thought; that would be to misunderstand the aim of this study. Rather, in looking to unravel this Gordian knot which cannot be chopped clean through we need to undermine the criticisms of Heidegger's philosophy that are wide of the mark. That is not to say that Heidegger's philosophy is only tangentially relevant to his political views, rather, the most distressing aspects of his political views are related to other aspects of his thought initially presented in *Being and Time*.

# 3

# Heidegger's 'Heritage': Philosophy, Anti-Modernism and Cultural Pessimism

*That Rickert and Frege associated with DPG and that, in their final years, they leaned to the political views of the extreme right, is important on other grounds, however. It has often been said that right-wing politics in Germany after the First World War was the product of a general hostility to reason and that it was associated with irrationalism in philosophy. This irrationalism has also frequently been considered the essential link between Heidegger's philosophy and his politics. It is certainly true that Heidegger criticized rationalism and that he subjected appeals to reason to withering attacks (though he always added that he was not an irrationalist). But these facts are insufficient for establishing an intrinsic connection between irrationalism, on the one hand, and right-wing and Nazi political views, on the other. The assumption of such a link may be refuted by the cases of Rickert and Frege. Though both men joined the DPG and subscribed to its political program, they also believed in the power of reason and strove to apply it in their philosophical work. Frege and Rickert were, moreover, by no means singular. Other German philosophers, such as Bausch, Hartmann, and Gehlen, similarly believed in science and reason and rejected the criticisms of philosophical antirationalists like Heidegger; at the same time they committed themselves to Nazi beliefs. Analyses that are based on the assumption of an intrinsic connection between irrationalism and National Socialism fall short of the mark because they explain little.*[1]

Much has been made of the tenor of Heidegger's rhetoric in the 1930s in particular. In many cases rather less than level-headed critics end up taking some of Heidegger's more inflammatory iterations as an excuse to tar the entire corpus with an unctuous layer of heavily nationalist, conservative revolutionary or even Nazi pitch. An indication that the preponderance of these discussions have wandered down the garden-paths of intellectual gossip, guilt by association and innuendo is the fact that so many sensational anecdotes are interspersed through these rants masquerading as proof or evidence. There is little question but that Heidegger's philosophy is influenced by its historical context, indeed, Heidegger himself would acknowledge this quicker than most. Nevertheless, Heidegger's titanic intellectual travails no more reduce to the crude jingoism of National Socialism than Aristotle's science of human affairs reduces to the martial aspirations of Alexander. Neither can Heidegger's philosophy be straightforwardly reduced to the work of the conservative revolutionaries!

There is a regrettable paucity of comprehensive *philosophical* attempts to tackle seriously the question of the intellectual, cultural and political milieu from which Heidegger emerged with a view to identifying some, at least, of the inspiration for and influences on some of his most important philosophical insights concerning technology, politics or indeed, modernity in general. Some might counter, of course, that Zimmerman's well-known study (*Heidegger's Confrontation with Modernity, Technology, Politics, Art*) serves such a purpose. However Zimmerman is frequently guilty of errant reasoning, buttressing much of his study with non-sequiturs and instances of the genetic fallacy.[2] Another attempt to situate Heidegger's philosophical corpus in some kind of intellectual and historical context was produced by Richard Wolin in *The Politics of Being*. Pierre Bourdieu and Lacoue-Labarthe also weighed in on the 'debate' at different times but all of these studies are laced with and indeed often hamstrung by a series of prejudices and interpretative handicaps. The problem with Wolin's work, for example, is that he hawks a somewhat undercooked Habermasian critique of Heidegger's thought oblivious to the fact that even the fully cooked dish served up by the Head-Chef himself has failed to cut any mustard with serious scholars of Heidegger's work. Wolin is an eloquent writer with an impressive grasp of the intellectual and political landscape of twentieth-century Europe; notwithstanding, he simply has an insufficient grasp of Heidegger's philosophy, relying excessively instead on a watered-down version *a la* Habermas and *that*, quite simply, is a recipe for an intellectual disaster. Other studies come to mind; Hans Sluga's book (*Heidegger's Crisis*) is well researched and interesting but it is not looking to deal with the problems that this study confronts while Charles Bambach's useful work in *Heidegger's Roots* simply overplays the strengths of its most important analyses by trying to prove that absolutely *everything* that Heidegger said and wrote reduces to his political obsession with rootedness and the concomitant intellectual and cultural heritage which he traces as a source for that motivation.

The aim in this chapter then is to examine the work of some of Heidegger's contemporaries, in particular, feted champions of the German Conservative Revolutionary movement; a movement, moreover, that was suffused with metaphors and rhetoric which Heidegger frequently borrowed. However, we shall then attempt to demonstrate the philosophical distance between these various figures (some of whom Heidegger counted among his friends)[3] and Heidegger's own work, thereby undermining the foundational premises of critics such as Adorno, Bourdieu, Wolin and Habermas concerning the 'generic' nature of Heidegger's 'early' thought.

As we begin this part of our investigation, it is crucial to bear one important fact in mind; Heidegger, more than anyone, wore his philosophical influences on his sleeve and, indeed, deliberately embroidered those voices, influences and tropes through his work. In doing so, Heidegger is remaining true to his hermeneutic convictions, as evidenced in *Being and Time*, and which he reaffirmed throughout his career. No one, least of all Heidegger, emerges from a vacuum – cultural, intellectual, historical, what have you. In his work, Heidegger self-consciously tries to demonstrate what is often unique in his vision while dealing with elements of his background, research and training which collectively shaped the way he responded to his situation. However, in the frenzied enthusiasm with which critics of Heidegger myopically trawl through his writings, gleefully netting tropes and motifs which evoke other thinkers and ideas, they rashly conclude that Heidegger's work ultimately reduces to nothing more than the reproduction of the same ideas, albeit in his own unique philosophical idiom. On the one hand then, Heidegger is credited with having identified the importance of context and history when it comes to understanding the nature of interpretation and yet at the same time he is seen as being incapable of any originality for the very same reasons. Once again, such strategies serve to conceal more than they reveal since Heidegger can easily be defended against such crudely formulated criticisms. The philosophical poverty of such approaches becomes all the more ironic as the explicit evidence that demonstrates the extent to which Heidegger committed himself to National Socialism continues to be discovered in recently published texts. And that same poverty is lamentable in that it fails to see that there are some genuinely problematic aspirations lurking in Heidegger's more important texts (which are rashly glossed by his critics) that dovetail at significant junctures with some of his most controversial claims concerning *das Volk* and rootedness (*Bodenständigkeit*). We will examine these substantive philosophical issues in Chapters 4 and 5.

\*\*\*\*

One of the issues that tends to jar readers and students of Heidegger, particularly those who profess to having been one-time enthusiasts when it comes to his criticisms of modernity (and technology/technicity in particular) is the apparent proximity of that work to the cultural pessimist/anti-modernist/conservative revolutionary rhetorical backdrop which they are sometimes less familiar with. I myself remember vividly the extraordinary impact which Heidegger's famous essay on the essence of technology had on me as a somewhat impressionable philosophy undergraduate. The novelty of Heidegger's approach, the perspicacity of the indictment of the technological mindset, the power of the insights concerning the alarming and dangerously insidious way that technology had infiltrated every level of our existence was not so much a breath of fresh air as a gale that blew through the cobwebbed cupboards of my intellectual indolence. In time I began to develop an appreciation for the philosophically intricate architecture of the essay, but that did not diminish the power of the surface rhetoric and ideas which had made such a profound impression on me as a young student.

One can imagine my dismay then when my attention was drawn to Jünger and his discussion of total mobilization and Spengler's critique of technicity; I was initially persuaded by the assessment of Habermas, for example, who gets considerable philosophical 'mileage' out of these associations, connections and resonances. Habermas dismisses Heidegger's confrontation with technology as little more than an all-too-familiar cultural pessimism and anti-modernism, typical of a class of German post-First World War 'mandarins'.[4] It is a recurring problem with critics of Heidegger: they point to overlaps between predecessors of Heidegger and some of Heidegger's own work and then suggest that what was putatively original in Heidegger's work, what strikes many as incomparably unique, is after all, nothing more than the discredited views of others repackaged in an abstruse prose. And this, of course, is the giant non-sequitur which Habermas, Adorno, Wolin, Bourdieu, Farias and Faye would have us swallow, albeit in a variety of dishes and seasoned according to their own prejudices. In short, according to these critics, because there are traces of other ideas and other movements in Heidegger's work, Heidegger's philosophy reduces to nothing more than a recapitulation of those same ideas and philosophical views!

## Adorno and the 'jargon' of German authenticity

The excessively polemical and often rash nature of Habermas's assessment of Heidegger's philosophy is consistent with a disappointing lack of genuine philosophical engagement not least as part of the invective levelled against Heidegger's criticisms of technicity.[5] As it turns out, Habermas's offhand dismissals of Heidegger's critical encounter with technology bear a strong resemblance to the various denunciations one discovers in the work of Adorno. Adorno is deeply suspicious of Heidegger's rhetoric and sees it as, fundamentally, of a piece with the jargon of authenticity which permeated German cultural and intellectual life. Habermas's criticisms to the effect that Heidegger's negative views regarding technology were derivative of a certain attitude specific to a class of 'German mandarins' then are clearly of a piece with Adorno's assessment. One finds comments very much to that effect, identical even in tone, throughout *The Jargon of Authenticity*. We have to conclude then that Habermas's own criticisms are disappointingly derivative in this regard, not only because they are variations on an earlier theme, but because they are variations on claims with little in the way of philosophical substance to begin with. Adorno may well have had sophisticated philosophical refutations of Heidegger cached away in his intellectual armoury, indeed, he confidently prophesied, according to Heidegger, that he would single-handedly destroy Heidegger's philosophical reputation inside five years.[6] And while his conspicuous failure to achieve this objective has no bearing on the merits (or lack thereof) of the arguments designed to accomplish as much, the arguments that he does in fact provide (if one can call them that) must be subjected to scrutiny.

*The Jargon of Authenticity*, among other things, is written as a sustained rejoinder to Heidegger's rhetoric of authenticity. And yet, in terms of the expected refutation of Heidegger's account of authenticity, the book is all bluster and style with little substance. Adorno's great weapon in his 'war' against Heidegger, as it turns out, is not to be found in his 'arguments' (one rarely finds any), rather Adorno's strength resides in his stunning rhetorical abilities. Interesting and eloquent as his forays may be, however, they don't offer much in the way of substantive criticism of Heidegger. Adorno's guerrilla tactics founder against the walls of the Heideggerian fortress and rarely, if ever, suggest even the merest breach. For our purposes, we find that Adorno's ambushes rely on the very tactics later employed by the likes of Steiner and Bourdieu, who, similarly, reduce some of Heidegger's most important notions to the anti-modernism of these same German mandarins invoked by Habermas in his polemic. For example, Adorno addresses something that Steiner has a similar gripe with in his well-known, and disappointingly jaundiced, introduction to Heidegger;[7] both are critical of what they see as an excessively romantic tendency in Heidegger's 'critique' of the modern technological world. For Steiner, Heidegger is a thoroughgoing agrarian and his views are excessively coloured by his obsession with the virtues of a peasant's life in the yawning shadows of forests and mountains. And, of course, when one reads Heidegger's account of his decision not to take the chair of philosophy in Berlin and the peasant's steadying embrace and a solemn stare that silently conveyed to him what the 'authentic' path was, one can of course see where Adorno and Steiner were coming from.[8] Notwithstanding, Heidegger's seminal meditation on the essence of technology is not somehow rendered ridiculous by such pretentious flourishes and gestures which Adorno dismisses as a kind of peasant kitsch.

In Adorno we find a surfeit of examples of shameless bandwagoning as he gleefully upbraids Heidegger's posturing. Take, for example, his quick aside upon quoting Heidegger himself in this context:

> 'And philosophical work does not take place as the spare-time activity of a crank. It belongs in the midst of the labor of farmers.' One would like at least to know the farmers' opinion about that.[9]

The problem with this kind of jibe, clever though it may be, is that it is nothing more than intellectual frivolity. These incessant attempts to win the imagined gallery have, in the end, nothing to recommend them in terms of philosophical merit. They are self-indulgent and irresponsible. Indeed Adorno's whole account of Heidegger's decision not to accept a chair of philosophy in Berlin, which admittedly provided the occasion for some rather farcical posturing on Heidegger's part, is recapitulated with all the unflinching acerbity of a comic but then left to stand as though it were representative of the deepest essence of Heidegger's confrontation with technology:

> His reflected unreflectiveness degenerates into chummy chit-chat, for the sake of the rural setting with which he wants to stand on a confidential footing. The description of the old farmer reminds us of the most washed-out clichés in plough-and-furrow novels, from the region of a Fressen; and it reminds us equally of the praise of being silent, which the philosopher authorizes not only for his farmers but also for himself.[10]

The problem in all of these cases, and even to a lesser degree in the more sober efforts of someone like Zimmerman, is clear enough; in identifying certain resonances between Heidegger's bucolic proclivities and the anti-modern cultural pessimism endemic to his German contemporaries, these critics take the further step of supposing that Heidegger's philosophy is nothing more than the reproduction of those same resonances, themes and ideas.

Neither is Adorno above the *ad hominem* attack. Indeed, he routinely cites Heidegger's provinciality and associated cultural attitudes and prejudices as being the ultimate catalysts for his philosophical positions:

> Whoever is forced by the nature of his work to stay in one place, gladly makes a virtue out of necessity. He tries to convince himself and others that his boundness is of a higher order. The financially threatened farmer's bad experiences

with middlemen substantiate this opinion. The socially clumsy person who may be partially excluded from society hates those middlemen as jacks of all trades. This hatred joins with resistance against all agents, from the cattle dealer to the journalist. In 1956 the stable professions, which are themselves a stage of social development, are still the norms for Heidegger. He praises them in the name of a false eternity of agrarian conditions: "Man tries in vain to bring the globe to order through planning, when he is not in tune with the consoling voice of the country lane."[11]

Again, this is a strategy which is all too common with critics of Heidegger; because some of his rhetoric smacks at some level of a kind of an anti-modernism which they associate with German conservative revolutionary views which in turn are seen as an obvious precursor to Nazism, they merely assume the offensiveness of the ideas Heidegger is trying to peddle. And, in a way, they do themselves a disservice since Heidegger's onslaught against modernity is genuinely flawed for a number of reasons which we will examine closely in the chapters that follow. However, to suppose that these are just the ravings of a German mandarin, or worse, some deluded Nazi hack, misses again the real problem we have to face and it is certainly easy enough to show how Heidegger's thought does not reduce to such a crass ideology.

There is no question that Adorno catches a whiff of something that's 'off' in Heidegger's rhetoric and, like so many of his contemporaries, is painfully sensitive to any association with the Blubo rhetoric of the day which Heidegger sutured onto his philosophy at different junctures. However, Adorno bases his analyses of Heidegger's highly questionable invocation of rootedness on the relatively unimportant and slightly pathetic paean to provincialism that is his radio address. That being so, he does identify one line in that piece which relates to a problem which we will examine in the context of Heidegger's philosophical writings concerning the authentic Dasein of a people and his concomitant conceptions of history, art and truth: 'One's own work's inner belonging, to the Black Forest and its people, comes from a century-long Germanic-Swabian rootedness, which is irreplaceable.'[12] Adorno could have developed a line of criticism here and related it to key aspects of Heidegger's philosophy. Alas, he fails to do so, and contents himself instead with *ad hominem* attacks and further examples of the genetic fallacy which Heidegger can all too easily be defended against.

## Bourdieu and Heidegger's ontological politics

We have two important sources concerning Bourdieu's assessment of Heidegger's philosophy and the discomfiting issue of the relationship between that philosophy and his political activities in the 1930s.[13] Given the rather jaundiced views of Bourdieu as we find them in his interview and the basic premise underlying his approach to the question, it is quite surprising that he took the trouble to write a book on the issue at all since his basic point in the interview amounts to the rather uninspired claim that Heidegger's philosophy is essentially a repackaging of the reactionary, anti-modern, conservative nationalism of his day, albeit cloaked in an almost impenetrable language.

However, if that is the ultimate measure of Heidegger's philosophical achievement, then the question of Heidegger's political allegiances is more or less irrelevant.

In Bourdieu's well-known book, he looks to situate Heidegger's philosophy such that his 'ontological politics' in the 1930s are perfectly consistent with and emerge rather predictably from the views he had been developing in the melting pot of cultural pessimism and a conservative revolutionary mindset which he would have been stewing in since his teens:

> Heidegger is close to the spokesmen of the 'conservative revolution', many of whose words and theses he consecrates philosophically, but he distances himself from it by inserting them in the network of phonetic and semantic resonance which characterizes the Hölderlin-style *Begriffsdichtung* of the academic prophet. All of which situates him at the antipodes of the classical academic style, with its several varieties of frigid rigour, whether elegant and transparent in Cassirer, or tortured and obscure in Husserl.[14]

Bourdieu explicitly describes Heidegger then as 'a conservative revolutionary in philosophy', something which is overly reductive and simplistic on our reading. Heidegger simply does not reduce to or overlap with Jünger or Spengler, for example, as readily as Bourdieu would have us believe, regardless of how many times he reminds us of the high esteem in which Heidegger held *Der Arbeiter*. It simply is not sufficient to try and reduce philosophical texts to biography, sociology or psychology and Bourdieu is inclined to shift between these registers as though he is fully entitled to do as much stating rather than demonstrating that

> There is no philosophical option – neither one that promotes intuition, for instance, nor, at the other extreme, one that favours judgement or concepts, nor yet one that gives precedence to the Transcendental Aesthetic over the Transcendental Analytic, or poetry over discursive language – which does not entail its concomitant academic and political options, and which does not owe to these secondary, more or less unconsciously assumed options, some of its deepest determinations.[15]

Bourdieu is completely subservient to his sociology of knowledge in this regard; it is also worth remarking that Bourdieu uses the very term (again pejoratively) to characterize Heidegger's criticism of twentieth century publicness and technology that we find in Habermas's summary dismissal (i.e. Mandarin):

> The opposition between *Eigentlichkeit*, 'authenticity', and *Uneigentlichkeit*, 'inauthenticity', those 'primordial modes of Being-there', as Heidegger says, around which the whole work is organized (even from the viewpoint of the most strictly internal readings), is a particular and particularly subtle retranslation of the common opposition between the 'elite' and the 'masses'. 'They', (*Das Man*, literally 'one') are tyrannical ('the real dictatorship of the 'they'), inquisitorial ('they keep watch over everything'), and reduce everything to the lowest level, the universal 'they' evade their responsibilities, opt out of their liberty: they live on 'procured' assistance, fecklessly depending on society or the 'Welfare State' which, especially

through 'social assistance' (*Sozialfuersorge*), looks after them and cares for their future on their behalf. One could list the commonplaces of academic aristocratism which recur throughout this oft-commented passage, replete with topoi on the agora as an antithesis of the *schole*, leisure versus school. There is a hatred of statistics (harping on the theme of the 'average') seen as a symbol of all the operations of 'levelling down' which threaten the 'person' (here called *Dasein*) and its most precious attributes, its 'originality' and its 'privacy'. There is a contempt for all forces which 'level down', doubtless with a particular disgust for egalitarian ideologies which endanger 'everything gained by a struggle', meaning culture (the specific capital of the mandarin, who is the son of his works), ideologies which encourage the masses to 'take things easily and make them easy'. There is also a revolt against social mechanisms such as those of opinion, the hereditary enemy of the philosopher, which recurs here through the play on *Öffentlichkeit* and *Öffentlich*, 'public opinion' and 'public', and against anything symbolizing 'social assistance', that is democracy, political parties, paid holidays (as a breach in the monopoly of the *schole* and meditation in the forest), 'culture for the masses', television, and Plato in paperback. Heidegger was to say this so much better, in his inimitable *pastoral* style, when, in his *Introduction to Metaphysics*, written in 1935, he set out to show how the triumph of the scientific-technological spirit in Western civilization is accomplished and perfected in the 'flight of the gods, the destruction of the earth, the transformation of men into a mass, the hatred and suspicion of everything free and creative' ...[16]

On the one hand, this simply parrots Adorno's heavy-handed derision of Heidegger, and indeed we find versions of the same criticism in Habermas, Steiner and Wolin too. And yet, Bourdieu thinks this kind of superficial reductionism is proof positive of the cogency of his story concerning the sociology of knowledge. One wonders, however, if Bourdieu's claim isn't staggeringly arrogant in its scope, since there seems to be little reason to suppose that his claims can be restricted to Heidegger, and, if they are not, then Bourdieu's position amounts to a rejection of the possibility of doing philosophy at all which is not a claim that warrants serious consideration. One might well ask why Bourdieu's own analyses are impervious to the historicizing and contextualizing he insists upon in terms of dismissing Heidegger's thought as simply the by-product of a series of cultural, political and historical features beyond his control? Bourdieu consolidates his own hermeneutic prejudices with a lofty summary and dismissal of Heidegger and his thought in the final lines of his text as follows:

> It is perhaps because he never realized what he was saying that Heidegger was able to say what he did say without really having to say it. And it is perhaps for the same reason that he refused to the very end to discuss his Nazi involvement: to do it properly would have been to admit (to himself as well as others) that his 'essentialist thought' had never consciously formulated its essence, that is, the social unconscious which spoke through its forms, and the crudely 'anthropological' basis of its extreme blindness, which could only be sustained by the illusion of the omnipotence of thought.[17]

Again, to recapitulate a variant of Lyotard's perspicacious insight, if Bourdieu's assessment is correct, then there really is no Heidegger controversy since we are not dealing with an important thinker and certainly nothing of philosophical substance is to be found in his thought. Or to put things somewhat differently, we are dealing with a very *different* controversy (which may interest some people), that is, the possibility that those of us who have been labouring away on Heidegger's thought for so many years have been on something of a fool's errand. Of course that is what some people would have us believe but it is not, I contend, the real issue that should animate people who become interested in this topic only to be dragged into the mudslinging that dominates the recurring 'controversy' which is really just a flimsy front for the ongoing hostilities between so-called analytic and continental philosophers.

## Zimmerman and the 'influence' of Spengler

In *Heidegger's Confrontation with Modernity*, Michael Zimmerman examines the development of Heidegger's thought through the 1930s, including the emergence of his critique of technicity, in the light of various intellectual, political and cultural factors that appear, so Zimmerman believes, to have forged Heidegger's particular brand of 'anti-modernism'. Zimmerman suggests that Spengler exercised a significant influence on Heidegger's 'mature' conception of technology and mass society noting that though Heidegger appeared to offer some clipped criticisms of Spengler's approach in *The Fundamental Concepts of Metaphysics*, he nevertheless presented an account of technological society which bore a marked resemblance to Spengler's descriptions. Unfortunately, as was Zimmerman's interpretative Achilles' heel in an earlier study,[18] there is a propensity to rely on tenuously established genealogies when it comes to Heidegger's paths of thinking. Zimmerman is inclined to paper over substantial cracks of incompatibility between Heidegger and his putative intellectual forebears (in this case Spengler) as he looks to amplify any and every possible affinity, no matter how superficial, as though crucial aspects of Heidegger's unique philosophical vision reduce directly to his intellectual, cultural and political heritage.

Zimmerman discusses Spengler's influence on Heidegger in a specific sub-section from Chapter 2 of *Heidegger's Confrontation with Modernity* – the sub-heading reads 'Heidegger's Critical Appropriation of Spengler in the Fight Against Modern Technology'. He frames his discussion with a truncated overview of Heidegger's brief discussion of Spengler in *The Fundamental Concepts of Metaphysics*. In these lectures, Zimmerman explains, Heidegger chose to 'disclose Germany's mood at the end of the 1920s' by examining the 'works of four representative authors – Oswald Spengler, Ludwig Klages, Max Scheler, and Leopold Ziegler. Heidegger's comments on Spengler and Scheler are particularly important.'[19] Zimmerman misjudges the tone of Heidegger's highly qualified remarks in this short section from *The Fundamental Concepts of Metaphysics* suggesting that Heidegger was largely in agreement with Spengler's assessment of things; in fact, this short section from Heidegger's 1929 lectures reads as a fairly straightforward criticism of Spengler, on Heidegger's part.

In short, Heidegger believes that the negative views of Spengler, similar to the views of others he examines from the same period, are 'correct' insofar as they recapitulate the negative side of Nietzsche's assessment, a view he reiterates much later in *What is Called Thinking*; but, as is often the case in Heidegger's critiques, the designation correct is not meant to indicate approval on Heidegger's part; Spengler is correct, but *merely* correct. We can see this even in the very passage that Zimmerman adduces from *What is Called Thinking* where Heidegger supposedly recapitulates the position Zimmerman attributes to him at the end of the 1920s:

> That people today tend once again to be more in agreement with Spengler's propositions about the decline of the West, lies in the fact that (along with the various superficial reasons) Spengler's proposition is only the negative, though correct, consequence of Nietzsche's word, 'The Wasteland grows.' We emphasize that this word is thoughtful. It is a true word.[20]

Heidegger is clearly not suggesting that Spengler has offered us a 'true word'. Rather, Spengler has a derivative, one-dimensional take on Nietzsche's true word and it is *Nietzsche's* true word that interests Heidegger. This is a reprisal of his criticism in *The Fundamental Concepts of Metaphysics* at the end of the 1920s. Zimmerman more or less acknowledges as much at the outset (almost as a throwaway remark) before stridently insisting that thoroughgoing overlaps obtain between the thought of Spengler and Heidegger concerning technology:

> For Heidegger, however, the decline of the West from the great age of the Greeks occurred not for biological or racial reasons, but for metaphysical and spiritual ones. By way of contrast, Spengler – influenced by Schopenhauer, Nietzsche, and Darwin – argued that the West's original drive for technological control and the subsequent decline of the West were related cycles in the 'struggle for life.' Heidegger countered that such 'naturalistic' interpretations of human life were products of the misguided metaphysical conception of man as the 'rational animal'.
>
> Despite disdaining Spengler's propositions and methods, early Heidegger began to conceive of his own work as an attempt to provide a philosophically sound account for the *symptoms* of decline popularized by Spengler.[21]

Already then, we can see an unwitting concession to the effect that the similarities between Spengler and Heidegger are superficial at best. After all, if two doctors simultaneously looking at the same symptoms in a given patient could only agree that they were actually looking at a patient with certain unmistakable symptoms but disputed the cause of those symptoms, we would, presumably, characterize these physicians as having *conflicting* views. For Heidegger as for many other twentieth century intellectuals, the impact of technology on society is plain for all to see. What is not so obvious are the actual causes of these various symptoms/effects and if Heidegger completely rejects Spengler's 'causal account', that is, his account of the genesis of the modern technological age, then they are in fundamental *disagreement*. It is *with these fundamental differences granted* that we can begin to examine the affinities between Spengler's account and aspects of Heidegger's criticisms of technicity with a view to understanding how Heidegger, as was his wont, absorbs various images, themes and metaphors from his background influences but deploys them in rather new and unique ways. And, indeed, Zimmerman himself points to many of the similarities which we examine in the course of our own investigation of *Man and Technics* below. One has to wonder then about the interpretative choices that Zimmerman makes in framing this discussion of the influence of Spengler on Heidegger's thinking; he wants to suggest that there are deep-seated affinities (that Heidegger himself acknowledges as much) along with a few disclaimers to the effect that Heidegger was critical of Spengler's biologistic conception of history; he then proceeds to elaborate on the similarities of their descriptions of the technological age: 'Despite his critique of Spengler, Heidegger was much indebted to his interpretation of modern technology.'[22] Ultimately then, while the surface similarities between Heidegger's descriptions of modern, industrial technology and mass society and Spengler's descriptions in *Man and Technics* are evident, the context within which Zimmerman presents these similarities is misleading and obfuscatory. It would be more accurate to say that despite their deep-seated, irreconcilable philosophical differences, there are nonetheless a series of images, themes and motifs concerning technology and mass society which both Heidegger and Spengler share.

\*\*\*\*

In *The Fundamental Concepts of Metaphysics*, Heidegger offers an extremely brief overview of the 'contemporary situation', 'popularly' understood, that is, mediated through the views of four influential figures: Spengler, Klages, Scheler and Ziegler. Heidegger essentially conflates the positions of all four as, ultimately, dependent on a fundamental opposition between life (soul) and spirit. Heidegger is quick to point out that his account of these figures is not in any way philosophically sufficient; that is, his account does not pretend to comprehensively undermine these positions theoretically. What interests Heidegger is how these positions have been mediated for popular culture through a kind of high journalism. And, when one looks at the readymade, popular understandings of these figures, Heidegger suggests that one finds a juxtaposition or tension between life and spirit at work in all of them. That is not to say that Heidegger does not have serious reservations concerning, for example, Spengler; rather, what interests Heidegger for the time being is the popular reception, if you like, of figures such as Spengler which he believes is symptomatic of a certain residual effect of Nietzsche's thought – the opposition between the Dionysian and the Apollonian:

> in Nietzsche an opposition was alive that in no way came to light in the four interpretations provided of our situation, but merely had a residual effect as material passed on, as a literary form.[23]

Heidegger does not wish to suggest that the four interpretations are thereby rendered useless; rather he is looking for the site where a confrontation proper with the four interpretations can take place:

> We know only that Nietzsche is the source of the interpretations we have mentioned. We are not saying this in order to accuse these interpretations of being

derivative or to detract from their originality in any way, but in order to designate the direction out of which an understanding is to be gained and to show where the place of the confrontation proper lies.[24]

And, Heidegger will conclude, the prevalence and influence of this type of cultural diagnosis indicates the emergence of a kind of high journalism as a substitute for the type of work which needs, so Heidegger believes, to be undertaken:

> We now ask anew: What does the fact that diagnoses of culture find an audience among us – albeit in quite different ways – tell us about what is happening here? What is happening in the fact that this higher form of journalism fills or even altogether delimits our 'spiritual' space? Is all this merely a fashion? Is anything overcome if we seek to characterize it as 'fashionable philosophy' and thus to belittle it? We may not and do not wish to resort to such cheap means.[25]

This may sound conciliatory, but we know from Heidegger's frequent pejorative remarks concerning newspapers and journalism in both his philosophical texts and indeed in his correspondence, that he was rather chary of the press and journalism itself as an intellectual medium. In his correspondence with Jünger, for example, he makes some rather unflattering comments concerning Jean-Michel Palmier's philosophical efforts suggesting that the author is better suited to journalism than to thinking and that he has already written far too much for someone so young.[26] Heidegger is essentially then rejecting these four interpretations of the contemporary situation, which have shaped the cultural and literary understanding of the present age as an age of decline, as weak derivatives of Nietzsche's philosophy and, fundamentally, as based on a misinterpretation of that philosophy:

> It does not require many words to see that here in Nietzsche an opposition was alive that in no way came to light in the four interpretations provided of our situation, but merely had a residual effect as material passed on, as a literary form.
> 
> Which of the four interpretations is the more correct in Nietzsche's sense is not to be described now. Nor indeed can we show here that none is correct, because none can be correct, insofar as they all mistake the essence of Nietzsche's philosophy, which for its part rests on strange foundations. These foundations indeed show themselves to be based on a quite ordinary and metaphysically highly questionable 'psychology'. Yet Nietzsche can afford that. Nevertheless, this is no *carte blanche*.[27]

## Oswald Spengler – *Man and Technics*

It would be disingenuous in the extreme, of course, to suggest that Heidegger was inured to the powerful cultural, political and intellectual influences which were percolating in Germany following the First World War up to and through the Weimar period. There was a surge of conservative revolutionary thinking along with a general sense of disaffection and betrayal characteristic of the *Dolchstoßlegende* mentality and Heidegger, for his part, was clearly sympathetic to elements of the conservative revolutionary movement. Indeed, when it suited his rather naked political ambitions and careerist objectives, he amplified any surface affinities with these movements, particularly in the early 1930s, as part of a concerted effort to ingratiate himself to the powers that be in the hope of scaling the ladder of university politics in Germany. Nevertheless, Heidegger steadfastly refused to embrace any of these movements in any kind of theoretically determinate fashion and, philosophically speaking, was clearly unimpressed with much of what they represented. Indeed, he often took a rather dim view of the philosophical capacities of the most prominent members of those movements. That is not to say that Heidegger didn't envisage a kind of political regime which would be compatible with his notion of an authentic historical community in ways which he was already trying to gloss in *Being and Time*, the inevitable failure of that endeavour notwithstanding. But Heidegger's views in this regard simply do not reduce to the views of the conservative revolutionaries!

In the case of Spengler, we already know that Heidegger was not overly enamoured with his philosophical vision in *The Decline of the West*. There are simply too many obvious problems with that text for Heidegger to have taken it seriously. It is, for many, *the* definitive German manifesto concerning cultural pessimism. However, the difficulties involved in trying to compare this work with any aspect of Heidegger's philosophy are innumerable and largely insurmountable. First and foremost, Heidegger would have been intellectually and philosophically appalled at Spengler's sprawling, inchoate, biologically deterministic outlook. One can readily identify surface elements of Spengler's text which opportunists might use in order to draw comparisons with some of the high-blown, rousing appeals for 'violence-doers' in *Introduction to Metaphysics*, for example, but such comparisons could never amount to anything more than interpretative cheap-shots; the distance between Heidegger's notion of pioneering individuals contending with the dynamic they find themselves thrown into and Spengler's advocacy of a kind of 'testosterone laced' Machiavellian 'virtù'[28] could hardly be greater. Spengler's subscription to an underlying biological determinism of sorts as part of his attempts to chart a steady decline is simply not compatible with Heidegger's philosophical vision in any of its evolving guises. In short, *The Decline of the West* is simply too unwieldy to lend itself to a ready comparison with Heidegger's work; it is, for the most part, philosophically incompatible.

We have to look elsewhere for something more amenable to comparison with Heidegger's work; the lesser-known volume, *Man and Technics*, which Spengler himself saw as performing something of a synoptic function for *The Decline of the West*, can serve our purpose more effectively. There are, in fact, a number of passages concerning 'technics' which anticipate Heidegger's characterizations of the technological landscape; then again, some of Heidegger's passages regarding standing reserve and Enframing recall much of what was, after all, a fairly prevalent anti-modernist suspicion of technology among a whole host of early twentieth-century European intellectuals. Nevertheless, Heidegger's extraordinary meditation on technology's essence doesn't neatly reduce to Spengler's musings in *Man and Technics* any more than it reduces to those complaints typical of a post-First World War German mandarin class.

For all of the surface similarities between their descriptions of 'technicity', Spengler and Heidegger offer very different accounts. Spengler's is a quasi-philosophical account and he clearly sees himself as indebted to what he views as a Nietzschean position – though one which is simultaneously biologistic. In a way, of course, it is no surprise to find Heidegger and other critics of technology sharing certain ideas and perhaps misgivings. To return to the example used earlier, two reports might overlap in their descriptions of the outward symptoms and ravages of some malady or other, cancer for example, and yet have very different views as to the cause of and indeed the appropriate treatment for that same disease! We would appear to be dealing with something like this in the case of Heidegger and Spengler: they are both looking at a world which has been significantly affected by technological development. The 'symptoms', as it were, are more or less evident. That is not to say that they necessarily agree either as to the best way to proceed or as to what is responsible for this technological explosion. Spengler argues, for example, that

> The unique fact about human technics, on the contrary, is that it is *independent* of the life of the human genus. It is the one instance in all the history of life in which the individual frees himself from the compulsion of the genus. One has to meditate long upon this thought if one is to grasp its immense implications. Technics in man's life is conscious, arbitrary, alterable, personal, *inventive*. It is learned and improved. Man has become the *creator* of his tactics of living – that is his grandeur and his doom. And the inner form of this creativeness we call culture – to be cultured, to cultivate, to suffer from culture. The man's creations are the expression of this being in *personal* form.[29]

We simply cannot ignore the fact that Heidegger would *never* accept that our relationship with technology is such that we are its 'creators' in the manner that Spengler suggests. It is not something which has emerged and evolved in a spirit of inventiveness, it is not simply a tool that we use (almost as a weapon, that is, a mere extension of our hands in a spirit of hyper creativity, as Spengler suggests) in order to further our aims as part of our tactics of living. That simply is not something Heidegger would concur with, or, even worse, advocate! Furthermore, regardless of how one ends up reading the account of authenticity in *Being and Time*, one can hardly suppose that Heidegger would assent to a rampant voluntarism which flew in the face of his protracted attempts throughout his work to achieve a resolute non-willing which eventually emerged as the notion of Releasement (*Gelassenheit*). Even if one were to argue, and many have, that Heidegger's account lapses into a kind of subjectivism in its own right in *Being and Time*, that is not to say that he advocates the rather naked, wilful subjectivism that permeates Spengler's account.

We can identify a fundamental difference in their conceptions of technology/the technological towards the beginning of Spengler's essay:

> *Technics is not to be understood in terms of the implement.* What matters is not how one fashions things, *but what one does with them*; not the weapon, but the battle.[30]

Spengler then doesn't really distinguish between modern technology and the older handwork technology of the ancient farmer or hunter-gatherer. Ultimately Spengler is interested in 'tactics', technics, are, for him, secondary. For Heidegger, conversely, modern technics, as a result of the revealing that holds sway (the essence of technology, i.e. *Gestell*, being a type of revealing) insidiously determines and shapes in advance the manner in which we arrive at goals which we develop tactics to try and secure.

There are numerous instances of that all-too-generic heroic fatalism which many of Heidegger's contemporaries succumbed to in the post-Weimar era. In a way, then, one can empathize with Karl Löwith's dismay upon witnessing those very motifs cropping up in Heidegger's work.[31] Habermas and Bourdieu are suspicious of these tropes as well since they are plainly evident in some of Heidegger's most suggestive writings from the 1930s. What might appear unique to readers of *Introduction to Metaphysics*, for example, doesn't appear nearly so unique when placed alongside passages such as the following:

> But each and every one of us, intrinsically a null, is for an unnamably brief moment a lifetime cast into that whirling universe. And for us therefore this world-in-little, this 'world-history,' is something of supreme importance. And, what is more, the *destiny* of each of these individuals consists in his being, by birth, not merely brought into this world-history, but brought into it in a particular century, a particular country, a particular people, a particular religion, a particular class. It is *not* within our power to choose whether we would like to be Sons of an Egyptian peasant of 3000 B.C., of a Persian king, or of a present-day tramp. This destiny is something to which we have to adapt ourselves. It *dooms* us to certain situations, views, and actions. There are no 'men-in-themselves' such as the philosophers talk about, but only men of a time, of a locality, of a race, of a personal cast, who contend in battle with a *given* world and win through or fail, while the universe around them moves slowly on with a godlike unconcern. This battle *is* life – life, indeed, in the Nietzschean sense, a grim, pitiless, no-quarter battle of the Will-to-Power.[32]

And what is needed in the face of this inexorable destiny is something like resolve, hardness, a warrior's grim defiance in the face of insurmountable odds – a willingness to throw oneself against destiny, to bare one's teeth to destiny with all the menace and contemptuous disregard of the beast of prey. The martial virtues are constantly celebrated by Spengler!

Notwithstanding, there are fairly obvious philosophical differences between Heidegger and Spengler here as well; for Spengler this destiny '*dooms* us to certain situations.' For Heidegger, our destining, the way we are thrown (in our era through the ordinances of *Gestell*) is 'never a fate that compels'. One cannot draw a straight line then from this blustery vision of heroic and predatory man, as envisaged by Spengler, to the violence-doer as described by Heidegger in *Introduction to Metaphysics*. These notions have, apart from the semblance of surface imagery and rhetoric, almost nothing in common philosophically. It is also worth noting that Spengler's attempts to recruit Nietzsche as something of an ally here are untenable. Nietzsche clearly sees his philosophy as one of affirmation and celebration, not one of heroic resignation. In embracing the dangerous character of life, one is liberated, not *doomed*. That is the paradox of Zarathustra's gift, the liberation one achieves once one embraces instead of resisting Zarathustra's most abysmal thought.

We continue to find in Spengler's essay a surfeit of examples of that heroic fatalism and figurative martyrdom which were so in vogue:

> *That* is his "world-history," the history of a steadily increasing, fateful rift between man's world and the universe – the history of a rebel that grows up to raise his hand against his mother. This is the beginning of man's *tragedy* – for Nature is the stronger of the two. Man remains dependent on her, for in spite of everything she embraces him, like all else, within herself. All the great Cultures are *defeats*. Whole races remain, inwardly destroyed and broken, fallen into barrenness and spiritual decay, as corpses on the field. The fight against Nature is hopeless and yet – it will be fought out to the bitter end.[33]

Again, we can see how one might be tempted to compare this passage of Spengler's with passages from *Introduction to Metaphysics*. Take for example this ostensibly similar passage from 'The Restriction of Being':

> Doing violence must shatter against the excessive violence of Being, as long as Being holds sway in its essence, as *phusis*, as emerging sway. But this necessity of shattering can subsist only insofar as what must shatter is urged into such Being-here, thrown into the urgency of such Being, because the overwhelming as such, in order to appear in its sway, *requires* the site of openness for itself. The essence of Being-human opens itself up to us only when it is understood on the basis of this urgency that is necessitated by Being itself. Historical humanity's Being-here means: Being-posited as the breach into which the excessive violence of Being breaks in its appearing, so that this breach shatters against Being. (IM: 173–4)

If we study Heidegger's passage closely, however, we begin to see that major philosophical differences obtain between Spengler's claims and what Heidegger is arguing above. Heidegger is wrestling again with a structural question which was to form the backdrop to nearly all of his work. One finds this notion of the interplay between Dasein as thrown and simultaneously solicited (as a thrown projector) already in *Being and Time*. Heidegger begins to tease out this notion in terms of a human awareness that finds itself already thrown into and absorbed by a technological, equipmental, project-oriented and project-disclosed world and, in turn, an awareness that projects on the basis of those interpretative moorings which are themselves indicative of the finite throwness of our shared existential situation. Heidegger revisits this structural constitution of human awareness and interpretation in *Introduction to Metaphysics*. The language is certainly recast at times to give it an apparent, and ultimately phony, affinity with the romantic, heroic nationalism which he identified with. But, at bottom, superficial resonances aside, the structural elements of Heidegger's account of the thrown/tragic nature of our existence, namely, our finitude (the way it shapes how we find ourselves and indeed how we can interpret at any given moment) are features of an ongoing attempt to try and accurately describe the interplay between presence and absence which first and only manages to emerge or become manifest through the disclosive activity of Dasein. Of course Heidegger is going to try and find a way to theoretically justify a valorization of his own particular conception of a German nation using this structural apparatus but that is an arbitrary move and one which, as we shall see, his own philosophy does not permit.

Spengler celebrates the notions of resolve and individuality in ways which again can easily be aligned with some of Heidegger's more inflammatory iterations concerning inauthenticity and publicness in *Being and Time* and *Introduction to Metaphysics*:

> The more solitary the being and the more resolute it is in forming its own world against all other conjunctures of worlds in the environment, the more definite and strong the cast of its soul. What is the opposite of the soul of a lion? The soul of a cow. For strength of individual soul the herbivores substitute numbers, the herd, the common feeling and doing of masses. But the less one needs others, the more powerful one is. A beast of prey is everyone's foe. Never does he tolerate an equal in his den. Here we are at the root of the truly royal idea of *property*. Property is the domain in which one exercises unlimited power, the power that one has gained in battling, defended against one's peers, victoriously upheld. It is not a right to mere having, but the sovereign right to do as one will with one's own. Once this is understood, we see that there are carnivore and there are herbivore *ethics*. It is beyond anyone's power to alter this.[34]

The first six lines of this passage immediately invite comparisons with similarly intoned invectives against mass society in Heidegger's work. One can see why critics, then, upon revisiting Heidegger's 'early' work following his shocking 'apostasy' in 1933[35], began to conflate some of that work with the themes of resolve and voluntarism which permeated the conservative revolutionary literature[36] and which we find again in this essay. Take for example some of the more 'suggestive' passages concerning *das Man* and publicness in *Being and Time*:

> In utilizing public means of transport and in making use of information services such as the newspaper, every Other is like the next. This Being-with-one-another dissolves one's own Dasein completely into the kind of Being of 'the Others', in such a way, indeed, that the Others, as distinguishable and explicit, vanish more and more. In this inconspicuousness and unascertainability, the real dictatorship of the "they" is unfolded. We take pleasure and enjoy ourselves as *they* [*man*] take pleasure; we read, see, and judge about literature and art as *they* see and judge; likewise we shrink back from the 'great mass' as *they* shrink back; we find 'shocking' what *they* find shocking. The "they", which is nothing definite, and which all are, though not as the sum, prescribes the kind of Being of everydayness.
> (BT: 164)

One can clearly see surface affinities between the sentiments expressed in the two passages. The fact remains, however, that Heidegger simply did not and would not advocate the homage to the 'Borgian' picture of predatory prowess proposed by Spengler. The carnivore's 'virtù'; a somewhat vulgar, naturalistic appropriation of Machiavellian prowess is at such a remove from anything Heidegger suggests that the tendency among some of his critics to simply lump his early work in with the worst excesses of the conservative revolutionary literature of the time beggars belief.[37] A suspicion of mass mentality and a disdain for democracy had smuggled their way into the mindset of many intellectuals and writers following the perceived catastrophe of the Weimar Republic. Again, we find in Heidegger traces of such themes, but Heidegger revisits these notions from the context of his confrontation with the history of philosophy. Heidegger flirts then with this aspect of the conservative revolutionary literature but very much against the backdrop of a long-standing philosophical concern with the nature of and/or inherent weaknesses of democracy.[38] It is in *this* context that Heidegger elects to interpret Heraclitus's fragments:

> They are incapable of bringing their Dasein to stand in the Being of beings. Only those who are capable of this, rule over the word – the poets and the thinkers. The others just reel about within the orbit of their caprice and lack of understanding. They accept as valid only what comes directly into their path, what flatters them and is familiar to them. (IM: 141)

But Heidegger's concerns here reflect his growing concerns with the difficulty of linking his philosophical vision with politics. The way beings (including ourselves) are revealed to and through us is something which should be reflected in our approach to politics, for Heidegger at any rate. How this is to be achieved is not something that he ever really manages to come to terms with, despite his enthusiasm in this regard in the early 1930s.[39] Heidegger is concerned with the capacity of certain pioneering individuals whose 'struggle' allows us to see the interplay of presence and absence and how being comes to presence and is revealed through our finitude/our temporal limits (as opposed to the tendency to simply allow being to be revealed to us as continuous presence) with a certain epochal character; in our epoch, through the ordinances of *Gestell*. Again, there is a danger here of stooping to apologetics; we have to be able to concede that there were jingoistic elements within Heidegger's rhetoric which were unfortunate and opportunistically designed to give the wrong impression to the right people. That is, Heidegger was looking for ways to make his philosophy *superficially* consonant with elements of the conservative revolutionary rhetoric which had been absorbed into the fabric of National Socialism. One doesn't want to exonerate Heidegger for this in any way; having said that, condemning his entire philosophical output from this period as contaminated to the core is excessive and overlooks the important continuities which knit together Heidegger's overall project from *Being and Time*, through this period and beyond.[40] One must also bear in mind, and this is something that we shall examine in some detail in subsequent chapters, that Heidegger will look to articulate his own political philosophy which he tries to relate to National Socialism but which is rather different in many respects to anything envisaged by his contemporaries. Our findings will come as cold comfort to those who were hoping to discover something altogether reassuring in the failure of Heidegger's attempts to combine his philosophy and his political vision; the fact that his philosophy doesn't reduce straightforwardly to Nazism or to the less salubrious intellectual elements of his day doesn't mean that what he endorses is something to be embraced. Heidegger's political vision, understood as the practical enactment of some version of his philosophy is grotesque and pernicious.

Heidegger discusses a number of Heraclitean fragments in *Introduction to Metaphysics*. For example, he spends some time discussing fragment 53. A conventional rendering of this fragment reads as follows: 'War is the father of all and king of all, and some he shows as gods, others as humans; some he makes slaves, others free.'[41] Spengler repeatedly offers observations concerning the natural rank of human beings which would seem to accord with a conventional reading of this Heraclitean fragment:

> As in every process there is a technique of direction and a technique of execution, so, equally self-evidently, there are *men whose nature is to command and men whose nature is to obey, subject and objects of the political or economic process in question.* This is the basic form of the human life, that since the change has assumed so many and various shapes, and it is only to be eliminated along with life itself.[42]

On the next page Spengler goes on to write:

> Finally there is a natural distinction of grade between men born to command and men born to service, between the leaders and the led of *life*. The existence of this distinction is a plain *fact*, and in healthy periods and by healthy peoples it is admitted (even if unwillingly) by everyone. In the centuries of decadence the majority force themselves to deny or ignore it, but the very insistence on the formula that 'all men are equal' shows that there is something here that has to be explained away.[43]

If one simply states that Heidegger invoked the Heraclitean fragment above (conventionally translated) and left it at that, then one may well be tempted to infer that Heidegger and Spengler are singing from the same hymn sheet. Consider, however, the way Heidegger himself chose to translate this fragment from Heraclitus:

> Confrontation is indeed for all (that comes to presence) the sire (who lets emerge), but (also) for all the preserver that holds sway. For it lets some appear as gods, others as human beings, some it produces (sets forth) as slaves, but others as the free. (IM: 65)

It is clear, from the translation alone, that Heidegger and Spengler are talking about different things. Spengler would most presumably subscribe to a fairly conventional reading of this Heraclitean fragment which would more or less accord with the passage from *Man and Technics* quoted above, while Heidegger would clearly resist this reading of the Heraclitean fragment. Heidegger elaborates on his understanding of Heraclitus arguing that

> The *polemos* named here is a strife that holds sway before everything divine and human, *not war in the human sense* … struggle first and foremost allows what essentially unfolds to step apart in opposition, first allows position and status and rank to establish themselves in coming to presence. (IM: 65 emphasis added).

Notwithstanding, Heidegger manages to muddy the waters in this already hoary context by invoking other notions from the Ancients which are dangerous (to say the least) in this context and represent an unambiguous attack on the democratic sensibilities of 'we' contemporary Europeans:

> Being as logos is originary gathering, not a heap or pile where everything counts just as much and just as little – and for this reason, rank and dominance belong

to Being. If Being is to open itself up, it itself must have rank and maintain it. Heraclitus's reference to the many as dogs and donkeys is characteristic of this attitude, one that belongs essentially to Greek Dasein. If people today from time to time are going to busy themselves rather too eagerly with the polis of the Greeks, they should not suppress this side of it; otherwise the concept of the polis easily becomes innocuous and sentimental. What is higher in rank is stronger. (IM: 141)

Heidegger is playing a dangerous game here; he is misrepresenting his position in a rather disappointingly disingenuous fashion. On the one hand, he is trying to qualify his attempts to rally to the heroic nationalism of the day with philosophical provisos which point toward what is really at stake, philosophically, in these texts. On the other hand, he is trying to dress his work in the manner of his contemporaries thereby recommending himself as the spiritual leader elect of the movement. Heidegger, as it were, wants the glass to be half full but half empty at the same time (to borrow a memorable phrase from Browning). There is no denying the opportunistic current running through this posturing on Heidegger's part. Nevertheless, as we shall see in the chapters to follow, Heidegger was willing to make some rather sinister remarks in his analysis of this particular fragment in one of his 1930s seminars which underlines the fact that his own political philosophy had a rather sinister streak running through it.

\*\*\*\*

There is of course an apocalyptic flavour to some of Spengler's descriptions and prognoses and again, there are elements of Heidegger's own criticisms of mass culture and the technological world which would seem in keeping with passages such as the following:

> Today we stand on the summit, at the point when the fifth act is beginning. The last decisions are taking place, the tragedy is closing. Every high Culture *is* a tragedy. The history of mankind *as a whole* is tragic. But the sacrilege and the catastrophe of the Faustian are greater than all others, greater than anything Æschylus or Shakespeare ever imagined. The creature is rising up against its creator. As once the microcosm Man against Nature, so now the microcosm Machine is revolting against Nordic Man. The lord of the World is becoming the slave of the Machine, which is forcing him – forcing us all, whether we are aware of it or not – to follow its course. The victor, crashed, is dragged to death by the team.[44]

We find echoes of this alarmist rhetoric in Heidegger's famous 1935 lectures but as we see again, there are important differences also:

> This Europe, in its unholy blindness always on the point of cutting its own throat, lies today in the great pincers between Russia on the one side and America on the other. Russia and America, seen metaphysically, are both the same: the same hopeless frenzy of unchained technology and of the rootless organization of the average man. When the farthest corner of the globe has been conquered technologically and can be exploited economically; when any incident you like, at any

time you like, becomes accessible as fast as you like; when you can simultaneously 'experience' an assassination attempt against a king in France and a symphony concert in Tokyo; when time as history has vanished from all Dasein of all peoples; when a boxer counts as the great man of a people; when the tallies of millions at mass meetings are a triumph; then, yes then, there still looms like a specter over all this uproar the question: what for? – where to? – and what then? [T]he spiritual decline of the earth has progressed so far that people are in danger of losing their last spiritual strength, the strength that makes it possible even to see the decline and to appraise it as such. This simple observation has nothing to do with cultural pessimism – nor with any optimism either, of course; for the darkening of the world, the flight of the gods, the destruction of the earth, the reduction of human to a mass, the hatred and mistrust of everything creative and free has already reached such proportions throughout the whole earth that such childish categories as pessimism and optimism have long become laughable. (IM: 40–1)[45]

Heidegger then concurs with the likes of Spengler insofar as the symptoms they catalogue indicate the presence of a serious underlying malady. But that seems to be as far as their accord goes. Indeed Heidegger explicitly distances himself from cultural pessimism in the passage above and Spengler is a clear target for some of his derogatory remarks here, dismissing 'pessimism', understood as a response to the contemporary situation, as 'laughable'.[46] Heidegger is thinking here of the levelling influence of *Gestell* – simply bemoaning a decline is utterly inadequate. Rather, Heidegger wants to get at the issue of how things are revealed to and by us in these ways through the ordinances of *Gestell*.

There are also descriptions of the effect which technology has had on our landscape which, as one might expect, sound rather similar to those we find in Heidegger:

> The picture of the earth, with its plants, animals, and men, has altered. In a few decades most of the great forests have gone, to be turned into news-print, and climatic changes have been thereby set afoot which imperil the land-economy of whole populations. Innumerable animal species have been extinguished, or nearly so, like the bison; whole races of humanity have been brought almost to vanishing-point, like the North American Indian and the Australian.[47]

Spengler goes on to lament our current predicament whereby

> We think only in horsepower now; we cannot look at a waterfall without mentally turning it into electric power; we cannot survey a countryside full of pasturing cattle without thinking of its exploitation as a source of meat-supply; we cannot look at the beautiful old handwork of an unspoilt primitive people without wishing to replace it by a modern technical process.[48]

Compare this with Heidegger's descriptions of equipmentality and our equipmental interpretation of nature and the world around us as early as *Being and Time*:

> The wood is a forest of timber, the mountain a quarry of rock; the river is water-power, the wind is wind 'in the sails'. As the 'environment' is discovered, the 'Nature' thus discovered is encountered too. (BT: 100)[49]

Heidegger has not as yet thematized this kind of instrumentality as problematic in its own right in *Being and Time*. Nevertheless, a life lived merely in the project-oriented, everyday world dominated by equipment, as a mere cog in a mass machine, was deemed ultimately inauthentic by Heidegger; one can surely then say that the seeds of his later thought were beginning to gestate here as opposed to the idea that the latter thought was a rejection or abjuration of this earlier discussion. In 'The Question Concerning Technology' Heidegger notes:

> a tract of land is challenged into the putting out of coal and ore. The earth now reveals itself as a coal mining district, the soil as a mineral deposit. The field that the peasant formerly cultivated and set in order [*bestellte*] appears differently than it did when to set in order still meant to take care of and to maintain … Agriculture is now the mechanized food industry. Air is now set upon to yield nitrogen, the earth to yield ore, ore to yield uranium, for example; uranium is set upon to yield atomic energy, which can be released either for destruction or for peaceful use … The hydroelectric plant is set into the current of the Rhine. It sets the Rhine to supplying its hydraulic pressure, which then sets the turbines turning. This turning sets those machines in motion whose thrust sets going the electric current for which the long-distance power station and its network of cables are set up to dispatch electricity. In the context of the interlocking processes pertaining to the orderly disposition of electrical energy, even the Rhine itself appears as something at our command. The hydroelectric plant is not built into the Rhine River as was the old wooden bridge that joined bank with bank for hundreds of years. Rather the river is dammed up into the power plant. What the river is now, namely, a water power supplier, derives from out of the essence of the power station. (QCT: 14–16)

Spengler's confident prediction of the imminent demise of technics/the technological world, however, seems a little naïve in retrospect and certainly is nowhere to be found in Heidegger's eschatological outlook. As it turns out, technology has proved itself far more flexible and resilient than Spengler supposed:

> The machine, by its multiplication and its refinement, is in the end defeating its own purpose. In the great cities the motor-car has by its numbers destroyed its own value, and one gets on quicker on foot. In Argentine, Java, and elsewhere the simple horse-plough of the small cultivator has shown itself economically superior to the big motor implement, and is driving the latter out.[50]

Heidegger was not nearly so confident of the imminent demise of technology. He was adamant of course that the technological nature of our world and the holding sway of Enframing was not 'a fate that compels', at the same time, even in his later proclamations concerning the prospects for humanity in the technological era towards the end of his life, Heidegger appeared anything but sanguine.

As we have seen briefly in Chapter 2 and has been discussed in detail elsewhere,[51] Heidegger's concerns with the technological age simply do not reduce to anything like what we find in Spengler. Heidegger is interested in the essence of technology which is nothing technological. His position is a philosophically sophisticated and nuanced one. There is no doubt that Heidegger has been influenced by and has absorbed the responses of people like Spengler to the technological advances which had begun to gather momentum at a frightening pace and, if we are to be fair, he is clearly sympathetic to elements of anti-modernism and a glorification of the bucolic in ways which resonate with some of the more unsavoury rhetoric of the day. But again, *Being and Time* itself can, if presented a certain way, seem like a carefully embroidered patchwork of threads from Aristotle, Luther, Kant, Dilthey, Husserl and Kierkegaard; that is certainly not to say that *Being and Time* reduces to such a patchwork. Heidegger's work eludes any such heavy-handed reductionism. Again, these interpretative strategies miss the real problems and, unwittingly, make it rather easy to get Heidegger off the hook.

## Ernst Jünger

In his preliminary remarks introducing Jünger's essay ('Total Mobilization') in *The Heidegger Controversy*, Richard Wolin notes that 'In the late twenties Jünger published over 100 essays in leading organs of Germany's conservative revolutionary movement ... thus establishing himself, along with figures such as Moeller van der Bruck and Oswald Spengler, as one of the movement's most celebrated and influential figures.'[52] Wolin is not alone in this conviction that Jünger exercised the greatest influence of all on Heidegger in terms of how Heidegger conceived of the effect of technology on the contemporary age.[53] In particular *Der Arbeiter* and 'Total Mobilization' are understood as proof positive of Heidegger's essential accord with Jünger's views on the technological age and, as Wolin explains, the essay

> represents a distillation of the argument of his book-length study of two years hence, *Der Arbeiter* – a work which enjoyed a tremendous commercial success and which, along with 'Total Mobilization,' represents a remarkable prefiguration of totalitarian rule.[54]

Wolin goes on to argue that

> The two works by Jünger, 'Total Mobilization' and *The Worker*, had an indelible impact on Heidegger's understanding of modern politics. In fact, it would not be much of an exaggeration to say that his 'option' for National Socialism in the early 1930s was based on the supposition that Nazism was the legitimate embodiment of the *Arbeitergesellschaft* (society of workers) that had been prophesied by Jünger and which, as such, represented the heroic overcoming of Western nihilism as called for by Nietzsche and Spengler.[55]

Wolin's subsequent claim, however, having attested to the enormity of the influence that Jünger exercised upon Heidegger (as he sees it), involves a gross misreading:

> In his lectures of the late 1930s, Heidegger would critically distance himself from Nietzsche's metaphysics. In the early 1930s, however, his relation to Nietzsche was far from critical. Instead, at this time, he clearly viewed the historical potentials of

the Nazi movement – its 'inner truth and greatness,' as he would later remark in *An Introduction to Metaphysics* (1935) – in a manner consistent with the doctrines of Nietzsche and Jünger; that is, as a resurgence of a new heroic ethos, a 'will to power,' that would place Germany in the forefront of a movement directed towards the 'self-overcoming' of bourgeois nihilism. Thus, following the argument set forth by Jünger in *The Worker*, in which 'the soldier worker' is viewed as a new social 'type' ('*Gestalt*') who is infatuated with risk, danger, heroism, and, as such, represents the antithesis to the timorous 'bourgeois,' Heidegger views Nazism as a Nietzschean-Jüngerian *Arbeitergesellschaft in statu nascendi*.[56]

It is not clear at all, however, that Heidegger's views on Nietzsche were entirely positive before the end of the 1930s. Heidegger's famous Nietzsche lectures provide the first occasion for us to see his in-depth assessment of Nietzsche and while Heidegger's admiration for Nietzsche is clear, he is also patently critical. Moreover, Wolin tends to conflate Spengler and Jünger with Nietzsche as though Heidegger's flirtation with aspects of the conservative revolutionaries was indicative of his commitment to a Nietzschean heroism in the manner adopted by Spengler and Jünger. And yet we can see clearly enough from Heidegger's remarks in *The Fundamental Concepts of Metaphysics* that Heidegger saw Spengler, for example, as operating with a rather superficial conception of Nietzsche's philosophy and that Heidegger is already critical of Nietzsche's philosophy in its own right. At the very least, then, Wolin is making things a little too easy for himself here since Heidegger was already critical of the misappropriation of Nietzsche in the work of Spengler and others in the early 1930s and was also beginning to worry over shortcomings in Nietzsche's own thought – supposedly when he held the opposite view, according to Wolin.

\*\*\*\*

## Total mobilization[57]

In 'Total Mobilization' Jünger is concerned with what came to light specifically in the First World War which he takes to have been unique amongst all previous wars:

> we will try to assemble a number of facts that distinguish the last war – our war, the greatest and most influential event of our age – from other wars whose history has been handed down to us.[58]

Already then we can see that for Jünger, the Great War is to be distinguished from all previous wars; as it turns out, the difference is going to relate to Jünger's own understanding of the role of technology and the concept of total mobilization. He prefaces the remarks to follow with an interesting aside which anticipates a famous exclamation from Heidegger in his own essay on technology's essence:[59]

> Let us leave aside the question of which spirit's realm rules over the optical illusion of progress: this study is no demonology, but is intended for twentieth-century

readers. Nevertheless, one thing is certain: only a power of cultic origin, only a *belief*, could conceive of something as audacious as extending the perspective of utility [*Zweckmaessigkeit*] into the infinite.[60]

Jünger then is reprising a theme which should seem familiar enough, that is, the prevalent misapprehension that technological advance represents 'progress' – 'progress' for the sake of 'progress'. Jünger suggests however that he wants to avoid any moralizing – in this he is in agreement with Heidegger who insists that the posture of the cultural pessimist is inadequate. And indeed, in characterizing the manner in which people seem to have been completely duped by the myth of technological progress, Jünger is close enough to some of the ways that Heidegger characterizes the all-consuming influence of *Gestell* which might well have been described as 'extending the perspective of utility into the infinite'.

One of the crucial defining features of the First World War for Jünger was the emergence of total mobilization. In previous wars there was 'general mobilization' but this was, for Jünger, very much a 'partial measure' and what set the Great War apart was the manner in which everything and everyone fell under the sway of a total mobilization:

> We can now pursue the process by which the growing conversion of life into energy, the increasingly fleeting content of all binding ties in deference to mobility, gives an ever-more radical character to the act of mobilization ... The events causing this are numerous: with the dissolution of the estates and the curtailing of the nobility's privileges, the concept of a warrior caste also vanishes; the armed defense of the state is no longer exclusively the duty and prerogative of the professional soldier, but the responsibility of everyone who can bear arms. Likewise, because of the huge increase in expenses, it is impossible to cover the costs of waging war on the basis of a fixed war budget; instead, a stretching of all possible credit, even a taxation of the last pfennig saved, is necessary to keep the machinery in motion. In the same way, the image of war as armed combat merges into the more extended image of a gigantic labor process [*Arbeitsprozess*]. In addition to the armies that meet on the battlefields, originate the modern armies of commerce and transport, foodstuffs, the manufacture of armaments – the army of labor in general. In the final phase, which was already hinted at toward the end of the last war, there is no longer any movement whatsoever – be it that of the homeworker at her sewing machine – without at least indirect use for the battlefield. In this unlimited marshaling of potential energies, which transforms the warring individual countries into volcanic forges, we perhaps find the most striking sign of the dawn of the age of labor [*Arbeitszeitalter*]. It makes the World War a historical event superior in significance to the French Revolution. In order to deploy energies of such proportion, fitting one's sword-arm no longer suffices; for this is a mobilization [*Ruestung*] that requires extension to the deepest marrow, life's finest nerve. Its realization is the task of total mobilization: an act which, as if through a single grasp of the control panel, conveys the extensively branched and densely veined power supply of modern life towards the great current of martial energy.[61]

Indeed, even in a post-Second World War publication such as *The Peace*, we find Jünger still insisting on the centrality and importance of this notion to any understanding of that particular period in the world's history:

> Behind the bloody battle lines, which for the first time welded the earth's ball with glowing bands, stretched the grey lightless depths of the army of workers. In them the greatest sum of human endeavor was produced that men have ever harnessed to one end.[62]

Heidegger himself describes how, under the ordinances of revealing issued through *Gestell*, everything everywhere is ordered to stand by, everything is revealed as resource to be used, on call and ready for use. In the passage above we read of a 'conversion of life into energy' and the way in which everything is reduced to its capacity to be 'mobilized'. However, Jünger looks to offer an historical and socio-political account for this situation where Heidegger sees all of this as the result of the unfolding of the history of Western Metaphysics. Granted, Jünger's descriptions and chronicling of the 'symptoms' bear a clear resemblance to both Heidegger and Spengler – what is called for under total mobilization is 'extension to the deepest marrow'; nevertheless, in his later essay (*The Peace*), Jünger proposes a causal account which Heidegger would again clearly oppose:

> In the course of these fateful years engagements were to take place which were far more terrible than the battles of materiel and fire of the first world war. For the man who believes he fights for ideas and ideals is possessed by greater ruthlessness than he who merely defends his country's frontiers.[63]

For Jünger, this explains some of the most obscene catastrophes of the Second World War in a way which Heidegger approaches rather from the standpoint of the growing dominion of *Gestell*:

> Over wide plains and fields the terrors of the elements vied with a technology of murder and unshakeable cruelty. There were areas where men destroyed each other like vermin and broad woods in which to hunt men like wolves. And one saw, cut off from all hope as if on a dead star, great armies go to their death in the horror chambers of pocket battles ... Even more somber becomes the picture of suffering in those places where the world turned into a mere slaughterhouse, to a flayinghouse whose stench poisoned the air far and wide.[64]

Indeed, Jünger's powers of description are chilling as he characterizes what we might describe as the symptoms of *Gestell* in the context of persecution and oppression:

> the way to the peaks had many stations. Particularly terrifying were the cold mechanics of persecution, the considered technique of decimation, the tracking and surveillance of the victims by means of lists and files of a police force which swelled into armies. It seemed as if every method, every discovery of the human mind had been transformed into an instrument of oppression.[65]

If we recall our discussion of Heidegger's essay on technology and his 'agriculture remark' we can see that Heidegger could easily be taken to be implying something quite close to what we find in Jünger's essay above. Again, the real difference emerges when one gets to the question of the forces at play in terms of explaining how it is that everything, including other human beings, could be revealed to us in these ways.

Returning to the earlier essay on total mobilization, we find that Jünger is also quick to identify the Russian five-year plans as relevant:

> For the first time, the Russian 'five-year plan' presented the world with an attempt to channel collective energies of a great empire into a *single* current.[66]

Jünger's descriptions of total mobilization in a wartime context are both vivid and compelling and one can easily see how much of an influence these ideas must have exercised on Heidegger as he began to consider the notion of technology and its impact on the twentieth century:

> Just as every life already bears the seeds of its own death, so the emergence of the great masses contains within itself a democracy of death. The era of the well-aimed shot is already behind us. Giving out the night-flight bombing order, the squadron leader no longer sees a difference between combatants and civilians, and the deadly gas cloud hovers like an elementary power over everything that lives. But the possibility of such menace is based neither on a partial nor general, but rather a *total* mobilization. It extends to the child in the cradle, who is threatened like everyone else – even more so.[67]

We can see a clear correlation between what Jünger says in the passage above and the various descriptions of mass society that we find even in *Being and Time* as well as the vivid characterizations of the manner in which *Gestell* operates as a challenging revealing such that everything everywhere is governed by the ordinances of this challenging revealing, where everything is challenged forth to reveal itself as stock, resource, that is, where everything is restricted to revealing itself in a functional context. Moreover, Jünger interprets the attempted genocide through the lens of total mobilization which clearly resonates with what we took to be Heidegger's views in his brief remarks from the Bremen lectures:

> From out of this waste of suffering where rise somberly the names of the great seats of murder where in a last and final frenzy they attempted to root out whole peoples, whole races, whole classes, and where leaden tyranny in league with technical efficiency celebrated endless bloody nuptials. These dens of murder will haunt man's memory to the end of time … If ever new pride fills us at the length and boldness of our flight, at our intellectual wings, our pinions of steel, it should suffice to cure us for a glance to be cast on the hordes driven like cattle to the graveyards and cremation ovens where the executioners waited. There they were stripped of their rags and slaughtered like shorn sheep. They were forced even to dig their own graves, if their murderers did not fill quarries and pit-shafts with the corpses which piled too fast.[68]

Heidegger, as we know, famously described the essence of technology as being operative when it came to the murder of inmates at the death camps using industrial means. And, we must concede then that Heidegger, like Jünger, sees technology as having a prominent explanatory role to play when it comes to thinking about the Second World War, the Holocaust and the state of the planet that survived the world war. However, Heidegger has a rather different 'causal' account in terms of what has allowed something like Jünger's total mobilization to take such a firm hold.

There is no denying that there are clear convergences between Heidegger, Spengler and Jünger. They are clearly all drawing attention to the way that mass society and technology have begun to monopolize our world, in a way, moreover, that seems entirely beyond any capacity for volition on our part. It seems clear that aspects of what Jünger describes in terms of total mobilization influenced Heidegger's own conception of modern technology. However, Heidegger quickly turns from the symptoms to the cause and begins to discuss the 'essence' of modern technology as a type of revealing and inserts it into his unique epochal story concerning the history of Western Metaphysics.

We have already discussed, both in this study and in earlier work,[69] the manner in which Heidegger thinks that the essence of technology is a kind of revealing, that is, a challenging revealing whereby everything is revealed to and by us through its constrictive lens. In the next two chapters we will examine how, in many ways, Heidegger is looking in the 1930s for a political regime which will allow us to halt the steady decline into a debased technocratic globalism. Heidegger explicitly recommends some combination of his own account of authenticity, writ large as the authentic Dasein of the *German* people, with a provincialism and ethnic chauvinism as the only salvation available for the planet. That is, Heidegger privileges, on a metaphysical and on some kind of ethnic level, the unique experience of suitably ethnically qualified Germans as being a superior kind of existence which would lead to a new German rootedness that could resist the tyranny of technology. Heidegger links these aspirations with aspects of National Socialist ideology which are deeply problematic and looks to his notions of historicity and authenticity to facilitate this uneasy union. It will prove an ill-conceived and ill-fated enterprise, of course, since Heidegger is ignoring the universal nature of the condition which allows for historicity and authenticity in the first place. However, in the putatively politically unproblematic 'later' work where Heidegger is supposed to have washed his hands of the unfortunate business of his brief, though disastrous, flirtation with politics, we find him returning to the question of how to respond to the levelling influence of *Gestell* whose dominion over the entire planet seems to have prevailed. Having said as much, it would still be a mistake to reduce key aspects of Heidegger's philosophy (which he tried to use as an undergirding for his political commitments) to cultural pessimism, anti-modernism or indeed to Nazi ideology since it simply doesn't reduce in that way. Heidegger's philosophy, as it turns out, cannot accommodate his politics on a theoretical level and even though he makes strident attempts to reconcile the two – his philosophy cannot be dismissed as so much crass ideology precisely because of the ultimate immiscibility of the two. It is a mistake then to simply suppose that because Heidegger is influenced by his conservative revolutionary contemporaries, trades in the *Blubo* currency of his day and invokes explicitly Nazi notions – his philosophy reduces to any of those particular ideologies. Heidegger has his own version of National Socialism in mind, which is to be based on key components of *Being and Time*'s theoretical apparatus, and is related to an ongoing confrontation with modernity and the history of Western metaphysics. This vision is run through with some shocking antisemitic undercurrents and an obscene ethnic chauvinism, as we shall see, and yet cannot be accommodated from within the theoretical parameters of Heidegger's thought. But it is imperative in that case to distinguish between Heidegger's philosophy and the political and intellectual movements he looks to hitch his philosophical cart on to in the 1930s. That is not of course to rally to the cause of those who insist on the irrelevance of Heidegger's politics to his philosophy. That is an obscenely disingenuous posture given Heidegger's pointed asseverations as to the fundamental connection between his philosophy and his political views.

Heidegger's views on technology, in particular the many symptoms of the 'technological condition', are clearly parasitic then on the views found in some of the literature which was to the fore of the conservative revolutionary movement. Notwithstanding, Heidegger's account as to how technology has had the impact on the contemporary landscape that it has enjoyed is operating in quite a different register to anything we find in Spengler or Jünger, for example. Moreover, what Heidegger proposes in terms of a 'response' is again something that seems unique to his own philosophy and, in particular, the notion of *Gelassenheit* as something which will foster a rootedness resistant to the tyrannical designs of *Gestell* in the technological age. That is not to say that Heidegger's philosophical posture in this regard is unproblematic, but we have to at least begin to identify where the real problems lie instead of perpetuating this interminable controversy by failing to deal with the genuine philosophical difficulties.

Heidegger was adamant to the end of his career that finding a way to respond to the manner in which the essence of technology governed how everything revealed itself to us was the greatest challenge facing us as human beings. Nevertheless, even though Heidegger's later philosophy is rarely seen as politically problematic, what we do in fact find when we get to Heidegger's own attempts at a 'response' is an unapologetic return to the notion of the authentic rootedness of a people. When we consider that Heidegger reiterates his concerns with the levelling influence of *Gestell* in his 1966 interview with *Der Spiegel* alongside his recalcitrant stance concerning democracy – it should, at the very least, give us pause!

## *Bodenständigkeit, Gelassenheit* and the Memorial Address

One of the terms most often invoked when discussing Heidegger's later philosophy is *Gelassenheit* (releasement) and yet, in one of his best-known discussions of this particular term as the appropriate response to the levelling influence of *Gestell* (the 'Memorial Address'), we find that the term is discussed very much in the context of an authentic rootedness (*Bodenständigkeit*) of the people. Ostensibly Heidegger's 'Memorial Address' was to be part of the celebration of the work of the local composer Conradin Kreutzer on what would have been his one-hundred-and-seventy-fifth birthday. However, Heidegger quickly begins to delve further and further into issues and questions which had become the central preoccupations of his thought. He begins to open up his address to wider themes within a few pages stating:

> What does this celebration suggest to us, in case we are ready to meditate? Then we notice that a work of art has flowered in the ground of our homeland. As we hold this simple fact in mind, we cannot help remembering at once that during the last two centuries great poets and thinkers have been brought forth from Swabian land. Thinking about it further makes clear at once that Central Germany is likewise such a land, and so are East Prussia, Silesia, and Bohemia.
>
> We grow thoughtful and ask: does not the flourishing of any genuine work depend upon its roots in a native soil?[70]

As we shall see in our discussion of the 'Origin of the Work of Art' in Chapter 5, there are distinct political ideas at play in Heidegger's conception of the work of art and already here Heidegger has introduced the priority and importance, in terms of the work of art, of homeland and rootedness in a native soil. Not only that, Heidegger reminds his audience that this is something which has clearly happened in certain parts of Germany. Heidegger goes on to ask 'Is there still a life-giving homeland in whose ground man may stand rooted, that is, be autochthonic?'[71] The plight of the German peoples in particular is raised here:

> Many Germans have lost their homeland, have had to leave their villages and towns, have been driven from their native soil. Countless others whose homeland was saved, have yet wandered off. They have been caught up in the turmoil of the big cities, and have resettled in the wasteland of industrial districts. They are strangers now to their former homeland. And those who *have* stayed on in their homeland? Often they are still more homeless than those who have been driven from their homeland. Hourly and daily they are chained to radio and television. Week after week the movies carry them off into uncommon, but often merely common, realms of the imagination, and give the illusion of a world that is no world. Picture magazines are everywhere available. All that with which modern techniques of communication stimulate, assail, and drive man – all that is already much closer to man today than his fields around his farmstead, closer than the sky over the earth, closer than the change from night to day, closer than the conventions and customs of his village, than the tradition of his native world.
>
> We grow more thoughtful and ask: What is happening here – with those driven from their homeland no less than with those who have remained? Answer: the *rootedness*, the *autochthony*, of man is threatened today at its core! Even more: The loss of rootedness is caused not merely by circumstance and fortune, nor does it stem only from the negligence and the superficiality of man's way of life. The loss of autochthony springs from the spirit of the age into which all of us were born.
>
> We grow more thoughtful and ask: If this is so, can man, can man's work in the future still be expected to thrive in the fertile ground of a homeland and mount into the ether, into the far reaches of the heavens and the spirit?[72]

Given what Heidegger had to say in the early 1930s, we cannot but shudder to see that in the 1950s he was to speak of Germans having lost their 'homeland' and having been driven from their 'native soil'. One wonders indeed if the vast numbers of Jews who were forced to flee Germany, or worse – were simply liquidated – are among the 'Germans' that he has in mind here? Though it seems clear that they are not! For one thing, they are not capable of being authentically German – something he makes patently clear in a seminar from the 1930s as we shall see in Chapter 5. Other Germans have lost their homeland for other reasons, in the main, because of the growing wasteland of industrial expansion and the lure of gainful, if soul-destroying, employment in the industrial districts. And even those that remain behind are enslaved by technological means of communication such as the television and the radio and the globalization that has ensued. All of this uproots Germans from the Earth and pulls the farmer, for example, away from the 'fields around his farmstead', 'the customs of his village' and 'the tradition of his native world'. And how are they [the Germans] to respond to this situation whereby they have been driven from their homeland or have migrated to the industrial districts or simply become enslaved to technology and uprooted from the farmsteads they yet occupy? How are they to respond to this 'loss of *rootedness*' that 'springs from the spirit of the age into which all of us [Germans] were born'? How 'can man's work in the future still be expected to thrive in the fertile ground of a homeland and mount into the ether, into the far reaches of the heavens and the spirit?' These are the pressing questions that Heidegger addresses in the course of his address, but again, very much in the context of the German people. Granted, one could easily begin to extrapolate from some of these comments in such a way as to suggest that they point to the way human beings in general have been uprooted. In other words, because of the way all of us are thrown into an historical world which is currently run through with the ordinances of revealing of *Gestell*, Heidegger's discussion of *Gelassenheit* is something which we can *all* in some way learn from as human beings. As we begin to excavate these ideas, however, and trace them back to Heidegger's philosophical views in the late 1920s and early 1930s, we see that Heidegger's views in this regard are not nearly so innocent as people might think.

We can further see here that in no way does Heidegger look to qualify his use of the term 'rootedness'. Some may want to argue that Heidegger is operating at quite a remove from the manner in which he deployed that term in the 1930s; however, it seems a pity if that is so not to qualify or explain whether and in what sense he is using this term in a highly qualified way here. As we shall see in what follows, Heidegger's earlier appeal to the authentic rootedness of a people was something he made very much in tandem with his political support for National Socialism. He openly identified this as a specific vocation of the German people who were to be understood as the most authentic of all peoples. Moreover, he insisted that certain people living within German borders did not qualify as German on the basis of a somewhat idiosyncratic ethnic chauvinism. To simply use the term rootedness then within the context of finding a way to respond to the rootlessness of the technological age, with nothing by way of qualification or clarification, seems at best an extremely injudicious oversight, at worst, rather sinister.

By the time Heidegger publishes *Gelassenheit* (which in English was given the title *Discourse on Thinking* and dates from about ten years after Heidegger's famous Bremen lectures out of which the essay on technology's essence emerged) he is explicitly invoking the notion of *Gelassenheit* as the appropriate posture for those who want to still think and yet remain free from the calculative mentality that holds sway under *Gestell*. In exhorting us to think meditatively, Heidegger wonders if our fate is not indeed one that compels: 'Or will everything now fall into the clutches of planning and calculation, of organization and automation?'[73] And the great danger, of course, as Heidegger had so vividly outlined in the famous essay on the essence of technology, is that the

> World now appears as an object open to the attacks of calculative thought, attacks that nothing is believed able any longer to resist. Nature becomes a gigantic gasoline station, an energy source for modern technology and industry. The relation of man to the world as such, in principle a technical one, developed in the seventeenth century first and only in Europe … The power concealed in modern technology determines the relation of man to that which exists. It rules the whole earth. Indeed, already man is beginning to advance beyond the earth into outer space.[74]

Heidegger goes on to write, and here we can see him becoming even more apocalyptic,

> In all areas of his existence, man will be encircled ever more tightly by the forces of technology. These forces, which everywhere and every minute claim, enchain, drag along, press and impose upon man under the form of some technical contrivance or other – these forces, since man has not made them, have moved long since beyond his will and have outgrown his capacity for decision.[75]

Not only that, Heidegger elaborates on our powerlessness in terms of will/agency in ways that he had begun to explore in the technology essay. He writes:

> No single man, no group of men, no commission of prominent statesmen, scientists, and technicians, no conference of leaders of commerce and industry, can brake or direct the progress of history in the atomic age. No merely human organization is capable of gaining dominion over it.
> Is man, then, a defenceless and perplexed victim at the mercy of the irresistible superior power of technology? He would be if man today abandons any intention to pit meditative thinking decisively against merely calculative thinking … For here we are considering what is threatened especially in the atomic age: the autochthony of the works of man.[76]

Autochthony is a translation of *Bodenständigkeit* which is also translated as rootedness and of course one cannot fail to notice the resonances with Heidegger's earlier use of the blubo rhetoric of the 1930s. Heidegger is clearly still committed, even in this seemingly innocuous piece from after the war, to some version of his own political understanding, one which involves a titanic confrontation with the technological age and the attempt to overcome calculative thinking (which, as we will see below, he directly links to the influence of 'world Jewry' in his private notebooks), which was in part what Heidegger had hoped for from National Socialism. Heidegger is openly suggesting to the audience here that the great challenge for thinking is to find a way to become authentically rooted in one's native homeland and that it is out of authentic homelands like Swabia, Central Germany, East Prussia, Silesia and Bohemia that the 'work of art has flowered in the ground' of its homeland. Furthermore, the meditative thinking and the concomitant notion of *Gelassenheit* which were to occupy centre stage for the rest of Heidegger's career are directly linked with the attempt to find the 'ground and foundation' for a new rootedness.

Heidegger had not really gone so far as to describe how we could successfully find an authentic relationship to technology in his earlier work. However, he certainly believed that it would depend on a people finding its authentic rootedness in the earth and resisting the rootless frenzy of the technological age. In his 'Memorial Address', however, Heidegger is quite confident that he can describe the comportment needed:

> For all of us, the arrangements, devices, and machinery of technology are to a greater or lesser extent indispensable. It would be foolish to attack technology blindly. It would be shortsighted to condemn it as the work of the devil.[77] We depend on technical devices; they even challenge us to ever greater advances. But suddenly and unaware we find ourselves so firmly shackled to these technical devices that we fall into bondage to them.
>
> Still we can act otherwise. We can use technical devices, and yet with proper use also keep ourselves so free of them that we may let go of them any time. We can use technical devices as they ought to be used, and also let them alone as something which does not affect our inner and real core. We can affirm the unavoidable use of technical devices, and also deny them the right to dominate us, and so to warp, confuse, and lay waste our nature.
>
> But will not saying both yes and no this way to technical devices make our relation to technology ambivalent and insecure? On the contrary! Our relation to technology will become wonderfully simple and relaxed. We let technical devices enter our daily life, and at the same time leave them outside, that is, let them alone, as things which are nothing absolute but remain dependent upon something higher. I would call this comportment toward technology which expresses 'yes' and at the same time 'no,' by an old word, *releasement toward things*.[78]

In a way, this is Heidegger's attempt to expand on what he was trying to do in the earlier essay on technology, namely, to build a free relationship to the essence of technology. The essence of technology, *Gestell*, is understood as the way that being reveals itself as meaningful in our current epoch in the history of being. Everything reveals itself to us through the ordinances of *Gestell* and everything is set upon to reveal itself, to offer itself up to us in those ways, including ourselves. A kind of interpretative sclerosis has set in then and the only possible response is to *once again* see how the manner in which the world reveals itself as meaningful, even through *Gestell*, is something that happens through us; it happens as a result of the way we are thrown and yet open to accept and reveal the world in that way and, in realizing it as a possibility and not a necessity, we begin to free ourselves from its constrictive grip on our interpretative capacities.

So, the great dangers which were to preoccupy Heidegger for a significant portion of his career before, during *and after* the war are directly related to the notion of rootedness. We read elsewhere of Heidegger's dismay at the 'hopeless frenzy of unchained technology and of the rootless organization of the average man' (IM: 40) and it may not strike us as all that significant that he uses the word rootless. But as we begin to pay attention, we find that this term goes deep into the Heideggerian confrontation with technology. And what is threatened more than anything in the technological age is our rootedness in the Earth. But Heidegger is flirting with danger here. After all, he deliberately wove together the notion of rootedness with the crass rhetoric of *Blut und Boden* when it suited his purposes in the 1930s and yet he uses the term here without apology or qualification. The question is, what does Heidegger mean by rootedness here and elsewhere?

One strategy, a strategy employed by Robert Metcalf in a very useful paper on the use of *Bodenständigkeit* in the Memorial Address, is to distinguish two uses of the term and its cognates.[79] Under that interpretation, the term has a phenomenological use in the 1920s, it is then used for rather less edified purposes in the 1930s before Heidegger reverts back to the phenomenological notion after the end of the Second World War. And though there is something compelling about Metcalf's account, it may in the end be a little too convenient and one can see how such an explanation might be dismissed as smacking of apologetics. There is no question but that Heidegger is sailing very close to the wind! Having said as much, it seems clear that Heidegger is genuinely philosophically concerned with uprootedness/rootlesssness as one of the major problems of the technological age. The difficulty here relates to the fact that at one point he envisioned his notion of rootedness as having distinct ethnic ramifications and he certainly never went out of his way to distinguish between his various uses of terms associated with rootedness, some of them clearly less salubrious than others. We can see then that Heidegger never entirely relinquishes some version of his own political philosophy – despite his sense of disenchantment with historical National Socialism which he sees as having been, in the end, not nearly revolutionary enough and disappointingly derivative. In the next two chapters we will look to trace the path to this later address (which still espouses some kind of commitment to the authentic vocation or destiny of the German people) back to its sources in Heidegger's philosophy. We must look to determine whether and to what extent that vision is embedded in his philosophy and, if it is, whether his philosophy can remain consistent and yet accommodate these political views. The second part of this study then will bring us back to *Being and Time*.

4

# The Authentic Dasein of a People

In the previous chapters we examined aspects of the Heidegger controversy where, it was argued, Heidegger's critics took a series of wrong turns. That is to say, in their haste to accuse Heidegger's work of latent Nazi sympathies, they focused on the wrong kinds of issues or even went so far as to precipitously dismiss his entire oeuvre as essentially a repackaging of the views of others. When it came to the issue of Heidegger's views on technology, many of the same critics simply misread the basic thrust and import of those views. In criticizing these *tendencies* within the 'affair' I am not for a moment suggesting that Heidegger is free from blame or that his thought is not somehow implicated. As I have said already, that strategy is precluded from the outset on the strength of Heidegger's own insistence on a profound relationship between his core philosophical views and his commitment in the early 1930s to National Socialism.

At the end of the previous chapter, we began to see how Heidegger's commitment to some kind of Germanocentrism had managed to survive all the way through to his later confrontation with the rootlessness of the technological age and his deployment of the notion of *Gelassenheit*. We further noted the disquieting reappearance of terms such as *Bodenständigkeit* and his insistence on the importance of artistic work being rooted in the native German soil of its homeland as the only possibility of salvation from a technological apocalypse for the West. In this chapter, we begin to excavate these seams in Heidegger's philosophy which *are* very much relevant to the political controversy and here we find ourselves in the midst of a veritable hornet's nest of difficulties which cannot be evaded. As we shall see below, Heidegger, in attempting to follow through on his broadside against egalitarianism and universalism looks to champion a version of provincialism which is worrisome in the extreme. Not only that, Heidegger himself looks to justify this move with an appeal to a disastrous interpretation of his own accounts of historicity and authenticity. More worrisome still, in a handful of passages in his private notebooks from the 1930s and 1940s and in seminars from the early 1930s, Heidegger tries to find a way to cobble together his concerns regarding *Gestell* and the concomitant problem of rootlessness with explicit antisemitic prejudices.

****

In what follows, we will examine Heidegger's outlines for the notion of an authentic community and the existential-ontological ground of such a community of mutual recognition. In doing so, we will look to show how Heidegger's account cannot consistently lend itself to the forms of 'rootedness', racism and antisemitism which he seemed to recommend without relying on a series of ultimately arbitrary moves. These types of discrimination, which Heidegger sees as an almost unavoidable consequence of being historical creatures, relate to an irreducible paradox which Heidegger's 'discovery' of historical man issues in. Within his own thought then, there is already a tension between those historical forces which shape our conscious awareness and thus infuse in us a sense of commitment, familiarity, community and belonging, and, at the same time, the *absolute* nature of the constitutive conditions which generate these commitments. In a way, Heidegger is resurrecting an old philosophical problem which Plato had examined in the *Republic*, namely, the inevitability of conflict when it comes to organizing any political community since to be human is, in a sense, to demand the right to favour one's own which, in the final analysis, cannot be reconciled with a universalizing account of fairness or equality! That in itself, however, does not pave the way for some kind of justifiable ethnic prejudice on the basis of historical or ethnic partisanship; rather what we can say is that Heidegger ignored the obligations he should have felt toward those who shared his own history in certain respects but who were looked on as a pariah people by other members of his community, namely, the Jews.

The irony is that we also find resources within Heidegger's own thought for a forceful condemnation of antisemitism and the Holocaust from the standpoint of their denial of the essence of human freedom, and therewith, the most important and exalted constitutive feature of human existence, namely our freedom-towards-death.[1] By denying the Jewish people this freedom as a people, their capacity, nay right, as a potential authentic community was denied them in the most depraved way. Indeed there are hints of such a criticism in Heidegger's iterations here and there and we will have to examine how this criticism might play out in terms of some of Heidegger's most fundamental philosophical insights concerning human freedom and the inveterately social character of existence. Again, however, we find that Heidegger failed some of his 'own' people in ways that the richness of his own thoughts on authentic historical community clearly proscribe!

## Heidegger and the authentic Dasein of a people

On Whit Sunday 1917, Heidegger pens a fascinating letter to his wife Elfride. One of the many significant remarks he makes points to a terribly difficult and, as it turns out, rather long-standing philosophical problem which, as I read things, is part of the motivation for Plato's *Republic* and is intimated again in the so-called Book X problem in Aristotle's *Ethics*. Heidegger writes that

> I cannot accept Husserl's phen[omenology]. as a final position even if it joins up with philos. – because in its approach & accordingly in its goal it is too narrow &

bloodless & because such an approach cannot be made absolute. Life is too rich & too great – thus for relativities that seek to come close to its meaning (that of the absolute) in the form of philosophical systems, it's a question of discovering the liberating path in an absolute articulation of relativity . . . The implacable necessity of a comparable engagement cannot be evaded today ... Since I've been lecturing, up to now I've constantly experienced these sudden reversals – until 'historical man' came to me in a flash this winter. (Heidegger. Freiburg. Whit Sunday, 1917)[2]

As we can see then, Heidegger conceives of his major breakthrough, even in his mid- to late twenties, as his discovery of 'historical man'; and, for better or worse, in a famous exchange with Löwith in Rome in the 1930s, he confirms that his notion of historicity in *Being and Time* stands as the philosophical underpinning to his commitment to National Socialism. Löwith reports:

I turned the conversation to the controversy in the *Neue Zuricher Zeitung* and explained to him that I agreed neither with [Hans] Barth's political attack [on Heidegger] nor with [Emil] Staiger's defense, insofar as I was of the opinion that his partisanship for National Socialism lay in the essence of his philosophy. Heidegger agreed without reservation, and added that his concept of 'historicity' was the basis of his political 'engagement.' (Karl Löwith. 'My Last Meeting with Heidegger in Rome, 1936')[3]

After *Being and Time* Heidegger had attempted to expand on his notion of authenticity and related notions, such as historicity, and makes references to the authentic Dasein of a people in various works, including *Introduction to Metaphysics*. He discusses this possibility, that is, the notion of an authentic Dasein of a people along structurally consistent lines to those we find in the accounts concerning authenticity, inauthenticity and solicitude in *Being and Time*. We are faced then with a number of challenges; first, we have to examine how Heidegger's notion of *Fürsorge*/solicitude is relevant to his account of authenticity before then asking whether the same difficulties which complicate the initial account of authenticity are going to trouble the idea or notion of an authentic Dasein of a people.[4] Ultimately, we may end up diagnosing Heidegger's political myopia in the 1930s as a consequence of his underlying inability to come to terms with the tension he articulates in his 1917 letter; he attempts to resolve that tension at the expense of Universalism and in favour of the relative, the provincial, but in a way which, I would contend, his own thought does not ultimately permit.

\*\*\*\*

In Section 26 of *Being and Time* Heidegger discusses the notion of solicitude (*Fürsorge*) and the related notions of leaping-in for someone (*für ihn einspringen*)[5] and leaping-ahead of them (*ihm vorausspringt*). Heidegger, at this point of *Being and Time*, wants to know what kind of 'identities' we have ordinarily, prior to any abstraction, when we are immersed or thrown into the world around us. His answer to this question relates to the compound structure that he has been examining, namely, being-in-the-world. Heidegger has argued that we live in an equipmental, project-oriented world.

In looking to describe the 'identity' of this everyday, busy, project-preoccupied Dasein Heidegger suggests that, already within the network of significations of our equipmentally oriented world, there is a clue to be discerned:

> In our 'description' of that environment which is closest to us – the work-world of the craftsman, for example, – the outcome was that along with the equipment to be found when one is at work [in Arbeit], those Others for whom the 'work' ["Werk"] is destined are 'encountered too'. If this is ready-to-hand, then there lies in the kind of Being which belongs to it (that is, in its involvement) an essential assignment or reference to possible wearers, for instance, for whom it should be 'cut to the figure'. (BT: 153)

Heidegger characterizes our interaction with Others as a liberating activity. We 'free' these entities which are 'like' us insofar as they are 'in'-the-world very much as we are when we encounter them. Heidegger observes, however, that when we first begin to consider our interaction with Others, we seem to be automatically oriented by our own Dasein and yet he looks to obviate any concerns that he is thereby sponsoring some kind of solipsism:

> even in this characterization does one not start by marking out and isolating the 'I' so that one must then seek some way of getting over to the Others from the isolated subject? To avoid this misunderstanding we must notice in what sense we are talking about 'the Others'. By 'Others' we do not mean everyone else but me – those over against whom the "I" stands out. They are rather those from whom, for the most part, one does not distinguish oneself – those among whom one is too. This Being-there-too [Auch-da-sein] with them does not have the ontological character of a Being-present-at-hand-along-'with' them within a world. This 'with' is something of the character of Dasein; the 'too' means a sameness of Being as circumspectively concernful Being-in-the-world. 'With' and 'too' are to be understood existentially, not categorially. By reason of this with-like [mithaften] Being-in-the-world, the world is always the one that I share with Others. The world of Dasein is a with-world [Mitwelt]. Being-in is Being-with Others. Their Being-in-themselves within-the-world is Dasein-with [Mitdasein]. (BT: 154–5)

Heidegger continues, arguing that we never in fact come across others as occurrent objects simply present at hand nor do we identify the other(s) as the distinct pole to oneself. Heidegger argues rather that our most immediate, typical experience of ourselves, takes place within our involved, project-oriented deportment as part of the 'group'; that is, we 'find ourselves' in the midst of some activity which relates us to others. Our most immediate sense of ourselves then, is as a member of some kind of human network or environment. We do not, in the first place, experience ourselves as remote individuals.

Having established this much in terms of the social constitution of Dasein, however, Heidegger makes a bizarre statement:

> The expression 'Dasein', however, shows plainly that 'in the first instance' this entity is unrelated to Others, and that of course it can still be 'with' Others afterwards.

> Yet one must not fail to notice that we use the term "Dasein-with" to designate that Being for which the others who are [die seienden Anderen] are freed within-the-world. This Dasein-with of the Others is disclosed within-the-world for a Dasein, and so too for those who are Daseins with us [die Mitdaseienden], only because Dasein in itself is essentially Being-with. (BT: 156)

The use of the word 'afterwards', in terms of how Dasein can be with others after initially being detached from them, sounds terribly problematic. It can read as though Heidegger is positing a primordial level of existence for Dasein which precedes or is antecedent to its existence with or involvement with Others. This seems to be a legitimate reading and yet it is patently incongruous with what he says *immediately* afterwards. In other words, if that is what Heidegger means, then the strength of his own characterization of the inveterately social nature of selfhood which emerges immediately afterwards would seem to outstrip the tenability of this anterior claim *and*, as it happens, there would appear to be a problem with his (implied) account of the barest and most foundational version of existential Dasein since being-with is existentially (existentially-ontologically) 'prior' to the Dasein that experiences the authentic *Augenblick*. Heidegger argues immediately afterwards that Dasein is *never* such that it is not already a being-with and yet we still have this curious claim to the effect that Dasein, in the first instance, is 'unrelated' to others but can be with Others afterwards. One *might* be tempted to read this as an allusion to Heidegger's understanding of the authentic *Augenblick* whereby one is momentarily 'alone', but this is to go against Heidegger's own explicit qualifications to the effect that one is alone as a creature that is a being-with insofar as that experience of being-alone is possible only as a creature that is existentially a being-with. But that means that that experience of aloneness is a deficient mode of our ineluctable 'being-withness', which means of course that even in our being-alone, as a deficient mode of being with, Dasein is in fact related to Others.[6]

In characterizing how we typically 'interact' with Others, we find that Heidegger reverts to a highly inclusive account of human existence which is more congruent with the account of Dasein as a being-with which preceded the confusing remark above. Heidegger characterizes our concernful dealings with others as *Fürsorge* or solicitude. Having introduced the notion of solicitude with respect to the manner in which we interact with and experience other people, Heidegger considers the various ways that that concern-for or solicitude can manifest itself, namely, as a leaping-in for or leaping-ahead of. What does it mean to leap-in for another person existentially? In a way, it is to deny the other their ownmost possibility – their freedom towards their ultimate horizon of finitude and thus a curtailment of their freedom. It is a way of dealing with another person that reflects a closing off of their authentic horizon, with its temporal hue, and to treat them in such a way as to conceal their innate potential.[7] In Heidegger's more general sense of authenticity and inauthenticity, to leap-in for would be to either usurp someone else's horizons and keep them locked within an existence characterized as continuous presence, as it were, or else to leap-ahead of and to see another person as similarly claimed and thus bounded by an horizon of finitude in their own right, thereby freeing the other for their own being-toward-death and recognizing in the other the same latent temporality which is constitutive of my own capacity to exist interpretatively.

If the notion of intersubjectivity, that is, authentic intersubjectivity, were something which Heidegger was going to expressly develop in *Being and Time*, there is enough in section 26 to suggest that it is something that would be cashed out in terms of leaping-ahead of another in an authentic relationship based on a reciprocal recognition of two people's mutual finitude. Even Dasein's most non-relational experience of its own finitude, which has a singularly individuating effect, cannot ultimately suppress its inter-connectedness. No matter how far the world of our everyday concern seems to recede from us during such an experience, we are still ultimately beings that are, only insofar as we are-in-the-world. And, to be-in-the-world, means to be a Dasein that is only insofar as it is a being-with. The only difference being that the light of our temporality is now refracted through those same structures of an everyday identity which we never really escape. We can now experience that world we inhabit more authentically and that means interpreting others more authentically as well. But none of this is the achievement of the isolated 'subject' in any traditional sense; rather it is a possibility that is available to Dasein when it experiences itself as a thrown projector. And, this, ultimately, would or should function as the theoretical backdrop to an authentic Dasein of the people which Heidegger glosses in section 74 of the same text and with *apparent* structural consonance in some of his later work.

To anyone who would express reservations over what appears to be a tendency at times toward solipsism in Heidegger's subsequent account of being-towards-death, he might well rejoin that he has already acknowledged that the very capacity to feel alone is merely a condition of our structural 'being-withness' whereby we experience a deficiency on the basis of the way we are existentially-ontologically constituted. But Heidegger yet maintains that the existential experience itself is characterized by a feeling of complete isolation and detachment. Clearly, Heidegger believes that his concession to the effect that the very capacity for 'aloneness' is only possible on the basis of our existential-ontological constitution as being-with is sufficient to forestall any solipsistic readings of his account of authenticity and to be fair, the gesture is made explicitly before the discussion of the authentic *Augenblick*. Notwithstanding, the discussion of this authentic experience itself is characterized existentially as something that leaves us feeling radically isolated and alone (which again, of course, is only possible on the basis of our constitution as *Mitsein*) and while this experience itself can function as the backdrop to an account of something like genuine intersubjectivity or empathy, it is still a phenomenologically impoverished account in some respects. Even within such an experience of extreme solitude, we can yet see something of our projection of 'otherness' as part of our very sense of self at work! It is not just an experience made possible by our existential constitution and a concomitant deficiency that relates to that constitution, rather the experience itself is not existentially an experience completely devoid of 'otherness'.[8] Heidegger, however, does not seem to agree, describing our confrontation with mortality as entirely individualizing, something utterly non-relational (*Unbezüglich*) and seems in the end to suggest that we cannot ultimately access another person's death as a substitute theme in terms of analysing that experience. Putting to one side, for the moment, my own reservations concerning Heidegger's scepticism regarding the relationality of our experience of finitude,[9] I would contend that his rhetoric and terminology with respect to the experience Dasein undergoes are somewhat tendentious and misleading in a way which undermines the theoretical underpinnings of his own Dasein story. Heidegger frequently affirms the exclusivity and the non-relational character of death as a possibility for Dasein:

> The full existential-ontological conception of death may now be defined as follows: death, as the end of Dasein, is Dasein's ownmost possibility – non-relational, certain and as such indefinite, not to be outstripped. Death is, as Dasein's end, in the Being of this entity towards its end. (BT: 303)

Granted, our everyday way of dealing with death, is very much in the mode of inauthenticity, that is, we 'process' everything in the mode of *das Man*. It is not something which we entertain as a genuine 'possibility' for our own Dasein. Rather death is something which is alien to us. Heidegger, in looking to retrieve the individual's most fecund existential possibility, wants to diminish the world of delusional everydayness as much as possible and this prompts an emphasis on a rather robust sense of solitary, anxious non-relatedness. However, this leads to something of an ambiguity in Heidegger's account since he can be seen to be suggesting then that what he wants to reject or undermine is the formal, structural notion of *Mitsein* which he characterized so positively earlier. And this of course cannot be what Heidegger means to achieve with his account of authenticity which is presumably why he reintroduces the caveats concerning the irreducibly social character of Dasein's existential-ontological constitution toward the end of the account of being-towards-death. What is crucial for Heidegger, of course, is the manner in which death as a possibility shapes our interpretative possibilities; it is formative at the most primordial, fundamental levels and this in turn is the clue needed for a fundamental ontology which appreciates the concealed backdrop to all disclosure and the recurring issue of an interplay between presence and absence. As an offshoot of this, Heidegger glosses or gestures at the possibility of an authentic life and an authentic community which would be based on the kind of authentic realization which is available to Dasein. We are individualized and socialized in the same stroke in terms of authenticity even if Heidegger hasn't quite formulated a terminology which captures this theoretical implication of his own account. Heidegger is clear at times that authentic being-towards-death is about rescuing the temporal backdrop to our interpretative existence from our immersion in the phony continuous presence of everydayness.[10] As Dasein's ownmost possibility, not to be out-stripped, anticipation of death is the experience that individualizes Dasein down to itself; but Heidegger cannot sever the structural ties to the others who, even in the authentic *Augenblick*, we are not entirely removed from; after all, the authentic self is merely an existentiell modification of the they-self. As such, Heidegger has to rescue the formal element of his account of the existential constitution of Dasein and reconcile it with the account of authenticity while trying to maintain this notion of non-relationality which harks back to the 'unrelated' nature of Dasein in section 26.

> The ownmost possibility is non-relational. Anticipation allows Dasein to understand that that potentiality-for-being in which its ownmost Being is an issue,

must be taken over by Dasein alone. Death does not just 'belong' to one's own Dasein in an undifferentiated way; death lays claims to it as an individual Dasein. The non-relational character of death, as understood in anticipation, individualizes Dasein down to itself. This individualizing is a way in which the 'there' is disclosed for existence. It makes manifest that all Being-alongside the things with which we concern ourselves, and all Being-with Others, will fail us when our ownmost potentiality-for-Being is the issue. Dasein can be authentically itself only if it makes possible for itself its own accord. But if concern and solicitude fail us, this does not signify at all that these ways of Dasein have been cut off from its authentically Being-its-Self. As structures essential to Dasein's constitution, these have a share in conditioning the possibility of any existence whatsoever. Dasein is authentically itself only to the extent that, as concernful Being-alongside and solicitous Being-with, it projects itself upon its ownmost potentiality-for-Being rather than upon the possibility of the they-self. (BT: 308)

As the non-relational possibility, death individualizes – but only in such a manner that, as the possibility which is not to be outstripped, it makes Dasein, as Being-with, have some understanding of the potentiality-for-Being of Others. Since anticipation of the possibility which is not to be outstripped discloses also all the possibilities which lie ahead of that possibility, this anticipation includes the possibility of taking the whole of Dasein in advance [Vorwegnehmens] in an existentiell manner; that is to say, it includes the possibility of existing as a whole potentiality-for-Being. (BT: 309)

We can see how, in these passages, Heidegger is trying to link his account back up to the notion of solicitude in section 26, in particular, his account of leaping-ahead for another Dasein. And we can see a kind of equivocation in what he is doing. On the one hand he writes that in the authentic *Augenblick*, all Being-with Others 'will fail us'. And yet he wants to maintain that 'if concern and solicitude fail us, this does not signify at all that these ways of Dasein have been cut off from its authentically Being-its-Self. As structures essential to Dasein's constitution, these have a share in conditioning the possibility of any existence whatsoever.' And then again he will insist that though death individualizes, it does so 'in such a manner that, as the possibility which is not to be outstripped, it makes Dasein, as Being-with, have some understanding of the potentiality-for-Being of Others'. In understanding the thrown nature of our own situation and the ultimate possibility which conditions every aspect of my interpretative existence I simultaneously see those from whom I never normally detach myself as similarly 'claimed'. But at the same time, this can almost read as a token gesture once he has gone almost too far in another direction with claims such as the following:

We may now summarize our characterization of authentic Being-towards-death as we have projected it existentially: anticipation reveals to Dasein its lostness in the they-self, and brings it face to face with the possibility of being itself, primarily unsupported by concernful solicitude, but of being itself, rather, in an impassioned freedom towards death – a freedom which has been released from the Illusions of the 'they', and which is factical, certain of itself and anxious. (BT: 311)

So Heidegger is emphatic that Dasein is existentially ontologically a being-with, and yet in the same section where he attempts to demonstrate as much he suggests that Dasein can be understood as being, in the first instance, unrelated to Others. He then proceeds to offer a richly inclusive account of the sociality of our existence and the authentic possibilities available in terms of engaging with others as finite transcendences in their own right in the mode of leaping-ahead. However, Dasein, always and for the most part is such that it has surrendered its identity to an inauthentic, anonymous group identity which he refers to as *das Man*/the they. And in the move to authenticity Heidegger describes how an awareness of our ineluctable finitude can rescue us from our 'lostnesss' in the collective, indistinct anonymous identity of everydayness. However, in doing so Heidegger seems to privilege again the notion of the intensely private, non-relational self which he has gone to considerable lengths to deconstruct as phenomenologically inappropriate. And in a way, this is already indicative of the struggle at the heart of Heidegger's thought in terms of the tension between the absolute and the relative or the universal and the immediate and is replicated in his disastrous attempt to gesture at an alternative political vision to modernity's universalizing aims by valorizing the provincial and the local in a way which is as unwarranted as the rhetoric of non-relationality and unrelatedness is to the project of *Being and Time*. The conditions which allow Dasein to become an individual are universal, their instantiation issues in an immediate historical context, but the conditions which shape that event are in a way absolute and are, simultaneously, the conditions for the possibility of mutual recognition; this is something which Heidegger had already seen in his letter to Elfride and it is a problem whose complexity he underestimated in the 1930s.

\*\*\*\*

So, given that Heidegger argues that human beings can be intersubjectively authentic, (and this would, presumably, function as the theoretical foundation for the notion of an authentic Dasein of a people) how are we to understand Heidegger's account of the authentic historical community? And can it be reconciled with the foundations we have unpacked above upon which it would have to be based? Heidegger certainly seems to suggest at times that his philosophy circumscribes the conditions for the authentic realization of an historical people, an authentic Dasein of a people. We find claims to that effect in the opening chapter of *Introduction to Metaphysics* for example. How then does an authentic historical community come about? And is there in fact, any sense, in which it can be thought to sanction the level of exclusion and provincialism which Heidegger felt justified in championing in the early 1930s in particular?

In *Introduction to Metaphysics*, we find Heidegger expanding on the notion of authenticity which he examined formally in terms of the individual Dasein in *Being and Time*:

> Our asking of the fundamental metaphysical question is historical because it opens up the happening of human Dasein in its essential relations – that is, its relations to beings as such and as a whole – opens it up to possibilities not yet

asked about, futures to come [*Zu-kuenften*], and thereby also binds it back to its inception that has been, and thus sharpens and burdens it in its present. In this questioning, our Dasein is summoned to its history in the full sense of the word and is called to make a decision in it – and this is not a derivative, useful application of this questioning in terms of morality and worldviews. Instead, the fundamental position and bearing of this questioning is in itself historical, stands and holds itself in the happening, and questions on the ground of this happening and for this happening.

But we still lack the essential insight into how far this asking of the question of Being, an asking which is in itself historical, intrinsically belongs to the world history of the earth. We said: on the earth, all over it, a darkening of the world is happening. The essential happenings in this darkening are: the flight of the gods, the destruction of the earth, the reduction of human beings to a mass, the preeminence of the mediocre. (IM: 47)

On the one hand, the possible emergence of an authentic Dasein of the people would seem to be something which is of the utmost concern for the people in general. And yet, Heidegger believes that this collective undertaking is the unique destiny of the German people since he persists in the hope that a different mode of revealing may emerge through this most metaphysical of all peoples as opposed to the debased technocratic societies of Russia and America:

This Europe, in its unholy blindness always on the point of cutting its own throat, lies today in the great pincers between Russia on the one side and America on the other. Russia and America, seen metaphysically, are both the same: the same hopeless frency of unchained technology and of the rootless organization of the average man. When the farthest corner of the globe has been conquered technologically and can be exploited economically; when any incident you like, in any place you like, at any time you like, becomes accessible as fast as you like … when time is nothing but speed, instantaneity, and simultaneity, and time as history has vanished from all Dasein of all peoples … there looms like a specter over all this uproar the question: what for? – where to? – and what then? (IM: 40)

As things stand with this passage, Heidegger would appear to be lamenting the state of Europe, squeezed as it is between the twin forces of American capitalism and Russian communism. And the only way out, it appears initially, is for Europe to somehow retrieve its spiritual strength. The nature of the decline is, as he was to say repeatedly through the 1930s and beyond, a kind of loss of roots, an uprooting or rootlessness which Heidegger identifies with Europe having lost its spiritual strength:

The spiritual decline of the earth has progressed so far that peoples are in danger of losing their last spiritual strength, the strength that makes it possible even to see the decline [which is meant in relation to the fate of 'Being'] and to appraise it as such. This simple observation has nothing to do with cultural pessimism – nor with any optimism either, of course; for the darkening of the world, the flight of the gods, the destruction of the earth, the reduction of human beings to a mass, the hatred and mistrust of everything creative and free has already reached such proportions throughout the whole earth that such childish categories as pessimism and optimism have long become laughable. (IM: 40/41)

Again this all very much sounds like a worldwide problem and that Europe, whatever he may mean by that, would have a decisive role to play in countering planetary technology. However, as Heidegger goes further, we see that there is a Germanocentrism at the heart of what he is doing:

> We lie in the pincers. Our people, as standing in the center, suffers the most intense pressure – our people, the people richest in neighbors and hence the most endangered people, and for all that, the metaphysical people. We are sure of this vocation; but this people will gain a fate from its vocation only when it creates *in itself* a resonance, a possibility of resonance for this vocation, and grasps its tradition creatively. All this implies that this people, as a historical people, must transpose itself – and with it the history of the West – from the center of their future happening into the originary realm of the powers of Being. Precisely if the great decision regarding Europe is not to go down the path of annihilation – precisely then can this decision come about only through the development of new, historically *spiritual* forces from the center. (IM: 41)

And Heidegger now links these ideas concerning the authentic Dasein of a people and its vocation specifically back to section 74 of *Being and Time*:

> To ask: how does it stand with Being? – this means nothing less than to *repeat and retrieve* [wieder-holen] the inception of our historical-spiritual Dasein, in order to transform it into the other inception. Such a thing is possible. It is in fact the definitive form of history, because it has its onset in a happening that grounds history. (IM: 41)

In the next chapter we discuss section 74 in *Being and Time* and the links between these ideas should become obvious. Heidegger, already before this 1935 text was weaving together ideas pertaining to fate and destiny which clearly anticipated some of the more worrisome rhetoric of the 1930s and this is made even more explicit in the 1933 to 1934 seminar *Nature, History, State*. Some may wish to argue that the fact that Heidegger never intended to publish the offending seminar which we also examine in the next chapter means that we should not place too much store in what we find therein. And, while I tend to agree that one shouldn't place such a seminar on the same footing as some of his more important philosophical texts, it is useful to see how Heidegger develops key notions from section 74 of *Being and Time* and *Introduction to Metaphysics* in a specifically political context.

A few passages later we find Heidegger deploying again the notion of rootedness:

> Through our questioning, we are entering a landscape; to be in this landscape is the fundamental prerequisite for restoring rootedness to historical Dasein. (IM: 42)

And it will be through the asking of the prior question to the fundamental question of metaphysics that Heidegger thinks that a path out of this dire situation will be found:

when we first ask the fundamental question, everything depends on our taking up the decisive fundamental position in asking it the *prior question*, and winning and securing the bearing that is essential here. This is why we brought the question about Being into connection with the fate of Europe, where the fate of the earth is being decided, while for Europe itself our historical Dasein proves to be the center.

Heidegger goes on to write that:

> Asking about beings as such and as a whole, asking the question of Being, is then one of the essential fundamental conditions for awakening the spirit, and thus for an originary world of historical Dasein, and thus for subduing the danger of the darkening of the world, and thus for taking over the historical mission of our people, the people of the center of the West. (IM: 52)

It seems clear then that Heidegger is reprising at the theoretical level a notion of Germanocentrism which was more nakedly problematic in some of his less-guarded iterations:

> when the spiritual strength of the West fails and the West starts to come apart at the seams, when this moribund pseudocivilization collapses into itself, pulling all forces into confusion and allowing them to suffocate in madness.
> Whether such a thing occurs or does not occur, this depends solely on whether we as a historical-spiritual Volk will ourselves, still and again, or whether we will ourselves no longer.[11]

We are left in little doubt then during the course of the opening section of *Introduction to Metaphysics* that Heidegger has the German people in particular in mind here.[12] However, we have to wonder as to whether his own theoretical underpinnings for authenticity permit him to make the various moves that he makes in terms of delimiting some kind of ethnic or cultural borders with respect to historical Dasein? If we operate from the platform of the discussion of Dasein, *Mitsein*, being-in-the-world and the notion of authenticity as an existentiell modification of our day-to-day existence as part of *das Man*, we have to wonder as to how Heidegger thinks himself theoretically justified in denying his shared 'history' with others within his own cultural and intellectual milieus. Why is the historical situation which unites him with Jewish colleagues, lovers and friends less authentic? This commitment to some of the blubo excesses of German nationalism is not necessarily entailed by Heidegger's account of authenticity or historical Dasein at all! Thus, we may be forced to attribute Heidegger's nationalist commitments to a kind of racism which, ultimately, cannot be reconciled with the theoretical framework upon which it is supposedly based. Having said as much, it must be recognized that Heidegger has genuine philosophical concerns with deracination, miscegenation, globalization, cosmopolitanism and internationalism. These are a part of his general confrontation with the project of modernity and we will have more to say on this toward the end of the chapter as we look to draw some conclusions. But one of the things which certainly *is* worrisome is the fact that Heidegger seems to advocate a kind of racism which is not perhaps based on the notion of biology, or race in that biologically deterministic sense, but a kind of spiritual racism which is deeply problematic in its own right.

To be authentic for Dasein involves a realization of our own finitude and the thrown nature of our existence in an historical world which is in turn projected by us and reflected even in the structures of everydayness. Seeing others as similarly thrown allows us to interact with them, not just in the disengaged manner of our inauthentic everydayness, but rather, given that we are never but with others in the first place, it allows us to interact with them as historical creatures very much as we are. And this in turn would have to be the undergirding for the ways in which a community would allow for authentic intersubjectivity. Heidegger attempts to map things out in this way in some of his political writings and speeches from the 1930s, but, alarmingly, he seems to resurrect some of the isolationist baggage of *Unbezogenheit* from section 26 of *Being and Time* and the notion of *Unbezüglich* from the account of being-towards-death. Heidegger's collectivist account is, as it were, the account of individual Dasein 'writ large', as the authentic Dasein of the people but remains encumbered with some of the baggage of non-relationality which complicates his account of authenticity in *Being and Time*.

During the period of his rectorship, while exhorting German people to support Hitler in the upcoming plebiscite concerning Germany's withdrawal from the League of Nations, we find Heidegger writing:

> This is not a turning away from the community of nations. On the contrary – with this step, our people is submitting to that essential law of human existence to which every people must first give allegiance if it is still to be a people. It is only out of the parallel observance by all peoples of this unconstitutional demand of self-responsibility that there emerges the possibility of taking one another seriously so that a community can be affirmed.
>
> The will to a true community of nations [Völkergemeinschaft] is equally far removed both from an unrestrained, vague desire for world brotherhood and from blind tyranny. Existing beyond this opposition, this will allows peoples and states to stand by one another in an open and manly fashion as self-reliant entities.[13]

Heidegger at times seems to suggest that the collective historical Dasein of a people functions as a singular entity in the manner of Dasein, that is, either authentically or inauthentically. And, if the account of the authentic Dasein of a people glossed in the passages above is an extrapolation structurally consonant with his own conception of authenticity in *Being and Time*, we are faced again with something along the lines of the problem we faced with the recalcitrant passage from section 26. In other words, Heidegger seems to want to invoke a kind of primordial level of isolationist self-determination, along historical lines, which is to serve as the condition for the possibility of a community of nations. But this kind of self-determining sovereignty as the precondition for any subsequent interaction at the level of individuals or communities seems to be incongruent with the existential ontological structure of Dasein while standing squarely in accord with the vexing notion of Dasein as being, in the first instance, unrelated to others (*Unbezogenheit*).

## Freedom toward death

In the foregoing we have discussed how Heidegger's authentic community might look and we have indicated how he himself erred on the side of singularity/relativity in ways which mirror the problems with the early account of authenticity. However, we have also seen how Heidegger's account is ultimately a universal one – the conditions under which someone is historicized are themselves universal. And, ironically enough, it is this very fact that allows Heidegger to subsequently condemn what happened to the Jewish community in one of the few explicit references to the Holocaust that he makes. Alas, Heidegger failed to follow this thought to its conclusion since, if he had, he would have realized that his own thought was not just inimical to biological racism but also to the sort of metaphysical/spiritual racism that he seemed to think in some sense justifiable.[14]

In 1949, during a series of lectures in Bremen, Heidegger provocatively notes (the infamous 'agriculture remark' occurs during the same series of lectures) that the victims in the death camps did not die, that their death had been denied them. The implication would appear to be that their capacity to be-towards-death was denied to them and, as such, we can understand them as being disposed of in a way which suppressed the most important well springs of a shared humanity. But this interpretation necessitates a concession to the absolute, universal nature of notions such as our historicity which are unavailable to the localizing move that Heidegger sometimes tries to make. In a lecture entitled '*Die Gefahr*' ('The Danger') Heidegger proclaims:

> Are there times when we could have noticed *the* distress, the dominance of distresslessness? There are indications. Only we do not attend to them.
> 
> Hundreds of thousands die in masses, Do they die? They perish. They are put down. Do they die? They become pieces of inventory of a standing reserve for the fabrication of corpses. Do they die? They are unobtrusively liquidated in annihilation camps. And even apart from such as these – millions now in China abjectly end in starvation.
> 
> To die, however, means to carry out death in its essence. To be able to die means to be capable of carrying this out. We are only capable of it, however, when our essence is endeared to the essence of death.[15]

What else is Heidegger invoking here if not the absolute precondition for any sense of authentic community, regardless of historical specificity? What else do we have here but the articulation of historical relativity or immediacy which can ground an individual and a community but which is ultimately universal/absolute? Heidegger is alluding here to one of his formulations of authentic human freedom. It may seem like a morbid account of freedom, but, in fact, it is very much construed as a positive possibility for human beings. We are inescapably finite creatures, and this is the horizon against which the world is affectively constituted for us. We are thereby understood, for Heidegger, as historical creatures and this, in part, is what he means by the claim that time is the meaning of being. That is, the hermeneutic conditions of our understanding of ourselves and the world reduce essentially to our sense of finitude; that is what being means for us. To be, for Dasein, means to be temporal. It is the ultimate delimiting condition for our interpretative understanding. This horizon is a horizon of possibility, according to Heidegger, and we are to understand our freedom in this light. Precisely what was stolen or denied the Jewish community by the perpetrators of the Holocaust (we can infer from Heidegger's remark) is their freedom (freedom so understood), their possibilities understood against the backdrop of a temporal horizon. Their possibility and future *im*possibility were taken away from them, their horizon as a community was expunged and they were plunged as existing creatures into a hell without horizons. As Heidegger puts it in the lecture itself:

> in the midst of these innumerable dead, the essence of death remains disguised … To be capable of death in its essence means to be able to die. Those that are able to die are first of all the mortals in the weighty sense of this word. Massive distresses innumerable, horrific undying death all about – and nevertheless the essence of death is disguised from the human. The human is not yet the mortal.[16]

In the end, and this is not at all to diminish the awful suffering of those who perished at Nazi hands, but in terms of the ultimate crime perpetrated against them, it was not just the act of execution itself that we should acknowledge; the collective erasure of their horizon is crucial as well![17] They were ejected from the world of solicitude and indeed most of them were reduced to 'horizonless' entities long before they reached their terminus. In other words, their historical horizon had been erased before they got to their point of execution. But what of the comparably oblivious poor souls who were murdered off the trains in a highly choreographed process which was designed to minimize anxiety? Well, in a sense, they were processed very much as animals on factory farms – where creatures are ushered along through a process with the minimum of fuss and are rendered lifeless as quickly as possible. Heidegger can be taken to be making something of a Kantian claim in that case – these people were duped into death almost as so many animals on a factory farm; they were treated as creatures en masse without horizons, not as ends in themselves, but mere quanta to be disposed of. And, in a way, there is an obvious link here to Heidegger's other remark in this context concerning the 'essential' similarity between the processing of bodies in death camps, factory farming and nuclear bombs in the unfortunately dubbed 'agriculture remark'. Heidegger is referring to the way in which the only considerations which have any purchase anymore are technological ones; everything is reduced to a series of technological and logistical problems to be solved using technological means whether we are dealing with the consumption of meat, genocide or military conflict.

Deprived of the spiritual oxygen upon which our capacity to entertain hope relies (to experience ourselves as historical beings, to anticipate and commemorate, to be creatures with a past and a future), those that were murdered in the death camps were rendered broken, docile creatures, like ruminants rambling aimlessly toward their slaughter. In a way, their execution had been carried out much earlier, long before they reached the gas chambers at Auschwitz.[18] For Heidegger then, the Jews in the death camps, by and large, did not 'die'. They were *put* to death, but they had already lost sight of their horizon and thus were rendered 'dead' long before they gasped for a last breath in the gas chambers. Their freedom toward death and thus their capacity to exist as free human beings and as an authentic community had been stripped from them. And in a sense, Heidegger is reinforcing, here, the absolute nature of the conditions which render any community relative or local as alluded to at the beginning of this chapter and the associated tension between the private and the public or the universal and the particular.

The notion of death figures rather prominently in *Being and Time*. Heidegger's interest is not a macabre fixation on moribund existence; rather he is interested in the way our understanding and interpretation of ourselves and the world around us is determined in advance by a series of constitutive conditions. One of the things which, whether we are aware of it or not, weighs heavily on the way we interpret the world around us, ourselves and other people is our inescapable sense of finitude. It is important to note however that Heidegger is not interested in our biological or even biographical death. Our actual demise is not something that really concerns him at all. Rather, Heidegger is interested in our temporality, the way our sense of 'possibility' is determined and limited in advance by our awareness of our own mortality. The futural, directional nature of our existence is already indicative of the temporal horizon within which we live; it is one of the constitutive conditions of our understanding of ourselves and the world around us. So it is not so much being-at-an-end that Heidegger has in mind, rather being-towards-the-end. Of course, for the most part, we look to suppress this part of our conscious existence and live in a kind of illusory state of continuous presence where death as a genuine interpretative possibility is precluded from our understanding of ourselves. It is not something which we, ordinarily, entertain as a genuine possibility for our existence. Nevertheless, Heidegger believes that some sense of this possibility is always constitutively operative and that despite our best attempts to evade any acknowledgement of it, we are still vaguely aware of its ominous 'presence' and this fact is attested to by the sense of anxiety we feel concerning our continued existence. Heidegger is convinced that this temporal backdrop to our interpretative awareness, our historicity, is crucial to any sense of living authentically and is constitutive of both our authentic and inauthentic existence. Being-free-for-one's-death, in a way then, is the ultimate type of freedom that a human can aspire to for Heidegger and it is the foundation for a community based on mutual recognition along the lines of leaping-ahead for the other in an environment where we are never anything but *Mitsein* to begin with. And it is this freedom which the Jews (as an historical community) can be understood to have been denied, denied in a way which Heidegger, from within the resources of his own thought, should be able to condemn as a crime against *any* historical community since it is a denial of the conditions under which any community can emerge as a free community.

This is what the Jews suffered at the hands of the Nazis according to this controversial statement from Heidegger – he holds the Nazis to account for the broken spirits of the inmates and others being ferried to their deaths from all over the continent! Their authentic human freedom as individuals and, thus, as a potentially authentic historical community, was denied them or suppressed as soon as their horizon, their freedom-toward-death was taken away. That weightless anchor which roots all of us in our lives, our historical horizon, was loosed from these people and they were left to drift desolately and disconsolately to annihilation. Alas, Heidegger is unable to see that this consequence of his own thought points to the extreme danger of privileging the historical instantiation of one community over another on the basis of conditions which, as he had already seen in 1917, are in a way *absolute*. Such a move is ultimately arbitrary and where Heidegger's mature thought seems to shy away (although even here things can be a little ambiguous) from such commitments, in the early and mid-1930s he was determined to justify such a move[19] – justify it in such a way, however, that it leads to a gross inconsistency in his own thought.

This brings us back to the issue raised earlier concerning historical man and a difficulty that the young Heidegger wrestled with which is as old as philosophy itself. How do we reconcile the human desire to prefer one's 'own' with the overarching demand for impartiality, universal justice and so on? We face an inevitable conflict no matter how we look to reconcile those incommensurable aspirations. In terms of modernity's universalizing aspirations, Heidegger remained a staunch critic and wanted to find some way to preserve the primacy of the immediate. But what allows the immediate, the relative, the historical situation to emerge involves conditions which human beings in general are subject to. And these are at once the grounds for the possibility of authentic intersubjectivity and cannot arbitrarily be the privilege of a particular class of people. Trying to negotiate between the absolute and the relative, as Plato saw with breathtaking acuity in the *Republic*, is the source of an inevitable conflict. The Enlightenment vision represents, for Heidegger (in the shape of liberal democracy and communism), a doomed attempt to resolve this conflict; Heidegger looks to find some kind of resolution convinced of the impossibility of that aim, but, in doing so, he tries to favour the historically relative in ways which his own account of authenticity cannot consistently allow.

So, in what sense does this difficulty which we have been discussing map onto the tension between the absolute and the relative which Heidegger identifies in 1917 and looks to resolve with his notion of historical man? Well, in speaking of historical man, the conditions under which the human being becomes historicized involve something like the discovery of oneself as a finite transcendence – as a thrown projector. As thrown in this way, one finds oneself as a particularized human being under the conditions of temporality which are determinative for each historical instantiation. However, Heidegger further wants to suggest that these are the conditions for something like authentic solicitude as well. Section 26 of *Being and Time* opens the door to the possibility of an authentic community of Daseins based on a mutual recognition of one's shared temporal constitution, that is, one's historicity. And we shall see that in section 74 Heidegger begins to put some meat on the bones of these ideas. But, in putting things in this way, Heidegger would appear to be saying that one can outline the conditions for the possibility of authentic co-existence. And yet, at the same time, Heidegger makes this curious claim to the effect that Dasein can, in the first instance, be such that it is unrelated to others. What this would seem to map onto is the idea that one can exist as a temporal or historical Dasein in such a way as to be individualized *first* before then turning to other Daseins. But this doesn't really tally with the account of Dasein as always and ever a *Mitsein*, that is, that being-with is constitutive of what it means for any human being to be in the first place. So, if Heidegger wants to find a way around the transcendental and the absolute, back to the provincial, he has to find a way to get back to the immediate and the historically relative but in a way which seems irreconcilable with the relevant theoretical underpinnings of his own thought.

In the end, the notion of historical man does not resolve the tension identified by the ancients, it merely restates it; Heidegger looks to favour the provincial in a way which is clearly problematic. That is not to say, of course, that there is anything wrong with having feelings of preference or partiality towards those with whom one identifies as part of a collective. The problem is that in confronting the universalizing tendencies of the project of modernity – one is not thereby warranted to treat those preferences as somehow justifiable in a more meaningful register. It is one thing to cheer for one's local team, but it is quite another to suggest that one team is entitled to more rights and entitlements than the opposing team. And given the personal and often significantly more than cordial nature of the relationship between Heidegger and numerous Jewish intellectuals – it seems unpardonable that he refused to see these people themselves as similarly claimed by the temporal and historical conditions which he was subject to or that he thought that any other cultural differences warranted anything substantive! In short, Heidegger completely oversteps the bounds of his own thought in supposing that the notion of historicity allows him to justify some of the political views he looks to champion. In the next chapter we will examine some of the ways that Heidegger tried to intertwine his political views with the notions of historicity and authenticity in ways which show him not only to be a committed Nazi but prone to ethnic chauvinism as well.

5

# Heidegger and Antisemitism

Towards the end of the previous chapter, we saw how Heidegger's thought was mired in a difficulty which he had been struggling with even as early as 1917, as expressed in a letter to his wife. Heidegger believed that his notion of historical man, or historicity, allowed him a way out of this impasse and instead of having to cede ground to the Moderns, he could absorb the worries of Plato and Aristotle and yet believed he could resolve the dilemma in such a way as would allow him to justify some kind of provincialism on theoretical grounds. We further saw how this attempt is ultimately doomed to failure on the basis of Heidegger's own account of the conditions which make us historical to begin with, that is, he relies on an appeal to a universal human condition which issues in a sense of historical specificity.

In this chapter, we shall look at the various ways that Heidegger 'campaigned' on behalf of his provincialist aspirations in the context of his commitment to National Socialism and in ways which have unmistakable antisemitic undercurrents at times. Again, this will not ultimately demonstrate that Heidegger's thought leads directly to antisemitism and should thus be extirpated from the canon; nevertheless, that does not absolve us of our duty to examine the issue since it is Heidegger himself who looked to buttress his ethnic chauvinism using resources from within his own thought. Demonstrating the failure of that attempt does not entirely exonerate Heidegger either; rather, what it indicates is the destitution of his thought in terms of building upon what his analysis of historicity at the theoretical level (in section 26 of *Being and Time* for example) entailed – namely, an injunction, almost Kantian, against ever treating others as 'means', or, in Heidegger's terms, never to deny them their essence, that is, their horizon, the capacity to be towards death, never, for example, to treat them as resources to be used or waste to be disposed of, precisely that aspect of the human condition which allowed him to condemn the treatment of inmates in the death camps as flying in the face of crucial principles of his own philosophy.

The question of Heidegger's antisemitism is one which deserves more sober treatment than it has hitherto enjoyed. Alas, even leaving to one side the agenda-driven sensationalism of a handful of cranks, the treatment of this issue has been largely anecdotal and gossipy. That is not to suggest that we can exonerate Heidegger – rather we should confront directly some of the most incriminating comments and actions of Heidegger while he was in a position to influence things under Nazi rule as Rector of Freiburg University along with all of the other evidence available from before and after that fateful period. This examination will clearly demonstrate, for example, that even so 'sensitive' a philosophical soul as Heidegger could become part of the 'establishment' once absorbed into the dynamics and hierarchy of the power structure that obtained. However, even worse than that, Heidegger was to go so far as to employ so loathsome a term as *Verjudung* in his correspondence from the early 1930s.[1] Some may argue that Heidegger's use of the term didn't quite reduce to the more repugnant forms of xenophobia which permeated Germany at that time, that the term was a generic one in Heidegger's mind, a shorthand reference to the levelling influence of cosmopolitan urbanity which he saw as a symptom of contemporary society's decadence.[2] But this is hardly sufficient to expunge this awful stain from his character; it doesn't mitigate or extenuate beyond putting things in a certain context. After all, to demonstrate that Heidegger wasn't quite the bloodthirsty, hate-mongering, latter-day Abraham of Sancta Clara should hardly seem necessary to anyone who thinks him an intellectual with a modicum of philosophical insight never mind a philosopher of the first rank![3] It was not so much that rabid antisemitism led Heidegger to seek a position which would allow him to persecute Jews; rather, once in a position where certain kinds of actions and postures were not just expected, but demanded, Heidegger proved himself a tractable and zealous Nazi. And, even were we to argue that Heidegger's hands were ultimately tied by the situation he found himself in (which would be an untruth to begin with), one's responsibility is not automatically discharged by circumstance. It seems reasonable to suppose that many of us would rarely put a foot wrong if difficult situations never arose; if doing the right thing was effortless, then which of us should falter? Evil isn't solely the commission of barbarous deeds by inhuman malefactors; of course such people do exist and they can perpetrate great wrongs, however, for the most part, evil and its outcomes are effected by and affect ordinary people. The attempt to render pathological the perpetrators of evil has the rather unfortunate effect of preventing us from ever understanding the lesson that history keeps trying to teach us, namely, that ordinary people, when placed in extraordinary circumstances, are as capable of great evil as they are heroism. As Christopher R. Browning writes in defence of his own efforts to understand the Holocaust through an historical study of a particular battalion of the Order Police:

> Another possible objection to this kind of study concerns the degree of empathy for the perpetrators that is inherent in trying to understand them. Clearly the writing of such a history requires the rejection of demonization. The policemen in the battalion who carried out the massacres and deportations, like the much smaller number who refused or evaded, were human beings. I must recognize that in the same situation, I could have been either a killer or an evader – both were human – if I want to understand and explain the behaviour of both as best I can. This recognition does indeed mean an attempt to empathize. What I do not accept, however, are the old clichés that to explain is to excuse, to understand is to forgive. Explaining is not excusing, understanding is not forgiving. Not trying to understand the perpetrators in human terms would make impossible not only this study but any history of Holocaust perpetrators that sought to go beyond one-dimensional caricature. Shortly before his death at the hands of the Nazis,

the French historian Marc Bloch wrote, 'When all is said and done, a single word, "understanding," is the beacon light of our studies.' It is in that spirit that I have tried to write this book.[4]

With respect to Heidegger himself, I am inclined towards the view that Heidegger *was* guilty of a moderate and indeed all too prevalent level of ethnic chauvinism; and, of course, 'the Jew' was the target of a great deal of German, and indeed European antipathy. Heidegger was, if you like, your garden variety, everyday racist. In other words, Heidegger's views, for the most part (and of course, in the context of his time) would have been those of many ordinary people not entirely unlike ourselves.[5] In our own time, while many of us don't necessarily have a problem with tinkers or travellers, foreigners or homeless people per se, we should ask ourselves whether we find that whispered words of prejudice secretly resonate with the slumbering prejudices of our own souls when our streets become strewn with shabby, recumbent figures grovelling for change, or when an encampment of travellers suddenly appears along our idyllic country lane, or, most 'egregious' of all, when we see a foreign person struggling in 'our' language to do a job that one of our 'nearest and dearest' would readily undertake in order to avoid the dreaded dole-queue?[6]

The fact that Heidegger's ethnic chauvinism wasn't quite the obscene racism of the likes of Streicher[7] does not in any way absolve Heidegger. In the first place, he should have known better; again, the relativity of historical man is in a way absolute; that is, 'the Jew' can have a history, a past and a future and thus the capacity to empathize and be empathized with every bit as much as the peasant who supposedly quashes the notion of him leaving the provinces to take up a chair in Berlin. And yet, as Peter E. Gordon notes in his review of the infamous black notebooks, Heidegger was willing to go so far as to describe the Jews, the Semitic nomads he criticizes in his 1933–34 seminar, as 'worldless':

> Machination was his preferred name for the technological force that Heidegger saw as dominating the modern world. The notebooks of the later 1930s are thick with dark ruminations on the rise of technology and its manifold consequences across the globe. *Machenschaft* appears with such frequency that it assumes a quasi-mythological status not unlike an ancient god. Heidegger brooded over 'the unconditional power of machination' and 'the complete groundlessness of things.' Occasionally, however, Machenschaft is embroidered with a more specific meaning: in an entry (circa 1939) he denounces liberalism, pacifism, and 'the rising power of Jewry.' The ascendency of the Jews belonged to 'the metaphysics of the West' that helped to spread both 'empty rationality' and 'a capacity for calculation.' Elsewhere he wrote that 'one of the most hidden forms of the gigantic and perhaps the oldest is the tenacious aptitude for calculating and profiteering and intermingling, upon which the worldlessness of Jewry is founded.'[8]

Quite clearly then, and certainly in private, Heidegger believed that his ethnic chauvinism was something which was related to his philosophy. In other words, Heidegger's concerns with rootedness and the urgency of the task of finding a way to resist the rootless frenzy of unchained technology was something that Heidegger connected to deeply troubling antisemitic prejudices and a more overarching ethnic chauvinism. Heidegger's philosophy looks to embrace a provincialism which has rather distressing implications. We have to ask ourselves then how far one should be willing to go for the sake of such provincial allegiance. After all, what of Heidegger's history away from the valley in Todtnauberg, in Marburg and Freiburg – the history of his own life at the academy and indeed his love affairs with the likes of Hannah Arendt as well as relationships with Jewish teachers, colleagues and friends? Where exactly are the lines of Heidegger's historical map to be drawn? On the ground we share with those we live and work with? Or those we live and work with and share certain ethnic identities with? How are such lines to be drawn? If not according to the manuals drafted by Nazi ideologues, then how would Heidegger have us draw those lines and, in the context of what his own actions and words seemed to betoken in that period, how can we not 'accuse'? The anti-modern suspicions of Heidegger are important and often penetrating, but surely we have to do a little better than Heidegger managed in this particular context.

## Nature, History, State

We turn now to Heidegger's infamous seminar from 1933–34 during the height of his activities as Nazi Rector of Freiburg University. And here we see, quite conspicuously, just how far Heidegger was willing to go in terms of pushing his account of historicity in the service of National Socialism. However, by way of keeping this seminar in context and in the light of the worries and reservations we expressed concerning *Being and Time* in the previous chapter, we shall first examine the way that Heidegger introduced some of these ideas in *Being and Time* itself. We return then to the question of historicity in light of some of the foregoing considerations and with one crucial point borne in mind: Heidegger himself insists that the basis for his political decision lay in the concept of historicity.

Section 74 of *Being and Time* has come in for renewed scrutiny in the last couple of decades as the extent of Heidegger's commitments to National Socialism became more widely known.[9] And though this section has caused a degree of unrest among commentators, it is very much in line with the interpretation we presented earlier concerning the manner in which Heidegger seemed to recommend an extrapolation from his account of authentic Dasein to something like an authentic Dasein of a people – an idea which he glosses in subsequent texts from the 1930s. Heidegger had earlier discussed the manner in which Dasein could exist authentically through anticipatory resoluteness. Resolving in this way allows Dasein to rescue itself from a complete immersion in a superficial, public, dispersed existence. Heidegger now pushes this idea further, however:

> As thrown, Dasein has indeed been delivered over to itself and to its potentiality-for-Being, *but as Being-in-the-world*. As thrown, it has been submitted to a 'world', and exists factically with Others. Proximally and for the most part the Self is lost in the 'they'. It understands itself in terms of those possibilities of existence which

'circulate' in the 'average' public way of interpreting Dasein today. These possibilities have mostly been made unrecognizable by ambiguity; yet they are well known to us. The authentic existentiell understanding is so far from extricating itself from the way of interpreting Dasein which has come down to us, that in each case it is in terms of this interpretation, against it, and yet again for it, that any possibility one has chosen is seized upon in one's resolution.

The resoluteness in which Dasein comes back to itself, discloses current factical possibilities of authentic existing, and discloses them in *terms of the heritage* which that resoluteness, as thrown, *takes over*. In one's coming back resolutely to one's throwness, there is hidden a *handing down* to oneself of the possibilities that have come down to one, but not necessarily *as* having thus come. (BT: 435)

Heidegger is returning then to an aspect of our throwness which he wants to develop – that is – that we are thrown into an historical situation which means that we inherit all manner of beliefs, mores and so on. He now refers to this as something that is handed down to us, our 'heritage'. Heidegger links this idea to the account of fallen everydayness which he had earlier unpacked; as someone thrown into a particular historical period, in a particular community with its own series of customs and conventions, its own identity – I am someone who, more or less unwittingly, has acquired a heritage. That is, many aspects of the way that the world is revealed to me and which I in turn project as part of my supposedly neutral understanding, have been handed down to me. As Heidegger argues, when we begin to pay attention to the way we exist as finite creatures, towards death, in the world around us, we begin to reflect on that world and see it in new ways; what we do not necessarily see, however, is the hidden '*handing down* to oneself of the possibilities that have come down to one, but not necessarily *as* having thus come.' He further tries to expand on the structural features of being-with which we examined earlier which are simultaneously the source of some confusion and tension within his own account as we saw above in our discussion of section 26:

If Dasein, by anticipation, lets death become powerful in itself, then, as free for death, Dasein understands itself in its own *superior power*, the power of its finite freedom, so that in this freedom, which 'is' only in its having chosen to make such a choice, it can take over the *powerlessness* of abandonment to its having done so, and can thus come to have a clear vision for the accidents of the Situation that has been disclosed. But if fateful Dasein, as Being-in-the-world, exists essentially in Being-with Others, its historizing is a co-historizing and is determinative for it as *destiny* [*Geschick*]. This is how we designate the historizing of the community, of a people. Destiny is not something that puts itself together out of individual fates, any more than Being-with-one-another can be conceived as the occurring together of several subjects. Our fates have already been guided in advance, in our Being with one another in the same world and in our resoluteness for definite possibilities. Only in communicating and in struggling does the power of destiny become free. Dasein's fateful destiny in and with its 'generation' goes to make up the full authentic historizing of Dasein. (BT: 436)

So Heidegger is folding together the idea of the structural constitution of Dasein as a being-with and the fact of our throwness insofar as what we are thrown into is a shared existential situation with not just the structural backdrop of our temporality but the cultural, political and historical heritage which has been shaped by that temporalizing process and through which we see ourselves, crucially, as having something like a shared destiny. And we can clearly see how Heidegger is here opening up his analysis and making it available for political interpretations in fairly obvious ways. But there seems to be nothing within this thought to suggest that we can include some but exclude others from this shared heritage; if it is a question of living in the same place and belonging to the same community at the same time, then, unless one wants to invoke ethnic differences as somehow significant in terms of becoming an authentic historical people, it would seem that anyone should be afforded a place within this notion of an authentic community. He continues:

> Only if death, guilt, conscience, freedom, and finitude reside together equiprimordially in the Being of an entity as they do in care, can that entity exist in the mode of fate; that is to say, only then can it be historical in the very depths of its existence.
>
> *Only an entity which, in its Being, is essentially* **futural** *so that it is free for its death and can let itself be thrown back upon its factical 'there' by shattering itself against death – that is to say, only an entity which, as futural, is equiprimordially in the process of* **having-been**, *can, by handing down to itself the possibility it has inherited, take over its own throwness and be* **in the moment of vision** *for 'its time'. Only authentic temporality which is at the same time finite, makes possible something like fate – that is to say, authentic historicality* … It is rather in Dasein's temporality, and there only, that there lies any possibility that the existentiell potentiality-for-Being upon which it projects itself can be gleaned *explicitly* from the way in which Dasein has been traditionally understood. The resoluteness which comes back to itself and hands itself down, then becomes the *repetition* of a possibility of existence that has come down to us. *Repeating is handing down explicitly* – that is to say, going back into the possibilities of the Dasein that has-been-there. The authentic repetition of a possibility of existence that has been – the possibility that Dasein may choose its hero – is grounded existentially in anticipatory resoluteness; for it is in resoluteness that one first chooses the choice which makes one free for the struggle of loyally following in the footsteps of that which can be repeated. (BT: 437)

So Heidegger quite clearly then wants to map his account of authenticity which, at times, appears to be discussed in relation to an individual Dasein, onto some protocommunity which would be bound by a shared destiny and fate. Only if Dasein has become authentic can it 'exist in the mode of fate … only then can it be historical in the very depths of its existence.' In coming to terms with our finite transcendence, we are able to become genuinely historical and thus to see ourselves as coming from 'a possibility of existence that has come down to us'. Heidegger elaborates then on what it might mean for Dasein to live authentically as an historical Dasein within a shared historical context where coming to terms with one's throwness involves taking up the possibilities that have been handed down to us. Seeing how we are thrown into and thus shaped and determined by our heritage, how a tradition is handed down to us (all of which occurs under the limiting condition of our finitude) is crucial to us existing authentically such that we can contribute to and share in an authentic community. So Heidegger appears to confirm the interpretation we volunteered earlier to the effect that the notion of authentic Dasein, understood as existing in a particular mode for the Dasein that is in-the-world, and, as such, Dasein as *Mitsein*, stands as the kind of individually realized version (though always already *Mitsein*) of authenticity which is structurally replicated at the collective level of the people. And here again we face the problems we mentioned earlier insofar as it is not at all clear that the conditions which lead to authentic existence and indeed co-existence as part of a 'people' are anything other than the transcendental conditions for the possibility of authentic co-existence and recognition. Nothing within this account warrants the *preference* for one tradition or heritage over another as though that preference was grounded in something that involved qualitative differences between peoples or communities. Nevertheless, if we are to be fair, even though Heidegger's account is leaning already in this direction, he shies away from explicitly saying as much in this particular text.

However, by the time we get to his infamous 1933–34 seminar, *Nature, History, State*, there can be little doubt about the deeply disturbing political currents flowing underneath these ideas. Heidegger offers a cursory overview of his conception of time and temporality during the course of one of the seminars right before he explicitly turns to the question of the state:

> We refer to this fundamental constitution of human beings as authentic time. As human temporality, it is the condition for the time of which we commonly speak. So there are two things that we understand as 'time':
>
> First there is the time with which we are used to reckoning, that time between 5 and 7 o'clock, *the* time in which the processes of nature and history occur. But then there is temporality in which man himself is.
>
> This is why in our consideration of history we 'quite spontaneously' introduced time. This does not mean the time that the historian can use to determine (and test) that in AD 800, Charlemagne was crowned emperor. No, we are talking about history as *our* past, as what was the fate of our ancestors and thus is our own. We do not understand time as a framework, but as the authentic fundamental constitution of human beings. And only an entity whose Being is time can have and make history. *An animal has no history.*[10] (NHS: 37, my emphasis)

Heidegger is beginning to link this notion of historical human beings, as a people, to the notion of the state he wants to champion and, in this context, he begins to weave the term *Volk* into his discussion. However, we can clearly see that Heidegger is revisiting the manner in which he had begun to develop these ideas in *Being and Time* insisting that he is not thinking here of time as a 'framework', rather he is thinking of human temporality and thus he is alluding to his account of authenticity. In thinking of history then, he is quick to note that he is not thinking of dates or chronology but rather in terms of time understood as the 'authentic fundamental constitution of human beings'. It is only as such an entity that we can be thought to be historical in the sense that Heidegger is trying to convey, after all 'only an entity whose Being is time can have and make history. An animal has no history.' And it is in terms of our authentic, historical nature as thrown Dasein that Heidegger believes we should begin to think of our capacity to belong to a state. We can see clearly enough now why Heidegger would have insisted to Löwith in the mid-1930s that his political views were derived from his notion of historicity. Heidegger now begins to think of this collective Dasein of a people, that is, the notion of historical Dasein writ large as the authentic Dasein of a people in terms of *Volk*:

> Now, which belongs to this state? – 'The people' [*das Volk*]. We must then ask what we understand by 'people,' for in the French Revolution they gave the same answer: the people.
> 
> This answer is possible only on the basis of a decision for a state. The definition of the people depends on how it is in its state.
> 
> To begin with, we established formally that the people is the being that *is* in the manner of a state, the being that is or can be a state. We then asked the further formal question: what character and form does the people give itself in the state, and what character and form does the state give to the people?
> 
> The form of an organism? Impossible, because when we ask about the state we are asking about the essence of man, and not about the essence of an organism.
> 
> The form of order? That is too general, since I can order everything – stones, books, and so on. But what hits the mark is an order in the sense of mastery, rank, leadership, and following. This leaves open the question who is master. In Aristotle and Plato, the question of the state begins with the question: who rules, who is permitted to rule?
> 
> But we should strive to gain a genuine knowledge of the state, so that the state may form our essence and thus come to power. (NHS: 38, 39)

So a people can only *be* a people 'in the manner of a state'; but what form does it take? A people cannot be understood in terms of the form of an organism since the question concerns the essence of 'man' not the essence of an organism; neither can it be the mere form of ordering, that is too general, one can order anything. So Heidegger suggests that 'an order in the sense of mastery, rank, leadership, and following' is the form that is needed. We know already from some of Heidegger's more notorious political statements from the 1930s that the kind of mastery and 'following' he has in mind is, at times, directly linked to the demand for blind obeisance to Hitler that the Nazis demanded. On other occasions he is fond of invoking Fragment 53 from Heraclitus, as we saw in the foregoing and shall see again below. Heidegger is again, however, trying to cobble this idea together with long-standing philosophical questions associated with Plato and Aristotle. He then begins to expand on the notion of *Volk* and we can hear distinct echoes of some of the ideas he was beginning to develop in section 74 of *Being and Time*:

> We therefore recognized it as an urgent task of our time to counter this danger in order to attempt to give back to *politics* its proper rank, to learn to see politics again as the fundamental characteristic of human beings who philosophize within

history, and as the being in which the *state* fully develops, so that the state can truly be called the way of Being of a people.

And with this we come to the entity that belongs to the state, its substance, its supporting ground: *the people* [*das Volk*] ... But closely related to this is a term such as 'public health' [*Volksgesundheit*], in which one also now feels the tie of the unity of blood and stock, the race. But in the most comprehensive sense, we use the term *Volk* when we speak of something like 'the people in arms': with this we mean nothing merely like those who receive draft notices, and also something other than the mere sum of the citizens of the state. *We mean something even more strongly binding than race and a community of the same stock: namely, the nation, and that means a kind of Being that has grown under a common fate and taken distinctive shape within a single state.* (NHS: 42/43, my emphasis)

So Heidegger on the one hand appears to have accepted the importance of notions of blood, stock and race in terms of the state and the people which is the 'supporting ground' of the state but, again, he wants to move away from the straightforward Nazi principles with which these terms would be associated. Heidegger then avoids straightforward biological racism – but that is not to say that he eschews any or all forms of racism; rather he opts for a different kind of racism, a 'spiritual' kind, if you will. He insists that he means something *more* than simply the bind that ties together 'race and a community of the same stock', rather, what he has in mind is the 'nation' and the nation is to be understood as 'a kind of Being that has grown under a common fate and taken distinctive shape within a *single* state.' In other words, a nation for him means the kind of authentic Dasein of a people which is the authentic or true community which he gestures at in *Being and Time* and looks to elaborate on subsequently. Not only that, Heidegger is now prepared to openly avow that not every people has such a state, that is to say, in a way, that not every people can be or is an authentic people:

The people that turns down a state, that is stateless, has just not found the gathering of its essence yet; it still lacks the composure and force to be committed to its fate as a people. (NHS: 46)

Moreover, in terms of an authentic people

growing with each other, they will set their meaningful historical Being and will against the two threatening powers of death and the devil – that is, ruination and decline from their own essence. (NHS: 49)

This is an unusual comment from Heidegger and it would seem precipitous to read too much into it as things stand. However, when we consider his comments concerning the need for an annihilation of the enemy lurking within the state in another of his 1930s seminars we can see how some might be tempted to suggest allusions to German Jews.[11] But, regardless of how we might speculate, surely none of us can still wish to split hairs when we read the passages some pages later where Heidegger writes:

Every people has a space that belongs to it. Persons who live by the sea, in the mountains, and on the plains are different. History teaches us that nomads have not only been made nomadic by the desolation of wastelands and steppes, but they have also often left wastelands behind them where they found fruitful and cultivated land – and that human beings who are rooted in the soil have known how to make a home for themselves even in the wilderness. Relatedness to space, that is, the mastering of space and becoming marked by space, belong together with the essence and the kind of Being of a people. So it is not right to see the sole ideal for a people in rootedness in the soil, in attachment, in settledness, which find their cultivation and realization in farming and which give the people a special endurance in its propagation, in its growth, in its health. It is no less necessary to rule over the soil and space, to work outwards into the wider expanse, to interact with the outside world. The concrete way in which a people effectively works in space and forms space necessarily includes both: rootedness in the soil and interaction.

Heidegger goes on to explain that a homeland is not yet a state:

The homeland becomes the way of Being of a people only when the homeland becomes expansive, when it interacts with the outside – when it becomes a state. For this reason, peoples or their subgroups who do not step out beyond their connection to the homeland into their authentic way of Being – into the state – are in constant danger of losing their peoplehood and perishing. This is also the great problem of those Germans who live outside the borders of the Reich: they do have a German homeland, but they do not belong to the state of the Germans, the Reich, so they are deprived of their authentic way of Being. – In summary, then, we can say that the space of a people, the soil of a people, reaches as far as members of this people have found a homeland and have become rooted in the soil: and that the space of the state, the territory, finds its borders by interacting, by working out into the wider expanse. (NHS: 56)

And, perhaps in the most incriminating passage of all, Heidegger dispatches altogether with the claims to collective authenticity of the Slavic and Semitic nomadic peoples:

For a Slavic people, the nature of our German space would definitely be revealed differently from the way it is revealed to us; to Semitic nomads, it will perhaps never be revealed at all. This way of being embedded in a people, situated in a people, this original participation in the knowledge of the people, cannot be taught; at most, it can be awakened from its slumber. (NHS: 56)[12]

There is no denying then that Heidegger was willing to profess views concerning the Jews, for example, which were reprehensible in the extreme and, on this question, more than any other perhaps, one must avoid the temptation to act as apologist on Heidegger's behalf. The strategy of Petzet, for example, can sound like the most obscene kind of apologetics imaginable.[13] Granted, what should be recalled is that, within the context of that period, for people who were close to Heidegger, he simply didn't exhibit any of the typical 'symptoms' of antisemitism which were so prevalent. Nevertheless, Heidegger clearly privileges a particular conception of the German people as the most authentic people and this conception, in this particular context, has unmistakable and explicit ethnic connotations even if they appear to be more than merely biological. When we consider how Heidegger was to underwrite the specific vocation of the German people as the most metaphysical of all peoples in texts such as *Introduction to Metaphysics*, we have to seriously call into question this aspect of Heidegger's thought rather than looking to make apologies for it. Heidegger very clearly states, after all, that to be 'German' doesn't even necessarily involve living within the borders of the state. There are German people who are forced to live outside the borders of their rightful homeland and thus Heidegger would appear to be championing the expansionist designs of the Nazi regime.[14] Not only that, Heidegger conceives of this German people as sharing in some kind of ethnic commonality, one which other 'peoples' who happen to live within Germany cannot share. And while I may well argue that Heidegger's attempts to justify such views ultimately fail from a philosophical point of view – that is not for a moment to suggest that these attempts are any less repugnant. It must also be kept in mind that Heidegger is striving all the while to link his philosophical account of authenticity with his political views through his particular conception of history; this is a concerted effort on Heidegger's part – not just a handful of flippant remarks. As we shall see below, Heidegger is still wrestling with some of these ideas, which have unmistakable political and ethnically chauvinistic undercurrents, throughout the 1930s; moreover, his attempts to articulate his political views through his unique philosophical lexicon are such that some of his supposedly more politically sanitary texts begin to appear far less innocent.

## The Origin of the Work of Art

Heidegger's famous essay on the origin of the work of art may seem a somewhat unlikely essay to discuss in terms of his political views; however, if we take the trouble, what we find, in an essay which is frequently hailed by Heidegger scholars as one of his most enduring classics, are traces of the political backdrop to his thoughts concerning historicity and the authentic Dasein of a people. And again, what is perhaps most troubling is Heidegger's failure to recognize that the conditions which allow for a people to identify themselves as historically and culturally specific are ultimately transcendental conditions which should ultimately allow the greatest room possible for inclusion rather than anything else. Alas, this is an implication of his own thought which Heidegger never manages to acknowledge. Granted Heidegger doesn't quite plumb the politically noxious depths of *Nature, History, State* or his notebooks from the period; notwithstanding, he clearly deploys the same rhetoric and ideas which he had invoked in rather more sinister contexts in other works.

We will not look to offer an exhaustive analysis of this influential essay here, we merely wish to examine it in terms of the implications it has for an understanding of the intersection of Heidegger's philosophy and his politics.[15] And, what we begin to see is that Heidegger's political views seep through even in the discussion of the role that the ancient Greek temple played in its own world-historical time – that time to which it genuinely belonged to a specific historical people. Heidegger is looking here for what the original nature of the work of art was, in what sense it could be understood as playing a role as a work of art and to this end he looks at what he holds to be a supreme early example of Western Art – the Ancient Greek temple:

> However high their status and power to impress, however well-preserved and however certain their interpretation, their relocation in a collection has withdrawn them from their world. Yet even when we try to cancel or avoid such displacement of the work – by, for example, visiting the temple at its site in Paestum or Bamberg cathedral in its square – the world of the work that stands there has disintegrated.
>
> World-withdrawal and world-decay can never be reversed. The works are no longer what they were. The works themselves, it is true, are what we encounter; yet they themselves are what has been. As what has been they confront us within the realm of tradition and conservation. Henceforth, they remain nothing but objects of this kind. That they stand before us is indeed still a consequence of their former standing-in-themselves. But it is no longer the same as that. Their former self-sufficiency has deserted them. The whole of the art industry, even if taken to extremes and with everything carried out for the sake of the works themselves, reaches only as far as the object-being of the works. This however, does not constitute their work-being. (OWA: 20)

Thus, as a site that we as tourists may visit, the temple or the cathedral no longer stands as the artwork it once did for the world which it itself allowed to come to presence in the strife between earth and world. The world that it once allowed to emerge for a people, where that people dwelled on the earth which allowed that world to come forth, is no longer the world of the temple that we visit in Greece or great cathedrals like the Notre Dame in Paris; it is no longer the 'artwork' it was for a people whose world emerged in its totality through that artwork. So these 'works' of art, if we are willing to grant that they are such, belong to another time and, in that sense, to another world:

> Where does a work belong? As a work, it belongs uniquely within the region it itself opens up. For the work-being of the work presences in and only in such opening up. We said that in the work, the happening of truth is at work. The reference to van Gogh's picture tried to point to such a happening. The question arose, in this connection, as to what truth might be and how truth could happen. (OWA: 20)

Heidegger mentions van Gogh's famous picture of shabby, perished-looking boots in the passage above[16] – earlier in the essay he tries to see how, as a work of art, van Gogh's picture of the shoes brings forth a world and allows people to see that world in its totality in a way that is almost unique to the work of art:

> From out of the dark opening of the well-worn insides of the shoes the toil of the worker's tread stares forth. In the crudely solid heaviness of the shoes accumulates the tenacity of the slow trudge through far-stretching and ever uniform furrows of the field swept by a raw wind. On the leather lies the dampness and richness of the soil. Under the soles slides the loneliness of the field-path as evening falls. The shoes vibrate with the silent call of the earth, its silent gift of the ripening

grain, its unexplained self-refusal in the wintry field. This equipment is pervaded by uncomplaining worry as to the certainty of bread, wordless joy at having once more withstood want, trembling before the impending birth, and shivering at the surrounding menace of death. This equipment belongs *to the earth* and finds protection in the *world* of the peasant woman. From out of this protected belonging the equipment itself rises to its resting-within-itself. (OWA: 14)

One can read this passage and immediately think of various poets who seem to try to evoke something concerning the powerful immediacy of our everyday world and how certain objects within that world can open up a region, a place to which we belong in some way; how such regions or places can allow us to identify ourselves as people and indeed as a particular person, shaped, moulded and perhaps wrought by the particulars of a place. As one reads Heidegger's description of the work boots, set against the backdrop of this rustic scene one conjures up similar images either from one's own past or from poetry or literature which look to show us various worlds using, as conduits, quotidian objects[17] that suddenly acquire or are restored to their historical context which allows us to see that worlding of the world in its totality. The work of certain Irish poets immediately springs to mind when one reads this passage. In particular, one can sense a certain resonance with some of Seamus Heaney's poems which explore agricultural life and the land. In 'Gifts of Rain' we find Heaney imagining a man wading through his rain-drenched fields on a suitably sodden Irish day – the land so swamped from the deluge that the old boundaries that demarcate the fields are submerged – 'A man wading lost fields breaks the pane of flood'.[18] Heaney's vivid descriptions of the man splashing through a lake of fields are wonderfully palpable and he has a capacity to convey the physical element of the effort in ways which Heidegger looks to communicate above. He goes on to describe the farmer's toil as he looks to retrieve some of his submerged crop:

His hands grub
Where the spade has uncastled

Sunken drills, an atlantis
he depends on. So

He is hooped to where he planted
And sky and ground

Are running naturally among his arms
That grope the cropping land.

In his own way, Heaney looks to depict a kind of strife between earth and world. And this is suggested clearly enough by the work of the spade; the world the farmer occupies is evoked by what the piece of equipment allows him to do, namely, to dig channels in the earth in which he sows the seeds of his crops, which, after the rain and sun of passing seasons ripen into a harvest; he depends on the weather and what nature brings in order to grow his crops – his world and Earth are united in a struggle to proffer grain and vegetables. He is also privy and subject to 'the silent call of the earth, its silent gift of the ripening grain, its unexplained self-refusal in the wintry field.' What is more, the farmer is claimed as part of the world that comes to presence in his toil on an Earth that sustains it all; as Heaney writes, 'he is hooped to where he planted'. And there is the undeniable call of the local, of the provincial which accompanies all of this; we are, if you like, 'rooted' in such ways. But Heaney imagines a desire to get out beyond the local to the Universal when thinking of the ways that water, rain and sounds can impregnate our present with a sense of another shared history, of a community living on a wider expanse of place and time:

> I cock my ear
> at an absence –
> in the shared calling of blood
>
> arrives my need
> for antediluvian lore.

In the immediacy of our rootedness in the local, Heaney sees a passage to the Universal, a desire to transcend the shared calling of blood to a shared calling of a universal kind. And yet, what he hears again in the water is the local, his own heritage:

> the tawny guttural water
> spells itself: Moyola
> is its own score and consort,
>
> bedding the locale
> in the utterance,
> reed music, an old chanter
>
> breathing its mists
> through vowels and history.
> A swollen river,
>
> a mating call of sound
> rises to pleasure me, Dives,
> hoarder of common ground.

Heaney hears the guttural sounds of his own heritage in the water of the river, Moyola[19], with its own unique cadence, 'bedding the locale in the utterance'. That is, in hearing the familiar sounds of a local river, he hears it 'breathing its mists through vowels and history'. And, in the midst of his foray out through the sound of the water to the wider echo sounds and frequencies, to a place perhaps where he can hear a 'voice eddying with the vowels of all rivers'[20], he is pulled back by the sounds of the local river to his immediate historical context.

One of Heaney's most important literary influences and an important figure in his own right in terms of his influence on twentieth century Irish poetry is Patrick Kavanagh who struggles with the issue of being a rural poet, a writer of the local, of the provincial and he dramatically distils these concerns in a short poem called 'Epic':

> I have lived in important places, times
> When great events were decided, who owned

That half a rood of rock, a no-man's land
Surrounded by our pitchfork-armed claims.
I heard the Duffys shouting "Damn your soul!"
And old McCabe stripped to the waist, seen
Step the plot defying blue cast-steel –
"Here is the march along these iron stones."
That was the year of the Munich bother. Which
Was more important? I inclined
To lose my faith in Ballyrush and Gortin
Till Homer's ghost came whispering to my mind.
He said: I made the Iliad from such
A local row. Gods make their own importance.[21]

Again, some of Kavanagh's concerns here are very much of a piece with Heaney's and clearly both poets are looking to articulate something that Heidegger is circling around in terms of the relationship between the universal and the particular. However, in the case of Heaney and Kavanagh, they seem to leave this as a tension, and an enriching one, without necessarily prioritizing one at the expense of the other. They sustain each other and are sources of mutual nourishment. The local is the gateway to the Universal and in looking out for what is beyond the regional, the provincial – we end up discovering it in the way the local obtains for others who are like us and yet different in specifically regional ways. But there is a kind of oscillation between these spheres; they require each other and must be sustained in a sort of perpetually reverberating tension and this in turn should serve as the backdrop to a profound respect for similarity within our multiplicity which would allow us to celebrate and embrace cultural, historical and ethnic diversity.

In terms of the passage just quoted from Heidegger's essay, it seems of a piece with his recurring celebration of the bucolic and all things agricultural and it seems to evoke something akin to the ideas and themes we have very briefly glossed in the work of these poets. That is, there doesn't appear to be anything necessarily exclusive to any particular region here and thus Heidegger could be thought to be opening a path to a non-specific regionalism. As we mentioned above, however, Heidegger also looks at the Greek temple (understood as a work of art) and wonders what its role as an artwork is. In interpreting the temple as a work of art, Heidegger begins to describe what its role is in the community and how it allows certain things to come to presence for a community and, furthermore, seems to want to suggest that that is what the work of art does and that it does so in a way that is regionally, culturally and historically specific.

So what is Heidegger trying to say? Well, for one thing, we begin to see that Heidegger's political views are lingering in the background. He introduces a conception of an authentic world-historical people that shares a vocation which clearly echoes some of his comments in texts such as *Introduction to Metaphysics* and some of the passages we have examined above. In some way, this particular temple, as Heidegger conceives of it, allows us to see the strife between earth and world and how a world comes to presence on the earth as the ground for world:

> It is the temple work that first structures and simultaneously gathers around itself the unity of those paths and relations in which birth and death, disaster and blessing, victory and disgrace, endurance and decline acquire for the human being the shape of its destiny. The all-governing expanse of these open relations is the world of this historical people. From and within this expanse the people first returns to itself for the completion of its vocation. (OWA: 20, 21)

Birth and death are, of course, simple biological occurrences and yet, we see how communities have ever and always looked to understand and interpret these events and commemorate and mark them with practices and rituals. These centralized practices become ways in which we identify ourselves as members of a community. And the practices themselves or the rituals and conventions which emerge around these events often become localized or regionally specific. Having said as much, what they look to celebrate, mark or explain are in fact universal features of human experience. As a consequence, one must beware of any attempt to valorize one type of practice over another as though it is based on a more authentic or genuine experience. And this is the constant danger inherent in Heidegger's deep-seated enmity towards Modernity. If we think back to section 74 of *Being and Time*, we can see that Heidegger is here elaborating on ideas that he first sketched in that section. In writing here of 'destiny' and the 'world of an historical people' Heidegger is reprising and expanding on views from his early work about the way a heritage is handed down to a people and handed to them in such a way that they can make it authentically their 'own'. And, this tradition-laden environment is something which they are thrown into and thus the community do not choose or decide in advance how things become meaningful to them. But one *can* respond authentically to this situation and embrace it as an historical people. No doubt, one could offer a very rich and compelling account of the role that communities play in terms of the way the rhythms and structures of our human existence are interpreted and handed down to us from one generation to the next which can in turn act as the foundation for a very strong sense of shared heritage, culture and identity. And, we can, of course, understand how one might feel quite partial to one's own homeland or community, even, dare we say it, to a 'people'. The problem again is the way in which Heidegger began to suggest that his own allegiances, in this regard, had more philosophical and theoretical justification and represented a *more* authentic type of human existence than that enjoyed by other communities and peoples with different ethnic backgrounds.

The temple further allows us to see the invisible stirring and striving of nature which sits as the backdrop to all of this. Through what human hand has fashioned, we see what has not been fashioned but what has come forth of itself, what the Greeks called *phusis*:

> At the same time phusis lights up that on which man bases his dwelling. We call this the *earth*. What this word means here is far removed from the idea of a mass of matter and from the merely astronomical idea of a planet. Earth is that in which the arising of everything that arises is brought back – as, indeed, the very thing that it is – and sheltered. In the things that arise the earth presences as the protecting one.

> Standing there, the temple work opens up a world while, at the same time, setting the world back onto the earth which itself first comes forth as homeland [*heimatliche Grund*]. (OWA: 21)

How things come to have their appearance and meaning for us *as* something is first given to us by the temple; it is not the case that the temple comes afterwards in terms of the priority of meaning. The various things that come to mean things as part of our world don't first exist for us and then we add the temple on to them as another present-at-hand thing afterwards. Rather, Heidegger argues, we should think of things the other way around:

> Standing there, the temple first gives to things their look, and to men, their outlook on themselves. This view remains open as long as the work is a work, as long as the god has not fled from it. So it is, too, with the sculpture of the god which the victor of the athletic games dedicates to him. The work is not a portrait intended to make it easier to recognize what the god looks like. It is, rather, a work which allows the god himself to presence and *is*, therefore, the god himself. The same is true of the linguistic work. In the tragedy, nothing is staged or displayed theatrically. Rather, the battle of the new gods against the old is being fought. In that the linguistic work arises from the speech of the people, it does not talk about this battle. Rather, it transforms that speech so that now every essential word fights the battle and puts up for decision what is holy and unholy, what is great and what small, what is brave and what cowardly, what is noble and what fugitive, what is master and what is slave (cf. Heraclitus, Fragment 53 in Diels, *Fragmente der Vorsokratiker*). (OWA: 21, 22)

It is worth noting that Heidegger specifically invokes the famous fragment from Heraclitus again here and it is a fragment to which he returned again and again in the 1930s. Heidegger discusses the fragment and the notion of *polemos* in *Introduction to Metaphysics* and in *Being and Truth*. As was mentioned above, in discussing the Heraclitean fragment in *Being and Truth* in particular Heidegger makes some rather sinister remarks and the fact that the same fragment appears in a similar context (i.e. in terms of the authentic Dasein of a people, the vocation and destiny of a people) but in an essay which supposedly concerns itself with the origin of the work of art is telling.

The work evokes a world then and Heidegger fairly clearly relates things back to the notion of religious dedication and devotion in terms of the way art in times past was supposed to function. It was a way in which the world was given its ultimate determinations in terms of meanings for a people. In the way that it allowed people to participate in a sense of the holy, it was a way of rendering the world meaningful, or better, of disclosing a world for the community. Heidegger now wants to examine this notion of world and, again, we can hear distinct echoes of *Being and Time*:

> World is not a mere collection of the things – countable and uncountable, known and unknown – that are present at hand. Neither is a world a merely imaginary framework added by our representation to the sum of things that are present. *World worlds*, and is more fully in being than all those tangible and perceptible

> things in the midst of which we take ourselves to be at home. World is never an object that stands before us and can be looked at. World is the always-nonobjectual to which we are subject as long as the paths of birth and death, blessing and curse, keep us transported into being. Wherever the essential decisions of our history are made, wherever we take them over or abandon them, wherever they go unrecognized or are brought once more into question, there the world worlds. The stone is world-less. Similarly, plants and animals have no world; they belong, rather, to the hidden throng of an environment into which they have been put. The peasant woman, by contrast, possesses a world, since she stays in the openness of beings ... – As a work, the work holds open the open of a world. (OWA: 23)

The work of art, understood as Heidegger wants to define it, allows us to see the way the world worlds for a community. It is something which is *not* transcendent, it is regionally specific. Out of its historical context, Heidegger would appear to be suggesting, it is no longer the same work of art since it does not involve the way the world emerges for an historical people.[22] On the one hand Heidegger appears to have conceived of certain artworks as helping a community to identify itself by allowing the way that that world bestows meaning to show itself. On the other hand, there appears to be nothing within this thought to justify the belief that one manner in which that happens for a people could be somehow more authentic or preferable to another. We further note that Heidegger again insists that the animal has no 'world' and what Heidegger means here, as he had argued in *Nature, History, State*, is that the animal is not historical so we again see the centrality of Heidegger's notion of historicity to his conception of a people and the world it occupies. When we consider further that Heidegger was to make comments insisting on the worldlessness of the Jews and their lack of history in his notebooks[23], one can see that Heidegger's political views and his antisemitism are never too far away during this period. In terms of the work of art and the role that 'world' plays, Heidegger writes 'The world is the self-opening openness of the broad paths and essential decisions in the destiny of a historical people' (p. 26). And, given that the way the world 'worlds' is crucial to anything having meaning for Heidegger, one wonders what the implications are for people who are worldless and without history? Obviously Heidegger's notion of truth is crucial to the idea of being becoming meaningful here and we note again the possible implications of the claim that 'Another way in which truth comes to presence is through the act which founds a state' (p. 37). Again, if we think back to *Nature, History, State* – we recall that Heidegger claims that:

> The people that turns down a state, that is stateless, has just not found the gathering of its essence yet; it still lacks the composure and force to be committed to its fate as a people. (NHS: 46)

The key again in all of this is the role that Heidegger's conception of history plays in the formation of a people. Even in terms of the work of art, Heidegger writes:

> Whenever art happens, whenever, that is, there is a beginning, a thrust enters history and history either begins or resumes. History, here, does not mean a sequence of events in time, no matter how important. History is the transporting

of a people into its appointed task [*Aufgegebenes*] as the entry into its endowment [*Mitgegebenes*]. (OWA: 49)

Heidegger is clearly weaving his political philosophy into the tapestry here insisting, in accordance with some of the claims in *Nature, History, State* for example, that history is not just a question of chronology, at least in the way that Heidegger conceives of it, rather history involves 'the transporting of a people into its appointed task as the entry into its endowment.' We have moved from a discussion of the work of art in its own right to the question concerning the authentic destiny of an historical people.

In the final few paragraphs of his essay, Heidegger shows his hand, as it were, and it becomes clear that he is talking about the way the work of art can function as a vehicle for his conception of being becoming meaningful for an authentic historical people, something which is the supreme destiny and fate of the German people. And the poetic prophet of this destiny is of course Hölderlin whom Heidegger will devote a number of his best-known lecture courses to in the late 1930s and early 1940s. Heidegger writes:

> Art is historical and, as historical, is the creative preservation of truth in the work. Art happens as poetry. This is founding in the threefold sense of bestowing, grounding and beginning. As founding, art is essentially historical. This does not just mean that art has a history, a history in the external sense that, in the passage of time, art appears together with many other things, and in the process changes and passes away, and offers changing aspects to the study of history. Art is history in the essential sense: it is the ground of history … The origin of the artwork – of, that is, creators and preservers, which is to say, the historical existence of a people – is art. This is so because, in its essence, art is an origin: a distinctive way in which truth comes into being, becomes that is, historical.
>
> We are inquiring into the essential nature of art. Why do we thus inquire? We do so in order to be able to ask properly whether or not, in our historical existence, art is an origin, whether, and under what conditions, it can and must become one. (OWA: 49)

The investigation into the artwork was simply a means or a vehicle for Heidegger to examine the interplay of art, history and truth which allows him to shift his focus to the question of poetry and the poetic. And, if one's suspicions were not sufficiently aroused before now, one should surely have guessed by this stage that Heidegger is going to invoke Hölderlin in terms of the poetically prophetic role he has to play for the German people if they are going to fulfil their authentic destiny as an historical people:

> Are we, in our existence, historically at the origin? Or do we, rather, in our relationship with art, appeal, merely, to a cultured knowledge of the past?
>
> For this either-or and its decision there is a certain sign. Hölderlin, the poet whose work still stands before the Germans as a test, put it into words when he said:
>
> Reluctant to leave the place
> Is that which dwells near the origin.

Schwer verlaesst
Was nahe dem Ursprung wohnet, den Ort.
(„The Journey," ed. Hellingrath, col. IV, p. 167) (OWA: 50)

If we consider then what Heidegger has to say concerning the only possibility of hope or salvation for the West in what at times almost seems like the acme of his vainglory, namely, his interview with *Der Spiegel* in 1966, we can see again that he never fully lets go of some version of his political philosophy.[24]

## The Self Assertion of the German University

The first public statement we have from the period of Heidegger's rectorship and membership of the Nazi party is the *Rektoratsrede* – 'The Self Assertion of the German University'. The address itself, though surprising in tone and despite being seasoned here and there with a series of distinctly Nazi tropes, is not quite the full-throated Nazi speech that is sometimes suggested.[25] This in part, perhaps, explains why writers such as Emmanuel Faye are keen to bombard us with images of the Nazi pomp and ceremony which adorned the occasion. The pictorial evidence of Heidegger marching in procession, led by uniformed members of the SS, on his way to an auditorium bedecked with Nazi flags is visually quite jarring! However, the text of the address itself demonstrates the intellectual and philosophical gymnastics Heidegger was capable of as he manages to give the illusion that he has weaved his own unique philosophical vision through the heart of popular strands of Nazi ideology.

Heidegger warms to his theme immediately insisting that 'The following of teachers and students awakens and grows strong only from a true and joint rootedness in the essence of the German university.'[26] And, Heidegger goes on to argue, 'This essence, however, gains clarity, rank, and power only when first of all and at all times the leaders are themselves led – led by that unyielding spiritual mission that forces the fate of the German people to bear the stamp of its history.'[27] So what is paramount as members of the academy is to be 'rooted in the essence of the German University' and this in turn can only come to pass when the leaders of the Academy are guided by the necessity of a spiritual mission which franks the destiny of the German people as their history. In order for the teachers and students to be 'authentic' members of the German academy then, they must first be guided by 'leaders' who, like Heidegger, are attuned and guided by the spiritual mission which is the historical destiny of the German people.[28] Already then, we can see an element of Heidegger's attempts at *Gleichschaltung* taking place but on the level of what will become his own understanding of genuine National Socialism. But, again, what we shall see here is how Heidegger is trying to link these ideas back to parts of *Being and Time* which we discussed above. What is crucial in terms of the university realizing its mission is that it reflect the notions of authentic history and destiny which Heidegger examines as part of his account of authenticity and historicity in *Being and Time* and then expands on in section 74 in ways that anticipate the notion of an authentic historical community in the early and mid-1930s.

****

We further notice the prominence of the word rootedness. Rootedness translates *Bodenständigkeit* which is sometimes rendered as autochthony as we discussed in a previous chapter. It is a rather worrisome word for Heidegger to use given the prevalence of the rhetoric of *Blut und Boden* at the time and yet, interestingly, even in some of Heidegger's least controversial texts from the 1950s where the notion of *Gelassenheit* supposedly takes centre stage, we found Heidegger again relying heavily on the notion of rootedness.[29] Here in his Rectoral Address we find Heidegger incorporating the notion of rootedness into his vision for the German university: 'The following of teachers and students awakens and grows strong only from a true and joint rootedness in the essence of the German university.'[30] The word rootedness had fairly obvious connotations in 1930s Germany, thus, Heidegger can immediately be seen to be making a political as well as an academic statement; by and large this is something taken to be more or less self-evident and therefore, not worth mentioning, and yet it seems important to note that Heidegger immediately was announcing himself not just as rector, but as *Nazi* Rector of Freiburg University. Granted, it may not have been the kind of Nazism that the Nazis themselves would have advocated[31] but he was certainly trying to pay lip service to it while looking to advance the political ideas he had been flirting with since the 1920s. Moreover, in his continual invocation of the qualities and importance of the highly influential and politically active student body, it is even superficially clear that Heidegger sees the university very much as part of a political, spiritual, and specifically German destiny, which is directly linked to National Socialism.[32] However, already within these early lines we can see Heidegger alluding to some of his own philosophical ideas which he had been trying to develop in *Being and Time*, in particular section 74, and that he was to return to rather crudely and disappointingly in the 1933/34 seminar *Nature, History, State* as we saw above. Heidegger describes a spiritual mission, the fate, not just of any people, but the German people and how, as a people, their fate is to 'bear the stamp' of their *history*.

He continues in this vein, expanding on what he had sketched in *Being and Time* but, in this instance, Heidegger is saying all of this in terms of the university's mission:

> We understand the German university as the 'high' school that, grounded in science, by means of science educates and disciplines the leaders and guardians of the fate of the German people. The will to the essence of the German university is the will to science as will to the historical mission of the German people as a people that knows itself in its state. *Together*, science and German fate must come to power in this will to essence. And they will do so if, we – this body of teachers and students – *on the one hand* expose science to its innermost necessity and, *on the other hand*, are equal to the German fate in its most extreme distress.[33]

What cannot be overlooked then is that Heidegger is very much explicitly conceiving of the German university as a political institution, in the service of the state, and that is tantamount to an admission that he conceived of it functioning as a Nazi institution. However, we can again see that Heidegger is weaving his own rather idiosyncratic version of National Socialism into the picture. After all, the science that should be the primary concern within the university is not to be understood as science has been hitherto construed, rather Heidegger has his own conception of science in mind. In order to really get at the essence of science we must

> place ourselves under the power of the *beginning* of our spiritual-historical being (*Dasein*). This beginning is the setting out of Greek philosophy.[34]

Pursuing things in this way, and, taking our cue from the Greeks,[35] we learn that

> Science is the questioning holding of one's ground in the midst of the ever self-concealing totality of what is. This active perseverance knows, as it perseveres, about its impotence before fate.[36]

Anyone familiar with Heidegger's work will immediately see that this is a thinly veiled reference to his own philosophy. At the end of the page he makes further reference to what will become some of the central concerns of his work in the 1930s and 1940s:

> Only if we resolutely submit to this distant command to recapture the greatness of the beginning, will science become the innermost necessity of our being (*Dasein*) ... But if we submit to the distant command of the beginning, science must become the fundamental happening of our spiritual being as part of a people.[37]

So we can see clearly enough now that it is Heidegger's philosophy which will serve as the springboard for everything that is to be achieved as a university, a people and a state. Not only that, the fragmented state of the modern sciences will be overcome through this more originary scientific questioning:

> Such questioning shatters the division of the sciences into rigidly separated specialities, carries them back from their endless and aimless dispersal into isolated fields and corners, and exposes science once again to the fertility and the blessing bestowed by all the world-shaping powers of human-historical being (*Dasein*), such as: nature, history, language; people, custom, state; poetry, thought, faith; disease, madness, death; law, economy, technology ... And the spiritual world of a people is not the superstructure of a culture, no more than it is an armory stuffed with useful facts and values; it is the power that most deeply preserves the people's strengths, which are tied to earth and blood; and as such it is the power that most deeply moves and most profoundly shakes its being (*Dasein*). Only a spiritual world gives the people the assurance of greatness. For it necessitates that the constant decision between the will to greatness and a letting things happen that means decline, will be the law presiding over the march that our people has begun in its future history.[38]

The link between this passage and some of the passages we examined in *Nature, History, State* is fairly obvious. And again, though Heidegger notes the importance of blood and earth, he is looking for a deeper bond that unites the German people and calls on them to fulfil their destiny, their vocation as an historical people. It seems further clear that Heidegger is revisiting the notion of the fate of a people and its future in *Being and Time* but Heidegger here explicitly uses the language of *Blut und Boden* in the same context. And, as I have argued, the incorporation of this aspect of National Socialism, no more than his attempt to champion the very notion of provincialism, is simply not warranted or justified on the grounds of anything we can find in his philosophy. Even more disconcerting in this instance is the arbitrary nature of Heidegger's invocation of the phrase (i.e. earth and blood); there is absolutely no philosophical or rhetorical warrant for the usage which indicates, again, an alarming capacity for opportunism. The substantial differences between Nazi ideology and Heidegger's own political vision (undergirded, so he believes, by his philosophy) notwithstanding, he himself clearly looks to make his own philosophical ideas chime with some of the most unmistakably Nazi concepts of the day. As such, we must challenge again anyone who, from the outset, wishes to insist on the necessary distinction to be drawn between Heidegger's philosophy and his politics. It may well be the case that we can, in the end, argue for such a distinction. Nevertheless, it is an argument that *needs to be made* since Heidegger himself avowed the inner relation between the two and here, again, makes it clear that he sees his political aspirations for the university and the German people as parasitic on or founded upon his philosophy.

## The Nazi Rector

Some of the most incriminating evidence against Heidegger in terms of his commitment to National Socialism dates from around the time of his tenure as Nazi Rector of Freiburg University. Given the mendacious nature of Heidegger's 'official story' concerning his rectorate, it is hard to find much to excuse much of his behaviour during this period. Heidegger proved himself a self-serving opportunist who jumped on the Nazi bandwagon for personal gain. In this he was, perhaps, no different to a whole series of other German academics in the early 1930s, but there is precious little consolation in that. Heidegger was already a famous and influential philosopher and wrote distressingly incendiary, pro-Nazi speeches for both the students and his teachers at the university. He privately maligned and vilified colleagues and reported them to the authorities. He traded in some of the most disgusting antisemitic rhetoric of the day and generally proved to be a thoroughgoing and committed Nazi. Whether we like it or not, the weight of the evidence and testimony dating from the period is undeniable. And, at least in this regard, both Farias and Faye concretely corroborate much of what others claim to already have known and what Hugo Ott had painstakingly chronicled in his political biography. There was a spike on the graph of Heidegger's Nazi sympathies then which doesn't entirely fit within the scheme of his philosophical concerns or the more moderate conservative revolutionary posture he displayed either side of that abysmal period. That is not to say that Heidegger didn't campaign on behalf of his ethnic chauvinism in his own philosophy; we have already seen how he did above. However, almost nothing there (apart from a handful of passages in *Nature, History, State* and the black notebooks) was quite so intemperate as the things he said and did in his capacity as rector. The great misfortune here is that Heidegger disingenuously posed as though his Nazi sympathies emerged from within the very fabric of his most enduring philosophical ideas. When one considers National Socialism as it existed historically, however, one cannot help but conclude that Heidegger knew only too well that existing National Socialism was fundamentally incompatible with his philosophical vision. As a result, Heidegger lobbied for his own private brand of National Socialism which was at quite a remove from the actual political movement. In doing so Heidegger has afforded ample ammunition to critics who wish to argue that his thought is Nazi to the core since he suggested as much at times himself. In this, however, there was as much, if not more, opportunism than philosophical substance! But, in view of what is at stake, that is not something that we can take as given, that is something that we must constantly look to show. Not least since Heidegger was very obviously trying to articulate a political philosophy for a period of time which was rather sinister in its own right. Neither should we look to diminish the level of Heidegger's misdeeds at the height of his Nazi involvement. In *Heidegger and Nazism* Farias recounts Heidegger's attempts to hobble the professional prospects and reputation of certain academics for 'political' reasons. For example, Heidegger took it upon himself to privately malign his one-time assistant, Eduard Baumgarten, while the latter was teaching at the University of Göttingen, a position he had to take after Heidegger took it upon himself to sabotage his position in Freiburg in the most loathsome and underhand way. In a letter sent to a Nazi functionary at the university, Heidegger writes:

> By family and spiritual attitudes, Dr. Baumgarten comes from that liberal-democratic circle of intellectuals gathered around Max Weber. During his time here, he was everything but a National Socialist. It surprises me that he is teaching at Göttingen. I cannot imagine on what academic basis he has earned his habilitation. After disappointing me, he became closely tied with the Jew Fränkel, who had been active at Göttingen and was later expelled. I suppose Baumgarten found some protection by this shift in affiliation. I deem it impossible to bring Baumgarten into the SA as well as to bring him into the teaching body. Baumgarten is a gifted speaker. In his philosophy, however, I think he is pompous and without solid and true knowledge. This judgment comes from my experience with him for two years. In the meantime, has there been a change in his political attitude? I am unaware of it. His stay in the United States, during which time he was Americanized, no doubt allowed him to learn much about the country and its inhabitants. But I have solid reasons to doubt the sureness of his political instincts and his judgment.[39]

Farias goes on to report that Heidegger sent the letter to 'the Führer of professors at Göttingen, Dr. Vogel, who put it in the archives with the notice: "not usable, filled with hatred"'.[40] Even the sensibilities of so devout and dutiful a Nazi as Vogel, it would seem, were offended by the unrestrained vitriol of Heidegger's letter! However, two years later, the letter resurfaced and appears to have been the primary cause of Baumgarten losing his job with a recommendation that he return to the United States. Baumgarten's wife was friendly with the secretary of the new Nazi functionary and arranged for Baumgarten to visit the office of the Nazi functionary at the university while the latter was away. And, it was during this visit that Baumgarten was able to view his dossier and transcribed the hateful letter from Heidegger.

There is an illuminating and indeed rather amusing appendix to Berel Lang's book on Heidegger's postwar silence concerning the Holocaust. The appendix contains the recollection of David Luban who met with Baumgarten in Freiburg a couple of months after Heidegger's death in 1976. The memoir is the record of meetings that Luban and a colleague had with Baumgarten over three days in mid-July. Baumgarten described to his visitors a rather disappointingly vainglorious character, obsessed with his reputation and with a capacity for jealousy and pettiness which were to cause Baumgarten considerable professional hardship and almost cost him his academic career altogether. Nevertheless, Baumgarten seems quite convinced that Heidegger's enmity towards him and the vicious letter he penned in an attempt to destroy Baumgarten's career had nothing to do with politics or antisemitism:[41]

> In 1935 his university career was threatened because of a letter of denunciation written by Heidegger. After the war Baumgarten advocated Heidegger's denazification, and Heidegger subsequently wrote him two reconciliatory letters. Baumgarten attributed his difficulties with Heidegger to personal animus rather than political conviction. In his view three incidents turned Heidegger against him.[42]

Baumgarten appears to have recounted a number of specific incidents which caused a rift between the two men and each of the incidents suggests a man [Heidegger] with bottomless reserves of vanity along with a disappointing capacity for jealousy, pettiness, vindictiveness and, at times, shameless opportunism. On one occasion Heidegger looked to have Baumgarten's stipend from Freiburg University revoked. On returning from America, Baumgarten's wife discovered that some money which she had earned and invested had not in fact been lost in the 1929 crash. The Baumgartens received a cheque for over $3,500 which was a huge sum of money by German standards at that time. They bought a house and Heidegger's wife was instantly smitten with the place, ordering their own architect to replicate the external proportions when designing their own house. Heidegger was incensed, accusing Baumgarten of gross impropriety and unjustly receiving a stipend when in fact he was quite affluent. Eventually the dean had to intervene and arranged a meeting to clear the air. Baumgarten explained the situation to Heidegger and the matter was resolved. Heidegger was rather grudging nonetheless, complaining that it still smacked of a certain 'American' attitude arguing that 'in Germany one still distinguished between putting aside money for one's family and purchasing a Schloss'.[43]

On another occasion, Heidegger was boasting of the rapturous response to his lecture ('What is Metaphysics?'). Baumgarten suggested that Friedrich Gundolf's laudatory remarks to Heidegger at the conclusion of the lecture might have been insincere. Such was Heidegger's obsessiveness and vanity that he sent Baumgarten on a mission to discover what Gundolf's genuine sentiments might have been. Baumgarten reported back that Gundolf's tone with Heidegger had been somewhat tongue in cheek – he had in fact made some derisory remarks, at Heidegger's expense, during the lecture. Heidegger's reaction is worth relating:

Heidegger got up from his desk and stood in the corner of the room whistling, a sign that he was barely under control. Baumgarten believed that Heidegger did not forgive him for this episode.[44]

There were other incidents, but one final episode sealed Baumgarten's fate with Heidegger. On this occasion it appears to have been a purely academic disagreement during one of Heidegger's private seminars. Nevertheless, it was to be the end of Baumgarten's association with Heidegger. Interestingly, on this account, and this is significant in terms of the rather sanguine picture of Husserl which Hugo Ott paints, Husserl appears to have been rather partisan and petty and not a little malevolently disposed towards his one-time protégé. Upon hearing of the row between Baumgarten and Heidegger which occurred early in 1932, before Heidegger had become a member of the Nazi party and Rector of Freiburg University, Husserl reacted in the most remarkable way: 'Baumgarten knew he was now finished with Heidegger. He went to Husserl and told him this. To his astonishment, Husserl rang for wine and toasted Baumgarten's liberation.'[45] The memoir goes on to describe Husserl as being in a state of jubilation at the fact that someone else had parted ways with Heidegger, which seems a somewhat cavalier attitude towards someone who has just had a very public spat with one of the most famous philosophers alive. At the very least, Baumgarten's recollection of this event suggests that Hugo Ott's characterization of Husserl as an innocent, humble, almost affably avuncular intellectual, entirely beyond reproach in his dealings with Heidegger, is something of a self-serving caricature for those who want to champion the great phenomenologist at Heidegger's expense. Husserl appears to have been rather self-involved and narcissistic in his own right.

Shortly after this incident, Heidegger, in a move which demonstrates a level of vindictiveness that beggars belief, wrote to the Lincoln Foundation, who paid Baumgarten's fellowship at the university, and declared him incompetent, which cost the younger man his living. It was Husserl who helped Baumgarten obtain a position in Göttingen and Baumgarten believed that Heidegger (in his infamous letter where he speculates as to how his 'enemy' could have obtained his position and suggests that his appointment had something to do with his association with 'the Jew Fränkel') made the reference to Fränkel only because Heidegger was not yet in a position to openly denigrate 'the Jew' Husserl, that is, that Heidegger was really alluding to Baumgarten's association with Husserl. As it turns out, Heidegger's remark was to be Baumgarten's salvation since he was able to swear an oath to the effect that he didn't know Fränkel which undermined the credibility of Heidegger's letter and allowed him to get his job back.

The memoir ends with a brief reflection on the meetings they had with Baumgarten, particularly in the context of Heidegger's malicious letter and his behaviour towards Baumgarten; it is an interesting retrospective and, perhaps, weakens the case of those who, in their case contra Heidegger on the issue of his antisemitism, rely heavily on the significance of his letter against Baumgarten:

> Heidegger's letter of denunciation reveals prima facie a man of substantial Nazi conviction. Baumgarten's portrait of Heidegger is different: it shows a man who was driven not so much by political or ideological passions as by personal pettiness,

more than usual vanity, and a desire for philosophical glory. (Baumgarten recollected that at one point Heidegger was working through a pile of Marxist writings so that he would be in a position to reign as *der deutsche Philosoph* no matter who prevailed in the ensuing political struggle. His portrait also reveals a man possessing a measure of – at least – social anti-Semitism.[46]

Hugo Ott, in his useful, albeit tendentious, biography of Heidegger manages to remain dispassionate in one of his discussions for just about long enough to get this particular point concerning Heidegger's antisemitism across.[47] On the question of Heidegger's antisemitism, in a rare moment of objectivity, Ott openly concedes that there is little evidence that Heidegger was a trenchant antisemite:

> One thing seems certain: if Heidegger subscribed to anti-Semitism, it was certainly not on the basis of the crude racial ideology embodied in Hitler's *Mein Kampf*, Rosenberg's world-view or Streicher's antics. Heidegger was too cultivated a man for that. How else could he have maintained a special relationship with the Jew Hannah Arendt over such an extended period of time, in flagrant breach of bourgeois convention? How else could he have brought in the Jew Werner Brock from Göttingen to be his personal assistant, because he thought highly of his abilities? Although he could not keep his assistant when he became rector, he did at least help him to make a new start in England. The available sources do not present a consistent picture.[48]

In terms of Heidegger's antisemitism, Ott refers to 'inconsistencies in the story'; despite the fact that Heidegger doesn't appear to have been motivated by a pronounced antisemitism, Ott takes very seriously some sporadic, anecdotal titbits from Husserl and one or two others concerning Heidegger's antisemitism. And, though these scraps remain completely unsubstantiated, Ott insists that they need nevertheless to be assumed to be documentary evidence. Ott's conclusion, in his capacity as historian, is that this demonstrates that there is a conflict of sorts between the various accounts. However, what he presents, in the end, is a conflict, on the issue of Heidegger's antisemitism, between the known facts and the 'countervailing evidence' supplied by hearsay and rumours. I would have thought that that at the very least should have indicated to the historian which direction his interpretative inclinations should lean. Not least since the context of his presentation of Husserl's allegation casts serious doubts on the credibility and motives of the aging and disillusioned phenomenologist. Ott's presentation of Husserl during the early 1930s, from his correspondence with colleagues and friends, reveals a man who was deeply affronted by the sudden realization that his one-time protégé did not take his mature philosophical project seriously and his remarks concerning Heidegger's own work, not least *Being and Time*, are the petty remonstrations of a wounded ego. And, it is from within *this* context that we suddenly hear Husserl add to the litany of grievances against Heidegger, namely, that he was becoming more and more antisemitic as well. And, yet, even though most of the evidence points to the contrary, that is to say, that Heidegger was not a typical, biological racist that supported the persecution of the Jews, we are nevertheless to take Husserl's throwaway remark as serious documentary evidence. The problem is that this is a lack of consistency on Ott's part since he is quite happy to dismiss any such unreliable evidence which might add favourably to Heidegger's defence.[49]

As we said at the beginning of this chapter, the issue of Heidegger's antisemitism is a delicate and sensitive subject and has been poorly handled during every recurrence of the Heidegger Affair. While Rector of Freiburg University, as even Ott is forced to concede, Heidegger didn't comport himself in the manner of a malicious antisemite or, by and large, even as someone possessed of that sort of bigotry, certainly not in such a way as to lead him to persecute or discriminate against his colleagues. The case of Baumgarten has typically been the trump card for critics of Heidegger here, and yet, we can see from Baumgarten's own testimony that he himself believed that Heidegger's actions with respect to him stemmed from a deep-seated pettiness and indeed a shocking capacity for ruthlessness. In Husserl's case, we know that Heidegger never barred his former mentor access to the library and while there was clearly increasing animosity between the two men, it seems clear that this was mostly as a result of intellectual differences between two arrogant intellectuals. What Heidegger demonstrated during his tenure as Rector of Freiburg was his commitment to some form of National Socialism – antisemitism does not seem to have played a major role in his activities as rector. However, that is not for a moment to say that Heidegger was free from blame or that his character is not forever besmirched with the stain of having privately endorsed one of the most enduring forms of ethnic chauvinism throughout history. In his private notebooks and his winter semester seminar as Rector of Freiburg University, we can clearly see that Heidegger's attempts to articulate a political philosophy, using the theoretical apparatus of his central philosophical ideas, was informed by and committed to ethnic chauvinism and, in particular, antisemitism. But, again, we are negotiating a treacherously thin tightrope here. It would still be misrepresentative to characterize Heidegger as some kind of closet philosophical Julius Streicher or to suppose that he discriminated against his Jewish colleagues, students and friends – that simply is not the case. There is nothing exculpatory in that, Heidegger's views are still blameworthy, but we must be clear on what we are holding Heidegger, the man and the philosopher, accountable for. As a man, for the most part, he was not guilty of gross transgressions against his Jewish acquaintances, even though they came to be horrified by his political views. As a philosopher he was committed to an antimodern politics with overt ethnically chauvinistic implications and he looked to use his own philosophy to articulate and defend that vision. But that effort failed precisely as a result of the refusal of that philosophy to allow itself to be successfully employed in that manner.

Given his not inconsiderable feelings of affection towards a number of Jewish students and colleagues, one *might* be tempted to suppose that Heidegger's antisemitic posturing was merely political opportunism, not least since much of the evidence against Heidegger here is from around the period of his rectorate. However, we simply cannot ignore the fact that Heidegger used terms such as *Verjudung*; he attacked his colleagues in letters to Nazi authorities for associating with Jews; he openly averred to Jaspers his conviction that there was a dangerous international alliance of Jews. And, more recently, we learn that Heidegger kept journals during the 1930s and 1940s which contain a handful of remarks that essentially echo what

Heidegger had said to Jaspers about a dangerous international alliance of Jews. So while it would be less than accurate to depict Heidegger as a bloodthirsty Nazi antisemite, we must concede that he subscribed to some form of antisemitism. Not only that – Heidegger very clearly thought that his ethnic chauvinism was something which he could justify philosophically using some of the core concepts of his own thinking.

However, specifically in terms of Heidegger's philosophy, can we find any philosophical support for the provincialism and anti-cosmopolitanism (which at the time had fairly obvious antisemitic implications) which he seemed to endorse in the 1930s in particular? The answer is, superficially at least, 'yes'! Heidegger's philosophy is profoundly concerned with problems of miscegenation, deracination and the concomitant influence of *das Gestell*. This set of concerns and criticisms would seem to dovetail readily with a sympathy for some form of the German antisemitism that was so prevalent at the time, not least when we consider that Heidegger, in his private notebooks at least, associates the steady increase of technicity and calculative rationality with 'World Jewry'. But Heidegger's philosophy itself is not, for all that, in any way shape or form antisemitic. And this is again where we are on the precipice of split hairs which yet span yawning divides. Heidegger's own version of rootedness and the concomitant suspicion of mass society and technicity were not really what Nazi ideologues had in mind when they flirted with anti-modern ideas; they were not thinking of deconstructing the history of Western Metaphysics, they were interested in the physical eradication of Jews and Bolsheviks. Granted, Heidegger was clearly suspicious of both the Jewish influence on Western culture as he saw it and remained terrified of communism to the end of his days. Notwithstanding, Heidegger's antisemitism seems incompatible with his own account of authentic historical communality. This tension also points to an insurmountable problem which predates Heidegger's account of authentic intersubjectivity but which rears its head again in that context: namely, how are we to reconcile our historical, 'rooted' existence with the demands that the 'other' constantly makes on us, or for that matter, on me? The boundaries, any time we look to delimit them, prove arbitrary and we may well find ourselves careering down slippery slopes! We have to concede then that Heidegger himself held deeply problematic political views and was inclined towards forms of ethnic prejudice which are inexcusable but which are, in the final analysis, at loggerheads with the theoretical foundations of his own philosophy. Certainly he looked to reconcile those views with aspects of his own account of historicity and authenticity at a theoretical level; the fact that he fails in that attempt and that we can therefore proceed with Heidegger's thought safe in the knowledge that it does *not* lead automatically to Nazism is not exactly to Heidegger's credit.

One unfortunate result of some of the revelations concerning Heidegger's antisemitism and ethnic chauvinism has been the kneejerk reaction of many critics. The Heidegger Controversy has been a contentious and emotionally charged issue from the beginning and so it is understandable that people who have something at stake in this debate might react a little rashly, rushing to reinforce opinions and conclusions which they have previously defended with some vigour. We see frequent examples of this in the way some of Heidegger's remarks in his private notebooks and previously unpublished seminars from the 1930s are adduced as proof positive that Heidegger's philosophy leads directly to Nazism. However, as we have seen in this study, that is not the correct inference to draw; what we can clearly see is that Heidegger genuinely did have very worrisome political views and that he was an antisemite (of some variety); we can also see that Heidegger thought that he could find a way to influence National Socialism according to his own private vision of that movement and that he could manage to justify all of this through the articulation of a political philosophy based on some of the core concepts of *Being and Time*. However, this does not demonstrate that Heidegger's philosophy leads directly to antisemitism or Nazism. Yes, Heidegger attempts to use his philosophy to offer a theoretical basis for his political views, but this attempt fails *because* his philosophy cannot sustain the undertaking. The notions of historicity and the related role of being-towards-death, the existential moorings of our situatedness in terms of the way we are thrown into the world are certainly key to understanding how we can feel rooted in a place, how we feel as though we belong to a community. And one can indeed see how a shared sense of identity might well emerge from this co-existence as part of the same historical community. That is still some way from being able to make ethnic distinctions on the basis of the universal human condition which is constitutive of how we find ourselves as historically specified creatures in various ways. If being-towards-death is what is pivotal to understanding how we are to be authentically free as human beings, then it is impossible to see how one ethnicity could possibly be thought to be better at being-towards-death than another, in any substantive way, on the basis of ethnic differences. What is more, if one finds oneself thrown into the same historical context as other people with a variety of ethnicities, then who is to say that we might not find ourselves as sharing in the historical destiny of our community? Heidegger believes that it is not enough to share a historical and topological context, to belong to the same community. In Germany, for example, he believes that Jews and Slavs could never authentically be part of a German nation while ethnically qualified Germans, who no longer live in Germany and therefore do not share the same historical or regional context, could certainly be part of the authentic German nation were they only allowed to relocate to Germany. However, in terms of his philosophy – whatever way we look at it – we simply cannot find a justification for Heidegger's ethnic chauvinism which means that his attempt to supply such a justification is based on an arbitrary prejudice which does not itself depend on any part of his thought.

# Conclusion

A number of times during the course of this study we have underlined the fact that the question that needs to be addressed is not so much whether Heidegger is a good philosopher or a charlatan; if he is in fact a charlatan, then his political views are of little consequence. And again, as should by now be patently clear, if Heidegger wasn't really a Nazi, then, in that case, there is really nothing for us to concern ourselves with, the controversy instantly dissolves. Moreover, if there is in fact *no* connection between Heidegger's philosophy and his political actions and views, then there would, again, be little reason for us to concern ourselves. After all, one could, I presume, be a brilliant logician or mathematician and whether or not one was a bigot, an antisemite or a Nazi would count for little since few would claim that that person's political views were integral to their notation or whatever theorems, paradoxes or proofs they might be credited with having discovered. And, no doubt, this would not be an issue that critics or commentators would devote too much time to. It may well be interesting for a biographer in terms of fleshing out the picture of that person's life, but it would not be an intellectual controversy or scandal.

This is not the case with Heidegger. Some, including Heidegger himself, have suggested that there is something of a vendetta against him, a witch hunt, undertaken by those who wish to find an easy way to reject a philosophy with which they disagree or find objectionable or threatening, for example.[1] And indeed, in the case of some intemperate commentators there is some truth to that. But that is not the entire story, not by a considerable distance. Given the very nature of Heidegger's philosophy and because that philosophy professes to being concerned with restoring the dignity of humanity to human beings,[2] the issue of his political views becomes rather more relevant. What is more, that same philosopher professed, from the beginning, that his political support for National Socialism was deeply rooted in some of the key notions of his most famous and, at that point certainly, his most important philosophical work – *Being and Time*! As a result, we *cannot* simply look to separate the philosophy and the politics as we might be willing to do with the likes of Frege. After all, it is Heidegger himself who implicitly enjoins us *not* to try to separate the two. This exculpatory strategy is precluded then by Heidegger's own words; that is to say, for those who would and have looked to avail of such a strategy, it is Heidegger himself that bars their way. Felix O'Murchadha argues (contra Thomas Sheehan) that the hermeneutic hindsight involved in insisting on the need to read Heidegger's works politically is tantamount to a claim that we must read all of Plato's dialogues in light of the Seventh Letter or that we should look at all of Aristotle's writings keeping his views on slavery and women firmly in mind. But this is a false analogy in that it can be dismissed as easily as one can dismiss the claim that Frege's work is influenced by his antisemitism.[3]

Heidegger himself explicitly professes a deep inner affinity between his core philosophical concepts and his political views – thus we cannot automatically dismiss as untenable any attempt to examine Heidegger's philosophical works from a political point of view! As we have already seen, Heidegger fairly obviously looked to articulate his own political philosophy using key notions from his own thought.

The question as to whether Heidegger can reconcile his political views with some of his central philosophical concepts is one which we took as remaining to be settled since deciding the matter in advance seemed illegitimate given Heidegger's own repeated insistence on an inner affinity. What I think we have shown is that there are serious problems with Heidegger's attempts to reconcile his philosophy and his politics. On the one hand this means that his philosophy does not in the end reduce simply to National Socialism or indeed to the more extreme elements of the conservative revolutionary outlook which he was clearly sympathetic to. However this is due to a *failure* on Heidegger's part, that is to say, it is down to the fact that Heidegger cannot succeed in what he sets out to do philosophically, namely, to resist modernity all the way down and to find a way to champion (at the philosophical level) extreme provincialism. And the reason he cannot realize this aspiration is due to the fact that Heidegger relies at the same time on a universal condition which is no more legitimate for one person or people than another.

What is more, Heidegger's refusal to acquiesce in a public auto-da-fé after the war shows that at some level he knew that any attempt to suddenly embrace Western democratic liberalism would be obscenely disingenuous.[4] That is not to say that his integrity is beyond reproach, I don't for a moment doubt that there was an element of hubris here as well. But one also has to concede that Heidegger proved himself a ruthless opportunist when the occasion presented itself and he had plenty of opportunities to make life a little easier for himself after the war but stubbornly refused to 'recant'. What he could not afford to do was to stridently deny that there was any philosophical relationship between his own original vision of National Socialism and his philosophy or to suggest that his philosophy could somehow be seen as compatible with Western liberal democracy since, as far as Heidegger was concerned, liberal democracy was a product of Western Metaphysics and Heidegger never concealed his antipathy for either; he was and remained a deeply anti-modern thinker. In this Heidegger saw further than those that subsequently piggy-backed his anti-modernist thought but found themselves scrambling for cover when the extent of Heidegger's Nazi involvement became more and more apparent as the decades went by. Heidegger himself realized only too well that his philosophy was premised on the very idea of the bankruptcy of modernity. He wanted to initially offer an alternative to any philosophical or political vision based on universal principles since he was convinced that that type of thinking was already doomed owing to its grounding in a metaphysics of presence which would ultimately issue in the age of technology, that is, the era of revealing governed by *Gestell*.

The Ancients had already seen how wrongheaded it was to approach moral and political problems in the same way that we attempted to make progress in the exact sciences. One way of reading Plato's *Republic* is almost as a political satire, an allegory designed to show the nightmare which might issue from an Enlightenment approach to the aspiration of a perfectly just regime. That Heidegger might have agreed with this way of looking at things is borne out by the fact that he himself saw Western Metaphysics as having led inexorably through modernity up to the twin technocratic evils of Western Capitalism and Eastern Communism and thus resisted modernity vigorously in his own work. Plato's *Republic*, understood as an allegory, can be seen to warn against the dangers of an absolute approach to the ideal regime since it issues in a nightmarish, communistic, closed society. Aristotle himself at the beginning of his science of human affairs suggests that one cannot approach ethical/political questions in the same way that one might approach questions in the exact sciences since they do not admit of the same level of exactitude, hence, a different kind of inquiry is called for.[5] In terms of this, admittedly reconceived, quarrel between the Ancients and the Moderns then, Heidegger can be seen to be very much on the side of the Ancients. The difference emerges when it comes to what one should do instead since neither Plato nor Aristotle tried to short-circuit the tension between the universal and the particular as readily as Heidegger did. And, alas, here we see that Heidegger's thought is both problematic and confused and, worse than that, that Heidegger himself looked to wring National Socialist prejudices out of parts of that thought that simply could not consistently be put to such service without taking all kinds of unlicensed philosophical liberties.

\*\*\*\*

For those who may counter that I reject the genealogical approach of many of Heidegger's critics before then accusing Heidegger of supporting and appropriating the very influences which I distance his philosophy from in my assessment of those same critics, I would say the following: I am making a different claim to these critics as well, who, to my mind are also bypassing the real controversy and are engaged in an exercise the success of which would merely show that there is no controversy at all – that is, that Heidegger's philosophy reduces to fairly obvious cultural and intellectual obsessions with *Blut und Boden* ideology. The problem is that things are not nearly as simple as that! I am not, then, trying to make things easier or more straightforward with this study, rather this is an *initial* attempt to demonstrate just how complicated and difficult this particular Gordian knot is and how resistant it will continue to prove to any of the blunt swords that have been wielded hitherto. Rather, the real controversy is that Heidegger looks to make a series of 'philosophical' moves based on notions such as historicity and authenticity to parallel some of his political views, but in ways which his own thought precludes. Precisely the move he wants to make in favour of the provincial and the local is supposedly buttressed by his powerful rejection of modernity and yet in the very place where he looks to situate the justification for such a move we find him relying on conditions which are the transcendental conditions for the possibility of any recognition or co-existence between any human beings at any time and of any race or creed whatsoever – namely the only 'fate' that we are *all* guaranteed – that we shall suffer death. Ultimately Heidegger's attempts to formulate such philosophical commitments in *Being and Time* rely on a universal condition.

And yet, at the same time, Heidegger's efforts to demonstrate how temporality and historicity give our lives the immediacy and context which cannot be bracketed from our investigations into human experience is a powerful challenge to the anaemic formalism of the accounts he resists. This is a very difficult and old problem; Heidegger wants to resist universalizing tendencies, but, in resisting those tendencies he goes too far in the other direction and overreaches the bounds of his own thought! His antipathy to modernity has the power to bring us to that powerful tension we find in the work of Plato and Aristotle – but his attempts to resolve the difficulties involved are not something which he can successfully carry off.

\*\*\*\*

Heidegger's cultural and political background is a continuing source of confusion and disharmony and, again, where the steadiest hands were needed, we have had far too much spasm and knee jerking. We have to try and steer a truer course than some of those who have previously tried to plough furrows in this rocky ground only to be derailed by each and every stone lying in the soil of Heidegger's cultural heritage. Moreover, as we hit those same rocks and stones from Heidegger's German background, we must avoid being thrown off track – wandering down paths strewn with examples of the genetic fallacy. The 'relish' with which writers such as Faye embroider the putatively Nazi jingoism sprinkled through Heidegger's rhetoric in the 1930s with anecdotal accounts of Nazi apparel, peasant caps and so on, smacks of an agenda which would gladly send the thought of one of the great philosophers of the twentieth century to its death on figurative gallows on the strength of the most tenuous associations. However, in rightly dismissing the dangerous propaganda of the Emmanuel Fayes of this world, many who would temper our criticisms of Heidegger and buttress the battlements against such assaults lose sight of what remains important – one of the most important thinkers of the twentieth century was himself immersed in and influenced by an ill-fated German conservative nationalism. However, as with so many of Heidegger's influences, he tended to absorb these ideas, motifs and resonances into the patchwork of his own rather idiosyncratic vision. Heidegger's 'heritage', German though it is, is no less Greek for all that and the *most* significant element of his own particular heritage is philosophical. And while we have to concede that the official story concerning Heidegger's Nazi activities, peddled by Heidegger himself, has been largely discredited, that does not mean that Heidegger's thought is gung ho fascism or that there are *no* elements of the official story that have any credibility whatsoever. What strikes one most as one reflects on the whole sorry business of Heidegger's failed attempts to weave together his philosophical and political views in the 1930s are the naked opportunism and egomania of the man – and this was brought home quite well in Baumgarten's recollections as reported in the appendix to Berel Lang's book on Heidegger's 'silence'. In his measured essay on the publication of the Black Notebooks, Gregory Fried correctly identifies a growing despair and disillusionment in Heidegger's reflections as he begins to realize that the Nazis have little or no interest in the revolution which he hoped for while other philosophical mediocrities, as Heidegger sees it, manage to scale the heights of academic prestige within the Nazi regime.[6] Heidegger's naïveté was *sufficient* for him to believe that from his position as Professor of Philosophy he could directly influence and determine the course that political events took during the Nazi regime and he was arrogant enough to feel betrayed and disillusioned when that turned out to have been an unrealistic aspiration. The naïve, would-be philosophical necromancer of Freiburg turned a withering, critical gaze on everyone and everything, while he retreated into his work and study, licking the wounds to his great yet fragile ego.

The following excerpts from Heidegger's letter to the Rector of Freiburg University following the war show something of Heidegger's mindset both during and after the war:

> However, I was nevertheless absolutely convinced that an autonomous alliance of intellectuals [der Geistigen] could deepen and transform a number of essential elements of the 'National Socialist movement' and thereby contribute in its own way to overcoming Europe's disarray and the crisis of the Western spirit.[7]

Heidegger goes on to write that:

> The practical efforts of the winter semester failed. During the few days of the Christmas vacation I realized that it was a mistake to believe that, from the basic spiritual position that was the result of my long years of philosophical work, I could immediately influence the transformation of the bases – spiritual or non-spiritual – of the National Socialist movement.[8]

Now, on the one hand, Heidegger has deliberately conceived this part of his letter (sent to the then rector) as an exercise in self-exculpation. He doesn't necessarily see his actions, so described, as in any way blameworthy since they were, he believed, in the best interests of the university, the students and, in keeping with the spectacular hubris which characterized all of his actions and deeds with respect to this issue, Western humanity. Seeping from every syllable of the letter quoted above are Heidegger's naked ambition and opportunism. Furthermore, his hubris is in fact so consumptive that he still remains blind to the gargantuan dimensions of his opportunism and egocentrism. Heidegger supposes that it was, at one time, reasonable to believe that a philosophy professor, with absolutely no experience in the arena of political machination, 'could immediately influence the transformation ... of the National Socialist movement.' Heidegger still expects us to identify with his 'cerebral', 'lofty' motives, and yet, in his thinly veiled appeal for sympathy, he betrays the shameless self-promotion, careerism and straightforward megalomania that determined his actions. Of course, in saying as much we are not accusing Heidegger of being a dyed-in-the-wool Nazi, replete with biologically deterministic views, but we are accusing him of both looking to piggyback the Nazi movement in its early years as a vehicle for self-aggrandizement and as having unmistakable messianic aspirations. Notwithstanding, Heidegger's intellectual heritage is, in the end, far more philosophical than political. If anyone suspects otherwise, they need only look at how disastrously inept Heidegger proved when venturing forth into the world of political affairs. He was clearly something of a novice in political terms and had no real facility for or understanding of politics.

His Rectoral address, while disappointingly Nazi in tone in a couple of places, is also terribly pretentious as 'political' documents go – which was undoubtedly part of how Heidegger conceived it. Having said as much, we must also concede that Heidegger clearly did try to find ways to manufacture a union of sorts between the problematic elements of his resistance to modernity and the elements of National Socialism which he thought were compatible with those notions.

Running through Heidegger's anti-modernism are very dangerous currents and this is something which is often not seen by those who have inherited and accepted features of his philosophical outlook, some of whom came to dominate European philosophy from around the middle of the twentieth century. And, one has to at least credit Heidegger with a kind of intellectual honesty (and wooden-headedness) on this issue following his disgraced return from his own 'Syracuse'; Heidegger understood very well how far the ramifications of his anti-modernism were to go and he was determined to give those ideas their due and remained opposed to democratic liberalism to the very end of his life.

\*\*\*\*

At times I have clearly defended Heidegger or his work against the less than moderate and, at least as I see things, ill-conceived denunciations and criticisms of his detractors. And, because of the apologetic character of some of the interpretations offered, the suspicion always looms that one is splitting hairs needlessly in order to salvage some aspect of Heideggerianism from the taint of Nazism. In other words, there is a danger that, in what may seem like interminable hair-splitting, contextualizing and qualifications, we end up sounding like revisionists who don't want to call a Nazi a Nazi. But that has certainly not been the aim of this study. There is no denying Heidegger's Nazism and there is a lot of troubling evidence stacked against him suggesting antisemitic proclivities as well. But, even with this much granted, we must make a better fist of all of this than has been hitherto achieved. Again, we run into examples of the genetic fallacy here which seem more and more prevalent in Heidegger studies, and not just on the issue of the political controversy – even when it comes to strictly theoretical discussions this problem recurs with disappointing regularity. The willingness to reduce Heidegger's work to earlier movements, thinkers and influences as though it amounts to no more than a reproduction of the work of his forerunners relies on a remarkable oversimplification. The fact that Heidegger was impressed by Kierkegaard is not tantamount to a demonstration that *Being and Time* is a reproduction of Kierkegaard's philosophy. Similarly, the fact that Heidegger's background and cultural views were heavily coloured by a particular bucolic, anti-modernist, anti-cosmopolitan outlook is not to say that Heidegger's philosophy is no more than a reproduction of local prejudices. And, while we can mine a great deal of important chronicled material and information from Victor Farias, for example, we must also do our utmost to steer clear of the rather juvenile reductionism, traduction and guilt by the merest association which characterizes Farias' efforts to demonstrate inveterate affinities between Heidegger's philosophy and his heritage, biography or cultural milieu as though his philosophy were as easily grasped from a brief study of his biography as wrestling with his most important texts. Granted, Farias has 'sociological' concerns which are better understood and articulated perhaps by the likes of Pierre Bourdieu. That is, he wants to emphasize the fact that the philosophy of Heidegger owes something to its heritage. Then again, this is something which both he and Bourdieu appreciate the importance of thanks in large part to the ground-breaking insights in this regard of Heidegger himself. Nevertheless, graphically expounding the virulent antisemitism of Abraham of Sancta Clara before reminding us of Heidegger's positive assessment of the same monk on two public occasions at which he was asked to offer some words is not *ipso facto* to demonstrate Heidegger's fundamental support for the baser elements of Abraham of Sancta Clara's xenophobia. Granted, Farias' disappointingly sensationalist and often intellectually ungainly psychological and philosophical 'profiling' of Heidegger is nowhere near the campaign of victor's moralizing and hate-filled propaganda spewing forth from the pages of Faye's notorious polemic, but it still creates as many problems as it purports to solve owing in large part to the rather naked agenda of the chronicler himself who is completely disillusioned with Heidegger and is desperate to reject both the man *and* his work for his association with National Socialism.

We must of course accept that Heidegger very clearly thought that there might be a way to justify, at the theoretical level, the ethnic chauvinism which he was clearly sympathetic to for a period of his life. We have seen that his philosophy simply is not as accommodating to this level of provincialism as Heidegger might have hoped and, in that sense, we can say that Heidegger's philosophy and political views don't map onto each other as readily as some of his critics suggest. Having said as much, we must constantly keep in view the fact that it was Heidegger who made this attempt and he was clearly and explicitly paving the way for some of these attempts as early as *Being and Time*. Thus, we cannot smugly insist on a fundamental discontinuity between Heidegger's philosophy and his political misadventure – as some of his most entrenched acolytes have done over the past few decades. After all, it was Heidegger himself who maintained openly that the basis for his political commitment to National Socialism was to be found in some of the central concepts of *Being and Time* and he was already beginning to tinker with these notions in ways that were and remain worrisome in that work. In the 1930s he makes a number of attempts to push this project forward and, what is more, one cannot help but cringe at some of the comments concerning native soil, homeland and rootedness in later works such as the 'Memorial Address', not least when one considers the manner in which Heidegger deployed those notions in the early and mid-1930s.

****

This brings us finally to what we can ascertain or determine with respect to Heidegger's antisemitism. Was it in fact the prejudice shared by some of the war criminals that were hanged for their role in genocide? To what extent can we charge Heidegger with complicity? Is it a complicity that is the World's shame? Europe's? Or is it the complicity of a host of Germans who stood idly by, who felt that there was a Jewish problem but perhaps would have looked to resolve it less drastically? For that complicity was itself disastrous! The question of Heidegger's antisemitism then is troublesome and, predictably, complicated. To the end of his life Heidegger continued to profess his admiration for and, in some cases, maintained close ties with, a number of Jewish intellectuals, not least Hannah Arendt. And yet, in conversation with Karl Jaspers, whose wife was Jewish, he once insisted that there was indeed a dangerous international alliance of Jews, a belief which he expresses again in his notebooks from the 1930s.[9] Heidegger's own wife was, by all accounts, fiercely antisemitic though Heidegger himself was not seen as such by any of his Jewish colleagues or friends; nevertheless, one wonders as to why it didn't present more of a problem to the couple given Heidegger's close relationships with Jewish students and colleagues.[10] Heidegger was occasionally brimming with Nazi braggadocio and would proudly don Nazi insignia and pins when in the company of Jewish friends and acquaintances who were suffering directly as a result of Nazi persecution. So, there is no denying that Heidegger was, at the very least, partially sympathetic to some form of antisemitism, regardless of how moderate some may have deemed it to be. In fact, Heidegger's antisemitism, I would submit, was very much of the garden-variety which has since been identified as shockingly prevalent throughout Europe during the early to middle part of the twentieth century. We are on the threshold of some very uncomfortable questions then, not least, the question as to how much of a role the quiet antisemitic prejudice of many Europeans played in facilitating elements of the Nazi plans for a final solution to the Jewish problem. In other words, the very day that the merest form of persecution according to race or ethnicity was allowed to proceed unchecked as official policy, did we not ultimately grease the tracks that carted millions to their deaths? What of the 'non-criminal' types who stood idly by? What of the 'Heideggers' of the Second World War who didn't favour genocide or persecution but who yet supported those who would have rid the world of the Jewish people as though they were a parasite or pest to be exterminated? Where do we ourselves, the accusers, the prosecutors, judges and jurors, in short – the victors – where do we draw the line when it comes to stretching necks? How many people who were never brought to trial in Nuremburg shared the same prejudices as those who suffered the long drop from a short rope? Once we had extracted our pound of flesh and vouched safe the historical narrative that would be disseminated and propagated, how many 'guilty' souls escaped the victor's noose? And yet, in terms of Heidegger, is such a 'defence' even feasible now that we have even more damning testimony from his private notebooks and seminars such as *Nature, History, State* from the early 1930s? When we see Heidegger privately relate his lifelong concerns with machination and the rootlessness of the technological age (the greatest problem we face as a species for Heidegger) specifically to 'World Jewry',[11] then what apology or gesture on behalf of the dead philosopher would satisfy us? If we did happen on a word of contrition in the manner of Pound, what good would it do us? Either the philosophy must be rejected or we can continue to work with Heidegger's philosophy, albeit with a heightened degree of caution.

# Notes

## Introduction

1. Richard Polt and Gregory Fried. 'Editors' Introduction'. In Martin Heidegger. *Nature, History, State: 1933–34*. Translated and edited by Gregory Fried and Richard Polt. London and New York: Bloomsbury, 2013, 1.
2. See Richard Wolin. *The Politics of Being*. New York: Columbia University Press, 1990, xi.
3. See page xviii of David Carroll's Foreword to Jean-François Lyotard. *Heidegger and "the jews"*. Translated by Andreas Michel and Mark Roberts. Minneapolis: University of Minnesota Press, 1990.
4. The case of Frege is sometimes mentioned in this context but I take it as more or less self-evident that this is not really an analogous case. Quite clearly, Frege's philosophical vision has little or nothing to do with any kind of political or ethical outlook. Heidegger's philosophy is not so obviously detached from the world we live in and it was Heidegger himself who insisted that his political decisions and outlook were based directly on the concept of historicity in *Being and Time*.
5. Of course that is precisely what some of the more partisan and less enlightened proponents of a certain brand of analytic philosophy would have us believe but it is not a view which I take seriously.
6. Heidegger, as we shall see in subsequent chapters, confirms as much to his one-time student, Karl Löwith, in Rome in 1936.
7. I realize that using this term in an unqualified way is to already beg the question for some; however, it seems to me that we cannot keep qualifying and apologizing for Heidegger's various antisemitic remarks in an attempt to exonerate him of this particular offence. In demonstrating that Heidegger was not one of Hitler's 'willing executioners' we are not thereby allowed to forgive him certain ethnic prejudices, ones which were nefarious and dangerous in their own right.
8. Heidegger's philosophical confrontation with technology ranks as among his most impressive intellectual achievements. And given that 'The Question Concerning Technology' is understood to be his most important text on the subject, we have to wonder as to the tenability of the criticism to the effect that Heidegger failed abjectly to say anything of note concerning the Holocaust when he was so eminently well placed to do so (philosophically at least). If some of Heidegger's most important philosophical work following the end of the Second World War is in fact a direct and philosophically profound attempt to deal with the Holocaust, then it was hardly a deafening 'silence', never mind a scandalous failure. That is not to say that Heidegger's numerous failures as a friend and colleague are thereby excused, but that is a different matter.
9. Christopher Browning. *Ordinary Men: Reserve Police Battalion 101 and the Final Solution in Poland*. New York: Harper Perennial, 1998, 160.

10   Marcuse levels this charge against Heidegger in their brief and rather strained correspondence immediately following the end of the Second World War. See *The Heidegger Controversy*. Edited by Richard Wolin. New York: Columbia University Press, 1991, 160.
11   Julian Young. *Heidegger, Philosophy, Nazism*. Cambridge: Cambridge University Press, 1998, 44.
12   Of course, there are some critics who would suggest that Heidegger's 'silence' and the cryptic attempts to map his views on technology onto the Holocaust were an appalling type of evasion on his part that betokened a moral failure of staggering extremes, a failure to fully see the culpability and repugnance of the Nazi regime.
13   One must concede, of course, that Farias helped to blow the lid off Heidegger's 'official story'. His exhaustive chronicling of materials from numerous archives completely shatters the myth that Heidegger tried to concoct concerning his Nazi involvement. The problem is that Farias quite often makes extravagant, sweeping claims about the basic structure of crucial philosophical texts such as *Being and Time*. He derives the basis for some of the more repugnant elements of Heidegger's day-to-day activities as a Nazi enthusiast, for instance, from the existential analytic. Furthermore, while all of the 'evidence' that supposedly supports the thesis that Heidegger was a thoroughgoing fascist with deep-rooted antisemitic, conservative nationalist sympathies is to be counted as significant, any evidence that clearly unsettles that thesis or else supports the view that Heidegger became a trenchant opponent of National Socialism as that movement developed and evolved is to be either discounted as incidental or is conveniently explained away. Notwithstanding, one has to estimate Farias' efforts a little higher than critics such as Derrida.
  In making this point, however, what commentators such as Sheehan failed to emphasize sufficiently in his protracted stand-off with Derrida *et al.* in *The New York Review of Books* was the extent to which critics such as Farias and Wolin manage to muddy the water that might have been 'cleared' with their purgative 'facts' as a result of their intrusive interjections as analysts of the relationship between those facts and Heidegger's philosophy. Indeed, many Heidegger supporters were quick to run to the *Meister*'s defence concerning the intricacies of his philosophy having forgotten in their haste that the incontrovertible facts assembled by Farias, for instance, stand as rather damning testimony in their own right and force us to rethink the connection between Heidegger's philosophy and his politics in ways that he himself had, through a strategy of evasiveness and deception, tried to preclude after the end of the war. What is perhaps most difficult to countenance is the extent of his frenzied, zealous support of an extreme provincial, Germanocentric and highly chauvinistic political outlook. At times, Heidegger seems utterly intoxicated with a kind of hysteria that was sweeping through the nation which is, to say the least, unsettling. Young cites Jaspers' observation to this effect: 'Jaspers reports the Heidegger of 1933 as in a state of "ecstasy" or "intoxication" (*vom Rausch ergriffen*)' (Julian Young. *Heidegger, Philosophy, Nazism*. p. 48).
14   I have tried to approach and read Faye's notorious book with an open mind. Alas, having studied the book with some care, I was dismayed to find that the only conclusion I could draw was that the author was waging something of a personal vendetta. More disappointing still have been his disingenuous token efforts at dialogue with philosophers who are genuinely concerned with confronting Heidegger's Nazi past. Any attempt to suggest that Faye's work is excessive or that his journalistic tendencies tend to outstrip the need for philosophical care, which

is about as charitable an estimation of his text as one could expect, is met with a salvo of *ad hominem* attacks. Ultimately, for Faye, the only reason one would disagree with him is down to a blind loyalty to Heidegger and a posture of denial. In his correspondence with Gregory Fried, Faye insists that commentators have universally failed to confront his close readings of Heidegger's own manuscripts which supposedly prove for once and for all that Heidegger was a committed Nazi; not only that, Heidegger's philosophy was clearly a front for a commitment to the worst excesses of what he refers to as Hitlerism. For example, in his correspondence with Fried, Faye expresses his disappointment that his adversaries fail to look at the incontrovertible evidence he provides and direct textual proof which corroborates his position. However, what we find by and large are highly dubious translations from previously unpublished manuscripts from the early 1930s. Faye goes on to offer terribly jaundiced and tendentious interpretations of the same passages with absolutely no concessions made as to the context of each of those passages sprinkled with repeated asseverations to the effect that he is offering undeniable proof for his position. He compounds these problems by continually proclaiming Heidegger's guilt by association with other Nazis; sometimes he simply has to be in the same city where some atrocity or other takes place in order for Heidegger to be complicit in the crime. And, of course, there are the countless non-sequiturs that Faye's 'arguments' are guilty of. And yet, when any mention is made of these unpardonable technical problems with his text, Faye simply goes on the offensive insisting that anyone who criticizes him in this way is a blind Heideggerian acolyte. Faye refuses to let the facts speak for themselves; his systematic, or better, closed system approach to Heidegger admits of no dialogue, not even with Heidegger's own texts. They are allowed to say nothing except what Faye interpolates and foists on them. As a consequence, all one can do is accuse the French author of gross intellectual negligence in calling for a figurative auto-da-fé which would be very much at home in the repressive society Heidegger supported for a period of time.

15   Even in his correspondence with his young wife, Elfride, Heidegger was critical of fundamental aspects of Husserl's work from the very beginning. Consider for instance the following asseveration from the young philosopher in 1917 in a letter to Elfride when Heidegger would only have just made Husserl's acquaintance: 'I cannot accept Husserl's phenomenology as a final position even if it joins up with philos. – because in its approach & accordingly in its goal it is too narrow & bloodless & because such an approach cannot be made absolute. Life is too rich and too great ...' *Martin Heidegger Letters to His Wife: 1915–1970*. Selected, edited and annotated by Gertrud Heidegger (R.D.V. Glasgow, Translator). Cambridge: Polity Press, 2008, 33.

16   Husserl had of course converted to Christianity as a younger man; he was baptized as a Lutheran in 1886 along with his fiancée.

17   Thomas Sheehan has two articles that discuss these topics in some depth; the earlier one in particular ('Everyone Has To Tell The Truth') specifically takes up the question of Heidegger's anti-Semitism. See Sheehan (1990, 1993). See '"Everyone has to Tell the Truth": Heidegger and the Jews'. *Continuum*, *I*(1), 1990, 30–44. 'A Normal Nazi'. *New York Review of Books*, XL(1–2), 1993.

18   See Chapter 3.

19   Pierre Bourdieu. 'Back to History: An Interview'. In *The Heidegger Controversy: A Critical Reader*, 269–70.

# 1 Re-assessing the 'Affair'

1. Jacques Derrida. *Of Spirit: Heidegger and the question*. Translated by Geoffrey Bennington and Rachel Bowlby. Chicago: University of Chicago Press, 1987, 109–10.
2. Julian Young. *Heidegger, Philosophy, Nazism*, 44.
3. In tandem with the Heidegger 'Affair' there is a longstanding 'debate' concerning the charge of obscurantism, which gained a little currency again with opportunistic critics keen to exploit matters at the height of the controversy surrounding Heidegger's political activities. Heidegger's work is really just the most visible target from within a tradition which certain philosophers from the Anglo-American tradition see as illegitimate. One still reads venomous polemics against what some commentators hold to be errant 'method' in Heidegger's work. Some of this criticism makes about as much sense as criticizing poets after Shakespeare for departing from the sonnet form as though poetry had to be structured according to the sonnet's parameters and is generally made by critics who refuse to ever take Heidegger seriously. Heidegger has continued to represent something of a *bête noire* for the analytic tradition as the interest in Heidegger continues to grow. For an example of the extremes which some critics have gone to in efforts to stem the tide of Heidegger's influence one need only look as far as Simon Blackburn's polemical overview both of Heidegger's work in general and *Contributions to Philosophy* in *The New Republic* (2000). It is typical of a certain strategy adopted during each recurrence of the controversy and involves jumping on the bandwagon of the Heidegger controversy in order to 'put a stake through the heart' of Heidegger's thought. As Heidegger proclaims in *Contributions to Philosophy*:

    > 'System' is only possible as a consequence of the mastery of mathematical thinking (in its widest sense). A thinking that stands outside this domain and outside the corresponding determination of truth as certainty is therefore essentially without system, un-systematic; but it is not therefore arbitrary and chaotic. Un-systematic would then merely mean something like "chaotic" and disordered, if measured against system. (*Contributions to Philosophy: From Enowning*. Translated by Parvis Emad and Kenneth Maly. Bloomington and Indianapolis: Indiana University Press, 1999, 45)

4. See Louis Clair's introduction in Ernst Junger. *The Peace*. Translated by Stuart O. Hood. Hinsdale, IL: Henry Regnery Co, 1948, 9–10.
5. It is instructive to note also that Caputo sees Heidegger's apotheosis of the Greek experience as a peculiarly Heideggerian theme as is the complete neglect of the Christian and Jewish traditions. See John D. Caputo. 'Heidegger's revolution: An introduction to an Introduction to Metaphysics'. In *Heidegger Toward the Turn*. Edited by James Risser. Albany: State University of New York Press, 1999.

    There are two points to be made here. First, the prioritizing of the Greeks and their tradition is scarcely an exclusively Heideggerian 'failing', one need hardly recount the litany of great thinkers who defer to the Greeks and no one else from the Western Tradition. Second, Heidegger has been more influential for Catholic/Christian theology than most other twentieth century philosophers. Heidegger remained interested in Christianity and other religions throughout his life and was still apt to dip his hand in the stoup at any chapel he passed when walking in the countryside since anywhere that so much praying was done, so Heidegger is reported to have said, the divine was bound to be present. Felix O'Murchadha makes a similar criticism against charges such as Caputo's in a recent book:

> Philosophy since its inception has challenged the deepest held beliefs of society. Clearly Heidegger challenged our belief in democracy and – not unrelated to that – our faith in progressive rather than abrupt change. Clearly there are fundamental dangers in such challenges as the experience of totalitarian regimes in the last century make abundantly clear. But to second guess thinking in the face of its risks is in the end to give up the philosophical enterprise itself. Hence, it is vital to consider Heidegger's relation to National Socialism in the spirit of Socrates and not in the spirit of the Athenian court. (Felix O'Murchadha. *The Time of Revolution: Kairos and Chronos in Heidegger*. London and New York: Bloomsbury, 2013, 174)

6  Wolin's heavy-handed editorial input in *The Heidegger Controversy* as well as his hugely problematic study – *The Politics of Being* (1990) – are frequently guilty of such a strategy.

7  Even toward the end of his career and in an interview which has often been discredited as little more than a PR stunt or exercise in damage limitation, Heidegger still averred that he remained unconvinced that democracy was the best type of political regime for 'managing' in the contemporary world: 'A decisive question for me today is: how can a political system accommodate itself to the technological age, and which political system would this be? I have no answer to this question. I am not convinced that it is democracy', Martin Heidegger. 'Only a God Can Save Us'. In *The Heidegger Controversy: A Critical Reader*. 104.

8  Wolin's attempt to avoid the excessive and tendentious nature of Farias' sensationalism gives way to a somewhat juvenile attack in its own right. Wolin's recounting of the response within French intellectual circles is consistent with that offered by a number of other commentators. However, in looking to discredit their various strategies, Wolin wants to rescue what is 'important' in Farias' work, namely, the continued emphasis on the fact that Heidegger was indeed a Nazi and that he remained sceptical concerning the tenets of liberal democracy for the rest of his life. Wolin suggests that we should 'let the facts speak for themselves', *The Heidegger Controversy: A Critical Reader*, 277. In other words, since Heidegger had philosophical reasons for supporting some version of National Socialism, his work is *ipso facto* corrupt to the core. Heidegger devalues the 'modern project of human autonomy' (ibid., 296), that is, modern liberal democracy and what Wolin refers to as 'the modern ideal of self-fashioning subjectivity'. In so doing, Heidegger's thought is even further debased. But again, this is hardly letting the facts speak for themselves. Wolin concludes that to criticize the model of 'self-fashioning subjectivity' is 'abstract, irrational, and sadly impotent', ibid., 296. But then again, why did Wolin trouble himself with Heidegger at all when it was clear to anyone with eyes to see or ears to hear that this was central to the Heideggerian project and his deconstruction of the metaphysics of the subject *from the very beginning*. He reprises this rhetorical tactic again in a 2003 review of Jean Grondin's biography of Gadamer. To have sympathies which are not gung ho liberal or 'leftish', particularly if one happens to have lived through Nazi Germany, is in itself an unforgivable shortcoming and puts a little meat on the bones of otherwise flimsy, speculative and circumstantial evidence of Nazi sympathies. See Richard Wolin. 'Socratic apology: a

wonderful horrible life of Hans-Georg Gadamer.' URL: http://www.bookforum.com/archive/sum/03/wolin.html

9   David Carroll cites Lacoue-Labarthe's view to this effect in his foreword to Lyotard's series of meditations entitled *Heidegger and "the jews"*: "as Lacoue-Labarthe argues, Nazism should not be treated as a madness or an aberration, for it did not come from another planet but emerged from within Western political thought and practice itself" (*Heidegger and "the jews"*, XX).

10  A good example of this is the incredulity and dismay that some of the more intimate details of Winston Churchill's life, for instance, are met with, more specifically, his prodigious capacity for alcohol. It was not unusual for Churchill to consume staggering amounts of Scotch each evening interspersed between the usual fare of wine and aperitifs which accompanied dinner before retiring with a pint of Scotch to his private quarters. There are also accounts of Churchill consuming bottles of wine with breakfast. These details concerning one of the twentieth century's true Western heroes embarrass us. For some reason we prefer to mythologize the past such that its important figures become more or less than human – deified superhuman heroes or contemptible inhuman creatures with inestimable capacities for cruelty. Both caricatures serve to deflect attention away from the fact that historical sagas, evil, and indeed bravery in the face of adversity, are played out by ordinary human beings with the same weaknesses, proclivities and strengths as the rest of us.

11  Alistair Cooke 1974. http://www.pbs.org/wgbh/masterpiece/series/cooke address.html.

12  *Heidegger and "the jews"*, xxi.

13  *Heidegger and "the jews"*, 52.

14  *Heidegger and "the jews"*, 52. Marcuse's exchange of letters with Heidegger touches on this issue also. Though one cannot help but think that Heidegger is missing the point of Marcuse's correspondence at times. Marcuse does not want Heidegger to offer a philosophical account as to the roots of Nazism. He wants a public confession, a willingness to recant his former Nazi heresy. If Heidegger even privately had made some gesture of acknowledgement that what happened in the concentration camps was indeed grossly heinous and barbaric, Marcuse might have been satisfied. However, in the absence of even so small a concession, and following years of silence, Marcuse is moved to warn Heidegger that one 'can only combat the identification of your person and your work with Nazism (and thereby the dissolution of your philosophy) if you make a public avowal of your changed views' (*The Heidegger Controversy: A Critical Reader*. 160).

15  Gregory Fried. *Heidegger's Polemos: From Being to Politics*. New Haven, CT and London: Yale University Press, 2000, 67, 68.

16  Jacques Derrida. *Of Spirit: Heidegger and the Question*, 32.

17  Philippe Lacoue-Labarthe. *Heidegger, Art and Politics: The Fiction of the Political*. Translated by Chris Turner. Oxford: Blackwell, 1990.

18  Even the most cursory web-search on Google France throws up countless newspaper articles in what has been a protracted and sensational saga. Highly polarized figures have continued to adopt contending positions through the press, routinely besmirching their opponents as either Nazi apologists or as second-rate intellectuals depending on the attitude toward Heidegger's philosophy and political activities.

19  George Santayana. *The Life of Reason*, Vol. 1. Scribners, 1905, 284.

20  One can hardly ignore the numerous counts of ethnic cleansing that have occurred since the Holocaust. Indeed we have heard repeated accusations to the effect that

politicians continue to play politics with people's lives and look to 'appease' while many thousands of innocent people are butchered.
21 Alistair Cooke, http://www.pbs.org/wgbh/masterpiece/series/cooke address.html
22 Of course Arendt struggles with the 'banality' question and is not comfortable with the idea that Eichmann was just a regular human being – that anyone could and would have done the same as he given the circumstances. However, so honest is her account of the proceedings of the trial and her impressions of Eichmann, that the indisputably non-singular, typical, un-extraordinary nature of Eichmann shines through. That is not, of course, to suggest that anyone could or would do the same, it is rather to say that we cannot always look to pathologize criminals as a way of explaining away their atrocities. Rather we must understand that sometimes, people who are entirely ordinary and unremarkable and who are yet responsible for their actions, can and will do dreadful things.
23 Michael E. Zimmerman. *Heidegger's Confrontation with Modernity, Technology, Politics, Art*. Bloomington and Indianapolis: Indiana University Press, 1990, 43.
24 Berel Lang makes this point as well. See Berel Lang. *Heidegger's Silence*. Ithaca, NY: Cornell University Press, 1996, 22.
25 See Marcuse's letter to Heidegger in *The Heidegger Controversy: A Critical Reader*, 164.
26 Michael E. Zimmerman. *Heidegger's Confrontation with Modernity*, 43. Julian Young touches on this issue as well arguing that

> Considerable support for Heidegger's analysis is to be found in the distancing, mechanistic, bureaucratic, dehumanising vocabulary of the Holocaust: the vocabulary of "final solution" and "extermination" – a term taken over from the vocabulary of vermin control (J. A. Topf & Sons who built ovens in which the murdered were burnt described them in their patent application as a 'process and apparatus for the incineration of carcasses, cadavers, and parts thereof'). (Julian Young. *Heidegger, Philosophy, Nazism*, 185)

27 We see this again, although it should hardly surprise us, in Emmanuel Faye's summary of his book on Heidegger in a 2006 article where he says that Heidegger claims that 'the concentration camps and mobilized agriculture amounted to the same thing', Emmanuel Faye, 64. Emmanuel Faye, 'Nazi Foundations in Heidegger's Work', *South Central Review*: 23, 1, Fascism, Nazism: Cultural Legacies of Reaction (Spring, 2006) 55–66.
28 Heinrich Petzet reports that in private conversation Heidegger condemned his activities as Rector and his association with the Nazis as the greatest stupidity of his life ('*die größte Dummheit seines Lebens*'). See Heinrich Wiegand Petzet. *Encounters and Dialogues with Martin Heidegger, 1929–1976*, 1983, 37.
29 Though a lot of ink and time is wasted on such *ad hominem* considerations, they are not all that philosophically relevant.
30 Safranski offers a sympathetic 'take' on Heidegger's attitude in this regard by reviewing his correspondence with Marcuse subsequent to the war: 'That he [Heidegger] should, on public demand, distance himself from the murder of millions of Jews – that Heidegger, rightly, regarded as monstrous. To do so would imply that the public considered him capable of complicity with the murder. His self-esteem demanded that he decline this unreasonable request.' See Rudiger Safranski. *Martin Heidegger: Between Good and Evil*. Translated by Ewald Osers, Cambridge, MA: Harvard University Press, 1998, 421. See also Heidegger's response

to Marcuse in *The Heidegger Controversy*: 'An avowal after 1945 was for me impossible: the Nazi supporters announced their change of allegiance in the most loathsome way; I, however, had nothing in common with them' (*The Heidegger Controversy*, 163).

31  Zimmerman summarizes the basic challenge of critics with respect to Heidegger's reticence when it came to National Socialism and the Holocaust after the war: 'Why, long after the end of World War II, did he continue to harbor such an ambiguous attitude toward National Socialism? Why did he express a reluctance, bordering on defiance, to condemn the Holocaust, or to grapple seriously with the historical and cultural anti-Semitic issues (not merely the metaphysical ones) that were obviously so central to National Socialism?', Michael E. Zimmerman. *Heidegger's Confrontation with Modernity*, 131.

32  For another example of a reading that intersects with my own here see Babette Babich. 'The Essence of Questioning After Technology: Techne as Constraint and the Saving Power.' *British Journal of Phenomenology* Vol. 30, No. 1, January/1999, 106–24.

## 2 The Essence of Technology and the Holocaust

1  Granted, one could argue that Heidegger deliberately tried to suppress this interpretation of his essay by modifying the remark significantly. However, that does not alter the fact that, when he was working on these issues and gave public lectures, he was of the opinion that his views concerning technology bore directly on the question as to how we should understand the Holocaust. And, given the way the remark has been used as something of a stick to beat Heidegger with since it first surfaced and has been, in my opinion, routinely misinterpreted in the secondary literature, perhaps it was initially a shrewd decision on Heidegger's part.

2  Martin Heidegger. 'Positionality'. In *Bremen and Freiburg Lectures: Insight Into That Which Is and Basic Principles of Thinking*. Translated by Andrew J. Mitchell. Bloomington: Indiana University Press, 2012, 27.

3  Some of the confusion here is no doubt precipitated by a hasty reading which ignores the fact that Heidegger uses the word 'essence' (and most especially in this essay) in a very specific and unique manner. The essence of something, as far as Heidegger is concerned, is not the underlying defining quality in virtue of which two objects can be called the same, at least not when it comes to the essence of technology. Rather the essence of these phenomena mentioned by Heidegger, the essence that he is looking to compare, is their *technological* essence and the essence of technology is a kind of 'revealing'.

4  In his translation of the Bremen lectures, Andrew Mitchell elects to translate '*Gestell*' as 'positionality' and Daniel Dahlstrom does the same in his recently published Heidegger dictionary. There is no doubt that 'positionality' brings to the fore aspects of Heidegger's term which might not seem as obvious with the word 'Enframing'. However, I am inclined to lean more toward the older translation since people by and large recognize it instantly as the word that translates '*Gestell*' and, in any case, the notion of framing something and the act of en-framing does, to my ear at least, carry the many and various resonances needed and indeed conveys a little more than the word 'positionality' on its own.

5   The first examples of factory farming were already in evidence in the 1920s when radical new methods were employed in the rearing of chickens.
6   See 'Only a God Can Save Us'. In *The Heidegger Controversy*, 105. Heidegger is here criticizing democracy and the Christian worldviews because of their failure to comprehend the essence of technology. If we consider that in the same interview he underlined his conviction that democracy could not accommodate itself to the technological age, we can see that Heidegger's overarching view remains the belief that the essence of technology is something which has yet to be properly understood.
7   One might wonder as to my decision to discuss Heidegger's 'agriculture remark' in the context of the later essay which he published instead of in the context of the lectures which he delivered in Bremen and elsewhere. After all, the lectures are now available with the remark that he made publicly when, in turn, he amended and sanitized the remark in the essay which he published. The reason for my choice is simple and based on my own hermeneutic principles when it comes to interpreting Heidegger's work: I simply consider it a matter of common sense to suppose that an essay or text that Heidegger elected to publish counts for more philosophically than his notes, seminars or indeed his lectures on the same issues. That is not at all to say that these resources are unimportant philosophically, that would be a gross over-statement. However, no more than with any other thinker, I think we have to hold that the work that they themselves worked and reworked and developed for publication as 'finished' philosophical texts simply must be closer to capturing what it is that they are trying to say philosophically than their notes, seminars or lectures on the way to the 'finished' article, as it were. Of course, one must nevertheless pay close attention to unpublished seminars and notebooks wherever we can with a view to fleshing out our understanding of the published text.
8   Again, it hardly serves our purpose to rehearse this abstract discussion in depth, we are really looking to offer a brief outline of the development of the essay such that we can appreciate how Heidegger arrives at the unusual notion that the essence of modern technology is a type of 'revealing' since it is this conviction that allows us to begin to understand the so-called agricultural remark as an 'epigraph' to this famous essay.
9   William Lovitt translates '*Hervorbringen*' as 'bringing-forth'.
10  And that is ultimately why Heidegger rejects the instrumental definition of technology as insufficient; it doesn't allow us to appreciate the essence of technology as a mode of revealing and, for Heidegger, the way things reveal themselves and are revealed goes to the heart of the matter.
11  Martin Heidegger. 'Only a God Can Save Us', 105–6.
12  That is not to suggest that the Jews were not the people to suffer most at Nazi hands, nor would I contest the view that the greatest antipathy amongst the Nazis was reserved for the Jewish people.
13  Daniel Jonah Goldhagen. *Hitler's Willing Executioners: Ordinary Germans and the Holocaust*. London: Abacus, 1997.
14  Of course this is to directly contradict Goldhagen's central claim in *Hitler's Willing Executioners*.
15  Heidegger was retrospectively critical of the term he coined for the essence of technology, namely, *Gestell* which is translated by Lovitt as 'Enframing'. The term is a little awkward since it is not as though Enframing works by 'framing' our image or picture of the world. Rather, we tend to see and interpret things in a way which has been 'filtered' beforehand. We are not only looking at something upon or around which a frame has been placed. Having said as much, I am still inclined to think

that the notion of Enframing is a slightly more inclusive word than what seems to be currently favoured by Heidegger scholars translating the term – 'positionality'.

16  The phrase in German reads: '*Endlösung der Judenfrage*'; literally – 'the final solution to the Jewish question'.

17  The closest we get to anyone worrying over the relevant issues in a way which might prove fruitful here has emerged in the functionalist interpretations of a number of well-known historians with respect to Hitler and the Third Reich against the intentionalist interpretations of others. Both camps sub-divide further into more and less radical versions of those positions. In terms of the Final Solution, the meeting in Berlin in 1942 and the countless incidences of mass murder in the Eastern regions which escalated in the lead up to the Wannssee Conference, both sets of historians have struggled with questions that begin to point in the direction we wish to go without ever quite getting there. Too often, these critics seem to either play something of a blame game, implicating Hitler down to the minutest degrees of intentionality for every instance of violence in the Third Reich or else they are so concerned with minimizing his role that they overlook the questions that need to be addressed which are implicit to that functionalism. And even those that steer a more moderate course on either side of this notorious divide, while eminently more measured and plausible in their speculations and analyses, are still not quite able to take the next step which should be taken. In short, the level of Hitler's complicity or responsibility is not what should concern us most; even were we to demonstrate that Hitler was more or less 'responsible', that would not explain why hundreds of thousands of Germans were willing to acquiesce in the genocidal aspirations of a 'monster'. Nor indeed does it make a huge amount of difference to our account if we can show that the blame can be spread over a wider pool of Nazi culprits. We are still left wondering why so many otherwise ordinary people seemed willing to participate in the greatest systematic slaughter of innocents in the history of the human race. At the same time, one feels a certain sympathy with some of the motives of the functionalists here; the feverish attempts to characterize Hitler as a diabolical necromancer who cast a spell over millions of people and indeed an army of auxiliaries and functionaries so as to manipulate them in the singular pursuit of his gruesome goals does him too much 'credit'.

18  http://www.writing.upenn.edu/~afilreis/Holocaust/wansee-transcript.html

19  Ibid.

20  The SS and the Order police had been experimenting with numerous methods of mass murder in the early 1940s during Operation Barbarossa. These various methods, which included mobile gas trucks, mass shootings and mass incineration of living people within sealed buildings were not ultimately sufficient for the scale of extermination envisioned by the German authorities. The gas chambers were to prove a major 'breakthrough' in terms of solving a 'logistical' problem of 'disposal' for the powers that be!

21  Ibid.

22  How German antipathy toward the Russians had evolved during the early part of the twentieth century again is not a question which we are trying to answer in terms of Heidegger's account of *Gestell*. However, it is important to note how readily the Russian POWs came to be looked on as simple waste to be disposed of as efficiently as possible.

23  Höss notes wryly at one point in his memoirs that the gas chambers were to be converted into bath houses once the mass extermination had come to an end. Rudolf

Höss. *Death Dealer: The Memoirs of the SS Kommandant at Auschwitz*, translated by Andrew Pollinger, edited by Steven Paskuly. New York: Da Capo Press, 1996, 37.

24 The attitudes of German soldiers, the SS and so on to Russian soldiers and indeed Russian citizens was as repugnant as their virulent antisemitic views. As Höss notes at the beginning of the chapter titled 'The Gassings', the decision had already been taken by the German authorities to exterminate the Russian POWs before the initiation of the plans for the Final Solution:

> Before the mass destruction of the Jews began, all the Russian politruks [Communist Party members] and political commissars were killed in almost every camp during 1941 and 1942. According to the secret order given by Hitler, the Einsatzgruppe [special troops of the SS] searched for and picked up the Russian politruks and commissars from all the POW camps. They transferred all they found to the nearest concentration camp for liquidation ...The first small transports were shot by firing squads of SS soldiers. (Rudolf Höss. *Death Dealer: The Memoirs of the SS Kommandant at Auschwitz*, 22)

25 Rudolf Höss. *Death Dealer: The Memoirs of the SS Kommandant at Auschwitz*, 155–7.
26 Ibid. 157.
27 *AUSCHWITZ*: Jean-Claude Pressac. *Technique and operation of the gas chambers*, The Beate Klarsfeld Foundation, 95.
28 *Death Dealer: The Memoirs of the SS Kommandant at Auschwitz*, 36–7.
29 'Kanada' was the name of the sorting area in Auschwitz where prisoners would sort through the luggage, clothes and belongings of the condemned. There was a good deal of pilfering involved; nonetheless, a vast quantity of gold, money and valuables were recovered. At that time Canada was seen as a land of abundance.
30 Of course, there are those who would express something very close to such a view today in the debates concerning the treatment and/or the rights of non-human animals. Nonetheless, Heidegger would almost certainly dismiss their foundational claims concerning the 'status' of animals in the 'world'.
31 The remark is from an interview Lacoue-Labarthe gave during a documentary on Heidegger. Philippe Lacoue-Labarthe. Interview in *The Ister* (Documentary). Produced and directed by David Barison and Daniel Ross. New York: First Run/ Icarus Films, 2004. Lacoue-Labarthe had made the same point in *Heidegger, Art, and Politics: the Fiction of the Political*. He uses the words 'scandalously inadequate' to describe Heidegger's remark concerning the 'essential' similarities between the Holocaust, agriculture, the atom bomb and blockades. See 34.

# 3 Heidegger's 'Heritage': Philosophy, Anti-Modernism and Cultural Pessimism

1 Hans Sluga. *Heidegger's Crisis: Philosophy and Politics in Nazi Germany*. Cambridge, MA: Harvard University Press, 1993, 99–100.
2 I should hasten to add that I am not lumping Zimmerman in with writers such as Faye or even Farias for that matter. Zimmerman's understanding of Heidegger is a long way ahead of either of those writer's grasp of his philosophy.

3   The extent of Heidegger's friendship with Ernst Jünger, for instance, was something which I did not fully appreciate until I began reading through their decades-long correspondence. See Martin Heidegger/Ernst Jünger. *Briefwechsel 1949–1975*. Klett-Cotta Verlag, 2008.
4   'Heidegger's critical judgments of "das Man", on the dictatorship of the public realm and the impotence of the private sphere, on technocracy and mass civilization, are without any originality whatsoever, because they belong to a repertoire of opinions typical of a certain generation of German mandarins'. Jurgen Habermas. *The Philosophical Discourse of Modernity*. Translated by Frederick Lawrence. Cambridge, MA: MIT Press, 1987, 140.
5   Of course one can well understand the frustration and outrage of Habermas; bear in mind that this is a man who suffered the lifelong ignominy of having been a member of the Hitler Youth Movement in his formative years. It is my belief however that Habermas routinely allows his emotions to govern his assessment of Heidegger. His normally sober and often tortuously meticulous approach to philosophical positions deserts him in his confrontations with Heidegger. He even fails to fulfil the most basic of all philosophical criteria in his criticisms of Heidegger, namely, 'consistency'. See Chapter 3 of Mahon O'Brien. *Heidegger and Authenticity: From Resoluteness to Releasement*.
6   'Als Adorno nach Deutschland zurückkam, hat er – man hat es mir berichtet – geäußert: In fünf Jahren habe ich Heidegger klein. Da sehen Sie, was das für ein Mann ist.' Richard Wisser. 'Das Fernseh-Interview' in Günther Neske (ed.), *Erinnerung an Martin Heidegger*. Pfullingen: Verlag Günther Neske, 1977, 283.
7   George Steiner. *Martin Heidegger*. Chicago: University of Chicago Press, 1991.
8   See Martin Heidegger. 'Why Do I Stay in The Provinces', translated by Thomas Sheehan. In *Heidegger: The Man and the Thinker*. Edited by Thomas Sheehan. Chicago: Precedent Publishing, 1981. In a footnote to his translation Sheehan notes that Heidegger's piece was published on 'March 7, 1934, a month after he had resigned the rectorate of Freiburg University. The passage Adorno refers to is the final paragraph:

> Recently I got a second invitation to teach at the University of Berlin. On that occasion I left Freiburg and withdrew to the cabin. I listened to what the mountains and the forest and the farmlands were saying, and I went to see an old friend of mine, a 75-year-old farmer. He had read about the call to Berlin in the newspapers. What would he say? Slowly he fixed the sure gaze of his clear eyes on mine, and keeping his mouth tightly shut, he thoughtfully put his faithful hand on my shoulder. Ever so slightly he shook his head. That meant: absolutely no! (Martin Heidegger. 'Why Do I Stay in The Provinces?', 29)

When one recalls a passage from *Being and Time* in the context of this piece, we may well end up wondering if there aren't other problems lurking in that text which have yet to be sufficiently addressed:

> *Is there not, however, a definite ontical way of taking authentic existence, a factical ideal of Dasein underlying our ontological Interpretation of Dasein's existence.* That is so indeed. But not only is this Fact one which must not be denied and which we are forced to grant: it must also be conceived in its *positive necessity*, in terms of the object which we have taken as the theme of our investigation. Philosophy will never seek to deny its 'presuppositions', but neither may it simply admit them. It conceives them, and it unfolds with more

and more penetration both the presuppositions themselves and that for which they are presuppositions. (BT: 358 emphasis in the first line is my own.)

9   Theodor Adorno. *The Jargon of Authenticity*. London and New York: Routledge, 2003, 43. Sheehan translates the same lines as follows: 'And this philosophical work does not take its course like the aloof studies of some eccentric. It belongs right in the midst of the peasant's work.' See *Heidegger: The Man and the Thinker*, 28.
10  Theodor Adorno. *The Jargon of Authenticity*, 44.
11  Theodor Adorno. *The Jargon of Authenticity*, 45. Adorno quotes Heidegger's *Der Feldweg*. Frankfurt-am-Main, 1956, 4.
12  Theodor Adorno. *The Jargon of Authenticity*, 43. The quote comes from two paragraphs where Heidegger is looking to underline the importance of his own 'rootedness' in his native soil to his philosophical views and, as we see again in his 'Memorial Address', this particular (and highly problematic) aspect of his political philosophy is something which he stubbornly adheres to until the end of his life:

> And this philosophical work does not take its course like the aloof studies of some eccentric. It belongs right in the midst of the peasant's work. When the young farmboy drags his heavy sled up the slope and guides it, piled high with beech logs, down the dangerous descent to his house, when the herdsman, lost in thought and slow of step, drives his cattle up the slope, when the farmer in his shed gets the countless shingles ready for his roof, my work is of the same sort. It is intimately rooted in and related to the life of the peasants.
>
> A city-dweller thinks he has gone "out among the people" as soon as he condescends to have a long conversation with a peasant. But in the evening during a work-break, when I sit with the peasants by the fire or at the table in the "Lord's Corner," we mostly say nothing at all. We smoke our pipes in silence. Now and again someone might say that the woodcutting in the forest is finishing up, that a marten broke into the hen-house last night, that one of the cows will probably calf in the morning, that someone's uncle suffered a stroke, that the weather will soon turn. *The inner relationship of my own work to the Black Forest and its people comes from a centuries-long and irreplaceable rootedness in the Alemannian-Swabian soil.* ('Why Do I Stay in the Provinces': 28, my emphasis)

13  Namely, Bourdieu's book – *The Political Ontology of Martin Heidegger*. Cambridge: Polity Press, 1991 and an interview – 'Back to History: An Interview', in *The Heidegger Controversy: A Critical Reader*.
14  *The Political Ontology of Martin Heidegger*, 54.
15  Ibid., 56.
16  Ibid., 79–80.
17  Ibid., 105.
18  See my discussion of Zimmerman's earlier work in Mahon O'Brien. *Heidegger and Authenticity: From Resoluteness to Releasement*. London: Continuum International Publishing Group, 2011, 78–81.
19  Michael E. Zimmerman. *Heidegger's Confrontation With Modernity, Technology, Politics and Art*. Bloomington and Indianapolis: Indiana University Press, 1990, 26.
20  *What is Called Thinking*. Translated by Fred D. Wieck, J. Glenn Gray. Harper & Row, 1976, 38.
21  Michael E. Zimmerman. *Heidegger's Confrontation with Modernity*, 26–7.

22  Michael E. Zimmerman. *Heidegger's Confrontation with Modernity*, 27.
23  Martin Heidegger. *The Fundamental Concepts of Metaphysics: World, Finitude, Solitude*. Translated by William McNeill and Nicholas Walker, Bloomington and Indianapolis: Indiana University Press, 1995, 74.
24  Ibid., 74.
25  Ibid., 77.
26  '*Der Verfasser aber ist begabter für den Journalism als für das Denken. Er hat für sein Alter schon zu viel geschrieben.*' (Ernst Jünger/Martin Heidegger *Briefwechsel*, 68) Jünger himself betrays a rather jaundiced view of journalism as evidenced by his response to the same letter from Heidegger:

> '*Das notierte ich als einen der Tiefpunkte deutscher Philosophie, wie seinerzeit Bauemlers Frage an Spengler: ob dieser nicht die Zeitungen gelesen habe?*' (Ernst Jünger /Martin Heidegger *Briefwechsel*, 69)

27  Martin Heidegger. *The Fundamental Concepts of Metaphysics*, 74.
28  The following is typical of Spengler's views in this context:

> Man is no simpleton, 'naturally good' and stupid, not a semi-ape with technical tendencies, as Haeckel describes him and Gabriel Max portrays him. Over these pictures there still falls the plebeian shadow of Rousseau. No, the tactics of his living are those of a splendid beast of prey, brave, crafty, and cruel. He lives by attacking and killing and destroying. He wills, and has willed ever since he existed, to be master. (Oswald Spengler. *Man and Technics: A Contribution to a Philosophy of Life*. Translated by Charles Francis Atkinson. Greenwood Press, 1976, 17)

29  Oswald Spengler. *Man and Technics*, 18.
30  Ibid., 9.
31  See Karl Löwith. 'The Political Implications of Heidegger's Existentialism'. In *The Heidegger Controversy: A Critical Reader*, 181.
32  Oswald Spengler. *Man and Technics*, 11.
33  Ibid., 23–4.
34  Oswald Spengler. *Man and Technics*, 15.
35  A number of Heidegger's students, many of them Jewish, have expressed their bewilderment at Heidegger's sudden and completely unexpected (as far as they were concerned) profession of support for the Nazis. Herbert Marcuse, in a well-known interview with Frederick Olafson in 1977 discusses this in depth at the beginning of the interview. See 'Heidegger's Politics: An Interview with Herbert Marcuse by Frederick Olafson'. *Graduate Faculty Philosophy Journal*, 6, 1 (1977).
36  Again, it must be pointed out that for Spengler we are ultimately doomed while his hero abstracts in a solipsistic manner which Heidegger simply would not advocate.
37  Admittedly, some of the passages from *Introduction to Metaphysics* where Heidegger interprets fragments from Heraclitus are less than helpful: 'If Being is to open itself up, it must have rank and maintain it. Heraclitus's reference to the many as dogs and donkeys is characteristic of this attitude, one that belongs essentially to Greek Dasein' (IM: 141).
38  Indeed, we see again in his infamous interview with *Der Spiegel* in 1966 that Heidegger remained firmly entrenched in his opposition to democracy to the end of his life:

> Meanwhile, in the past thirty years it should have become clearer that the global movement of modern technology is a force whose scope in determining history can scarcely be overestimated. A decisive question for me today is: how can a political system accommodate itself to the technological age, and which political system would this be? I have no answer to this question. I am not convinced that it is democracy.

See Martin Heidegger. 'Only a God Can Save Us'. In *The Heidegger Controversy: A Critical Reader*, 104.

39  Again, it has to be noted that Heidegger was deliberately trying to give his project at least the resonance of the rhetoric of the day. I can think of no justification for this attempt on Heidegger's part beyond a rather insalubrious private ambition to put himself into the uppermost echelons of German university politics.
40  Neither is that grounds for dismissing the entire corpus as a celebration of Hitlerism, as Faye has argued in his notorious diatribe.
41  Richard D. McKirahan. *Philosophy Before Socrates*. Indianapolis: Hackett Publishing Company, Inc., 1994. 10.82(53), 124.
42  Oswald Spengler. *Man and Technics*, 32.
43  Ibid., 33.
44  Ibid., *Man and Technics*, 46.
45  Although it is interesting to note the occurrence in this famous passage of a rhetorical question which is more or less identical to the one we find in Spengler's earlier work. We find Spengler discussing the technical onslaught of the 1800s as follows:

> Movement on these paths we call Progress. This was the great catchword of last century. Men saw history before them like a street on which, bravely and ever forward, marched 'mankind' – meaning by that term the white races, or more exactly the inhabitants of their great cities, or more exactly still the 'educated' amongst them. [B]ut whither? For how long? *And what then?* [I]t was a little ridiculous, this march on infinity, towards a goal which men did not seriously think about or clearly figure to themselves or, really, *dare* to envisage – *for a goal is an end.* (Oswald Spengler. *Man and Technics*, 10)

46  Heidegger makes a similar point in 1966 when he responds to his interviewers concerning the urgency of the crisis in the age of technology: 'Pessimism, no. Pessimism and optimism are attitudes which we are trying to consider, and they do not go far enough' ('Only a God Can Save Us', 105).
47  Oswald Spengler. *Man and Technics*, 47.
48  Ibid., 48.
49  It is indicative of a certain interpretative prejudice of Zimmerman for example that in making a similar comparison between these observations of Spengler's and some of Heidegger's utterances, that he chooses only remarks from Heidegger's essay concerning technology and not the comments to this effect to be found in *Being and Time*. This is consistent with Zimmerman's belief that *Being and Time*'s account of equipmentality was guilty of an instrumentalism which the later Heidegger was looking to disavow and is part of his overarching discontinuity thesis which I have discussed elsewhere. See Mahon O' Brien. *Heidegger and Authenticity: From Resoluteness to Releasement*, 78–81.

50  Oswald Spengler. *Man and Technics*, 48.
51  For a detailed discussion of Heidegger's well-known essay on technology see Mahon O'Brien. *Heidegger and Authenticity: From Resoluteness to Releasement*, Chapter 4.
52  Richard Wolin. *The Heidegger Controversy*, 120.
53  Zimmerman appears to hold similar views in *Heidegger's Confrontation with Modernity* and focuses more of his attention on Jünger than Spengler in terms of the key influences on Heidegger's political views and specifically his evolving concerns over the increasing role of technology in our lives. In responding to a highly condensed version of this chapter in a presentation where I looked to compare Spengler's *Man and Technics* with Heidegger's views in texts such as *Introduction to Metaphysics* and 'The Question Concerning Technology', Karsten Harries dismissed the influence of Spengler as negligible but also insisted that Jünger's influence was indispensable to an understanding of Heidegger's views on technology. My own view is that Heidegger is influenced by both and that he shares many of the views concurrent to a generation of conservative revolutionaries in Germany; but again here, we must avoid the recurring tendency to reduce Heidegger's philosophy to these sources or influences completely.
54  Richard Wolin. *The Heidegger Controversy*, 120.
55  Ibid., 121.
56  Ibid., 121–2.
57  In his somewhat self-serving account of his activities as Rector of Freiburg University, Heidegger confirms the importance of Jünger's views in 'Total Mobilization' and *Der Arbeiter* for his view of the world historical situation:

> A pointer may suggest how I saw the historical situation even then. In the year 1930 Ernst Jünger's article 'Total Mobilisation' ('*Die totale Mobilmachung*') had appeared: in this article the basic features of his book *The Worker* (*Der Arbeiter*), which appeared in 1932, announced themselves. Together with my assistant Brock, I discussed these writings in a small circle and tried to show how they express a fundamental understanding of Nietzsche's metaphysics, in so far as the history and present of the Western world are seen and foreseen in the horizon of this metaphysics. Thinking from these writings and, still more essentially, from their foundations, we thought what was coming, that is to say, we attempted to counter it, as we confronted it. At the time many others also read these writings; but together with many other interesting things one also read, one laid aside without comprehending their far-reaching import. (Martin Heidegger. 'The Rectorate 1933/34: Facts and Thoughts'. Translated by Karsten Harries, *The Review of Metaphysics*: 38, 3 (March 1985) 484)

58  Ernst Jünger. 'Total Mobilization'. In *The Heidegger Controversy*, 123.
59  In 'The Question Concerning Technology' Heidegger famously declares that 'There is no demonry of technology' (QCT: 28).
60  Ernst Jünger. 'Total Mobilization', 124.
61  Ernst Jünger. 'Total Mobilization', 126.
62  Ernst Jünger. *The Peace*. Translated by Stuart O. Hood. Hinsdale: Henry Regnery Company, 1948, 21–2.
63  Ibid., 24.
64  Ibid., 24–5.

65  Ibid., 27.
66  Ernst Jünger. 'Total Mobilization', 127.
67  Ibid., 128.
68  Ernst Jünger. *The Peace*, 29–30.
69  See Chapter 4, Mahon O'Brien. *Heidegger and Authenticity: From Resoluteness to Releasement*.
70  Martin Heidegger. 'Memorial Address', *Discourse on Thinking*. Translated by John M. Anderson and E. Hans Freund. Introduction by John M. Anderson, Harper & Row, New York, 1966, 47.
71  Ibid., 48.
72  Ibid., 48–9.
73  Ibid., 49.
74  Ibid., 50.
75  Ibid., 51.
76  Ibid., 52–3.
77  Again this is very close to his formulation in 'The Question Concerning Technology' which we mentioned above. See QCT, 28.
78  'Memorial Address', 53–4.
79  Robert Metcalf. 'Rethinking "Bodenständigkeit" in the Technological Age'. *Research in Phenomenology* Vol. 42. No. 1 (2012): 49–66.

## 4 The Authentic Dasein of a People

1  Indeed, the same resources within Heidegger's account should have been sufficient for him to see the absolute untenability of any form of ethnic chauvinism.
2  Martin Heidegger. *Martin Heidegger: Letters to his wife 1915–1970*. Selected, edited and annotated by Gertrud Heidegger. Translated by R. D. V. Glasgow, Cambridge: Polity Press, 2008, 33.
3  Karl Löwith. 'My Last Meeting with Heidegger in Rome, 1936'. In *The Heidegger Controversy*, 142.
4  The reason we examine Heidegger's discussion of solicitude (*Fürsorge*) is pretty straightforward; in section 26 of *Being and Time* Heidegger basically glosses the outlines for something like authentic intersubjectivity and we can clearly see something like the theoretical underpinnings for the moves that he is going to want to make in section 74 of *Being and Time* and subsequent texts. It will also show us clearly enough that Heidegger is going to paint himself into something of a corner, one which he cannot get out of and one which, in the end, bars the political aims he wishes to fortify with philosophical foundations.
5  Macquarrie and Robinson concede in their notes to this section that 'it would be more idiomatic to translate "für ihn einspringen" as "intervene for him", "stand in for him" or "serve as deputy for him"; but since "einspringen" is to be constrasted with "vorspringen", "vorausspringen" and perhaps even "entspringen" in the following paragraphs, we have chosen a translation which suggests the etymological connection.' See Translator's Note 1. Martin Heidegger. *Being and Time*. Translated by John Macquarrie and Edward Robinson. Oxford: Blackwell, 1962, 158.
6  In previous work I have looked to offer a charitable reading of this somewhat jarring line in Heidegger (see Mahon O'Brien. 'Leaping Ahead of Heidegger: Subjectivity

and Intersubjectivity in *Being and Time*'. *International Journal of Philosophical Studies*, Volume 22, Issue 4, (October 2014)). After all, Heidegger seems to look to qualify the line immediately afterwards so it's unlikely that he simply had some kind of lapse back into the type of Cartesian subjectivism which he so vigorously resists. But, at the same time, in the same way that it is tempting for critics of Heidegger to read such lines in a way that makes Heidegger appear rather foolish – we must also resist the temptation to make things too easy for ourselves.

7   And, as we shall see below, this is going to help clarify what Heidegger means in his rather unsettling comment about the murder of innocents in the death camps in a 1949 series of lectures.

8   That is not necessarily to adopt either a Levinasian or Sartrean view of things – though I think both of them can sense a potential problem in Heidegger's account. However, it seems to me at least, that if we were to push Sartre's account a little and claim that even before any other person catches us in the act of spying, that one already has a sense of being a spy in a way which reduces to and yet transcends the self and that this is something that is reflected in the notion of Dasein as always and ever *Mitsein*, then we have a way of forestalling what appears a lop-sided privileging of non-relational Dasein in the account of being-towards-death.

9   Again, it seems as though precisely what many of us can share is a mutual fear in the face of a death which we can imagine very much as our own; surely, that, in part, is what film-makers, artists, writers and dramatists are taking for granted as they try and bring us right into the mind of someone facing their death. Notwithstanding, we must nevertheless acknowledge that many people facing death describe and feel a very intense sense of isolation and loneliness. But that is to confirm precisely the inveterately social nature of Dasein once more since we are describing an anticipation of the complete loss of being-in-the-world and the concomitant sense of co-belonging and being-with. And this is something that we can imagine and empathize with when we are confronted with someone who is facing death.

10  "Death is Dasein's ownmost possibility. Being towards this possibility discloses to Dasein its ownmost potentiality-for-being, in which its very being is the issue. Here it can become manifest to Dasein that in this distinctive possibility of its own self, it has been wrenched away from the 'they'. This means that in anticipation any Dasein can have wrenched itself from the 'they' already. But when one understands that this is something which Dasein 'can' have done, this only reveals its factical lostness in the everydayness of the they-self." (BT: 307).

11  Martin Heidegger. 'The Self Assertion of the German University'. Translated by William S. Lewis. In *The Heidegger Controversy: A Critical Reader*, 38.

12  Not only that, Heidegger often privileges a particular conception of a specific ethnic group. The reasons for this conviction seem of a piece with the kind of romantic view of German culture and language which we find in Fichte's *Addresses to the German Nation*, though Heidegger's views certainly cannot be thought to reduce to Fichte's and indeed, in places, Fichte can appear more moderate. Indeed, as we shall see in the next chapter, Heidegger specifically appeals to the notion of German people not yet living within Germany's borders while openly ignoring people living within those borders that he begins to treat as non-German, namely, German Jews.

13  Martin Heidegger. 'German Men and Women'. In *The Heidegger Controversy*, 48.

14  Berel Lang points out that Heidegger continually defended himself against the charge of biological racism by pointing to the fact that he had close alliances with numerous Jews. See Berel Lang. *Heidegger's Silence*. New York: Cornell University

Press, 1996, 69. Of course this is a familiar strategy – akin to that used by many people accused of homophobia, for example.
15 Martin Heidegger. 'The Danger'. *Bremen and Freiburg Lectures: Insight Into That Which Is and Basic Principles of Thinking*, 53.
16 Ibid., 53–4.
17 Of course there were 'degrees' of success in this levelling, homogenizing system of deprivation and dehumanization. This attempt at demoralization through deprivation could not be presumed to have laid waste to the affective interpretative horizon of any and every person exposed to the extreme campaign of degradation enforced by the Nazis. As a result, there were attempts to offset any potential reaction or resistance on the way to the gas chambers.
18 There were those perhaps whose horizon remained before them until close to the end and for those poor souls the terror at the end must have been unbearable. The end of the 'process' for the executed souls whose bodies shuffled wearily into death chambers signalled the final death rattle of a slow, tortuous spiritual crucifixion.
19 We will look at Heidegger's various attempts to achieve as much in the next chapter.

# 5 Heidegger and Antisemitism

1 Emmanuel Faye quotes a letter from Heidegger from before the early 1930s in which, ironically enough, he recommends the awarding of a grant to Eduard Baumgarten; we will have more to say concerning Heidegger's relationship with Baumgarten later:

> What I could only hint at in my report, I can say more directly here. Nothing less is at stake than the ineluctable realization that we find ourselves facing the following alternative. Either we restore genuine forces and educators emanating from the native soil to our German spiritual life, or we abandon it definitively to the growing Jewification, in the broad and the narrow sense of the term. (Emmanuel Faye. *Heidegger: The Introduction of Nazism into Philosophy*. Translated by Michael B. Smith, New Haven and London: Yale University Press, 2009, 34)

In his notes, Faye states that the quote is from a letter to Viktor Schwoerer.
2 The most worrisome fragments from Heidegger's Black Notebooks have been in circulation since before their official publication in German earlier this year. These same passages continue to draw the most attention since Heidegger makes a number of remarks within them which clearly show him to have held antisemitic prejudices. Take for example the following remark:

> But the temporary increase in the power of Jewry has its ground in the fact that the metaphysics of the West, especially in its modern development, served as the hub for the spread of an otherwise empty rationality and calculative skill, which in this way lodged itself in the 'spirit' without ever being able to grasp the concealed domains of decision on its own. (GA: 96; 46–7. I am grateful to Richard Polt for sharing his excellent translations of a number of passages from GA 94, 95 and 96.)

For Heidegger then, there was a Jewish problem, one of global proportions, and it was directly related to the levelling influence of *Gestell*.
3   Daniel Goldhagen's hugely problematic and controversial study, *Hitler's Willing Executioners*, is relevant on this issue. Part I of his comprehensive study involves a detailed attempt to establish the inveterate eliminationist, antisemitic mindset of ordinary Germans from the Middle-Ages right up until the period before the Nazi party assumed power. See Daniel Jonah Goldhagen, Part I: 'Understanding German Antisemitism: The Eliminationist Mind-Set'. In *Hitler's Willing Executioners: Ordinary Germans and the Holocaust*. London: Little, Brown and Company, 1996.
4   Christopher Browning. *Ordinary Men*, xvii–xviii.
5   In a panel discussion of Jeffrey Van Davis' documentary on Heidegger (*Only a God Can Save Us*) which was to precede a day-long conference on the Black Notebooks, Karsten Harries argued that Heidegger's use of the term *Verjudung* needed to be put in context – insisting that the word was very much in everyday circulation. While that is undoubtedly true, it does not mean that we should not be terribly disappointed that Heidegger subscribed to the conventional, antisemitic prejudices of his day and was resolved to find a way to justify those prejudices philosophically. See https://www.youtube.com/watch?v=hMizd8GplEA
6   This is a particularly offensive type of discrimination and readily displays the self-satisfying, delusional nature of some of these beliefs insofar as the same jobs were often there all along for the same 'nearest and dearest' who, as it turned out, thought the same jobs or occupations beneath them, opting instead for the dole queue. That is not to say that there is anything wrong with being unemployed; it can happen to any of us. But the idea that the only reason that any of our family members or friends end up on the unemployment line is as a result of the influx of foreign workers is a type of myopic self-delusion which goes hand in hand with rather malevolently xenophobic views!
7   Julius Streicher was the founder and publisher of *Der Stürmer* – an aggressively antisemitic newspaper which was an important mouthpiece for Nazi antisemitic propaganda. Streicher was tried for and convicted of crimes against humanity as part of the Nuremburg trials and was executed in 1946.
8   http://www.nybooks.com/articles/archives/2014/oct/09/heidegger-in-black/
9   Johannes Fritsche has written a book-length study on the notion of historical destiny (which is at the heart of section 74 in particular) in *Being and Time* and while the author rightly identified this as something that needed to be examined in terms of Heidegger's commitment to National Socialism, the book itself is tendentious and less than convincing for the most part. Much of Fritsche's work resembles Faye's strategy of guilt by association and argument by assertion instead of compelling exegesis. See Johannes Fritsche. *Historical Destiny and National Socialism in Heidegger's 'Being and Time'*. Berkeley and Los Angeles/London: University of California Press, 1999.
10  Heidegger goes further here than he had in texts such as *The Fundamental Concepts of Metaphysics* and insists that the animal has *no* world where he had earlier suggested that the animal is 'poor' in world.
11  In *Being and Truth*, while discussing the Heraclitean notion of *polemos* we find the following chilling passages from Heidegger:

> An enemy is each and every person who poses an essential threat to the Dasein of the people and its individual members. The enemy does not have

to be external, and the external enemy is not even always the more dangerous one. And it can seem as if there were no enemy. Then it is a fundamental requirement to find the enemy, to expose the enemy to the light, or even first to make the enemy, so that this standing against the enemy may happen and so that Dasein may not lose its edge.

The enemy can have attached itself to the innermost roots of the Dasein of a people and can set itself against this people's own essence and act against it. The struggle is all the fiercer and harder and tougher, for the least of it consists in coming to blows with one another; it is often far more difficult and wearisome to catch sight of the enemy as such, to bring the enemy into the open, to harbor no illusions about the enemy, to keep oneself ready for attack, to cultivate and intensify a constant readiness and to prepare the attack looking far ahead with the goal of total annihilation. (Martin Heidegger. *Being and Truth*. Translated by Gregory Fried and Richard Polt. Bloomington and Indianapolis: Indiana University Press, 2010, 73)

12  Felix O'Murchadha makes a spirited, if ultimately unsuccessful, attempt to defend this aspect of Heidegger's thought in his recent publication *The Time of Revolution: Kairos and Chronos in Heidegger*:

A people are those who understand themselves as "we" in terms of a common historical moment. Being a people is a decision, a decision with respect to a historical situation in which, as a people, 'we' find ourselves. As such, the uniqueness and singularity of a people has nothing to do with race. There is no actuality to point to – neither race, nor citizenship, nor cultural traditions, nor activities etc. … – but rather a decision concerning a 'mission and a vocation' (*Auftrag und Sendung*) in which we find ourselves.

As we can see from the passages just quoted from *Nature, History, State* – this defence of Heidegger begins to ring a little hollow. The fact that Heidegger appears to reject Nazi biologism does not mean that he is not antisemitic or that he is not an ethnic chauvinist. Heidegger's putative 'racism' is, as O'Murchadha points out, not biologistic – though it bears repeating that Heidegger acknowledges the importance of 'stock' and 'race' in terms of becoming an authentic historical people. However O'Murchadha and others who thus argue that a non-biological racism is impossible since the very notion of 'race' is biological to begin with are dissembling to an extent. If we should condemn any form of prejudice based on religion, nationhood, or ethnicity, for example, then the fact that someone doesn't discriminate exclusively on the basis of innate biological differences but on the basis of these kinds of differences doesn't mean that they are somehow immune from criticism. O'Murchadha, however, uses this rhetorical sleight of hand to exonerate Heidegger here:

It is unfortunate that in many cases those who criticize Heidegger's Nazi engagement do not exercise the principle of charity in their interpretations and seem too easily to move from disinterested philosophers to prosecutors. A case in point is with respect to the concept of 'people'. It seems clear that Heidegger cannot be accused of biologism with respect to race or people, and as such appears to part company with the Nazis on a fundamental issue. In response to this, Tom Rockmore speaks of Heidegger's 'metaphysical theory of racism'. But, as Julian Young points out, racism is irreducibly a biologistic concept and as such to speak of metaphysical racism is, strictly, to speak nonsense.

It seems, however, that in lambasting critics who fail to adopt a principle of charity in reading Heidegger that O'Murchadha goes too far in the other direction:

> That Heidegger displays a certain chauvinism with respect to the German nation and language is clear and that he, sometimes uncritically, takes up the Romantic myth of a special bond between the Germans and the Greeks is equally so. It is important, however, to see that this is a 'spiritual' bond; what Heidegger sees in the German language and history is the possibility to take up a historical mission.

Again, this defence doesn't really seem to succeed when we read what Heidegger has to say in the passages from *Nature, History, State* concerning Jews and Slavic peoples. Moreover, he makes it clear that Germans not currently living within the borders of Germany, as opposed to people (who would have viewed themselves as German) living within Germany but who happen to be 'Jewish', for instance, could clearly be a part of the authentic German nation in ways that Jews could not and surely one cannot explain that fact away or make apology for it as O'Murchadha does. When Heidegger is still willing to claim in his 1966 interview with *Der Spiegel* that the French cannot truly think or philosophize unless they do it in German (which is what Heidegger claims to have been told by a cluster of obsequious French sycophants who championed his cause after the war), that their own language is debased and not, if you like, as pure, then what kind of claim is that? Surely it represents a form of bigotry and chauvinism which needs to be condemned and which is clearly related to his attempt to intertwine his philosophy with National Socialism in the 1930s. Hence, one really cannot accept O'Murchadha's recommendation that we simply ignore Heidegger's Germanocentric bigotry and ethnic chauvinism since it *was* clearly part of his political outlook and he tried to use the very notions that O'Murchadha artfully unpacks concerning authentic historical community to try and offer a philosophical foundation for these political views. O'Murchadha may well argue, and on this we might agree, that these notions, if they are based on key notions from *Being and Time*, for example, cannot be made *exclusionary* in such ways. That is *not* to say that Heidegger didn't try to use these notions in these ways or that all of these discussions are entirely neutral. O'Murchadha writes

> This mission is one which concerns the question of being not because that question is only one of concern for the German people, but because the Germans have the vocation – as the Greeks once had – to pose the question of being and to do so again in a new beginning. I submit that the latter claim should move us more genuinely to an ironical smile than to outrage; there is nothing in the claim which can in any way be said to be either racist or imperialist.

The fact of the matter is that Heidegger *did* believe that the German people in particular had a *special* destiny and that they represented the possibility of an authentic historical community which would necessarily exclude other non-German ethnicities and this was very obviously related to Heidegger's support for National Socialism. Granted, Heidegger rejected biologism on its own – but that does not mean that he didn't discriminate and I would contend that what is important is that he discriminated against whole races of people on the basis of ethnic prejudices which he suggested were not based solely in blood but, in fact, a bond that ran even deeper, deep enough that it could bind people who lived outside Germany's borders but would exclude many who lived within its borders. It is not that Heidegger didn't value the importance of 'blood' and 'stock'; rather these notions were not enough. He wanted an ethnicity that ran even deeper which would necessarily exclude, for example, the Jews. And it was in the service of precisely *this* repugnant aspiration that Heidegger put his concept of an authentic historical community bound by a shared mission and destiny and that, I feel compelled to write, is no laughing matter. To be fair, O'Murchadha's book appeared before some of the more notorious publications from the last couple of years including the recently published notebooks from the 1930s. Hence, we must allow that the author might be inclined to amend his views if he were to write his book again. Nevertheless, even having granted that much, there was enough incriminating evidence before the appearance of the Black Notebooks, for example, to disincline one to offer such extreme apologetics.

13 In a slightly odd publication (*Encounters and Dialogues with Martin Heidegger, 1929-1976*), Heinrich Petzet recalls his many encounters and conversations with Heidegger and is keen to rehabilitate the image of his hero. In terms of Heidegger's antisemitism, Petzet simply explains away Heidegger's apparent antisemitism insisting that Heidegger was not in any way a racist but rather wanted to resist the cosmopolitanism of certain Jewish intellectual circles but that this did not imply any serious underlying antipathy toward the Jews on Heidegger's part. Lee Braver is closer to O'Murchadha in the way he looks to defend Heidegger against the charge of antisemitism:

> In the later work history reaches all the way down, so that not just our vocations but our nature changes with history and culture. Now if this is true, then we do not all possess the same timeless nature but are determined from the ground up by the society we grew up in. *Being and Time*'s Kierkegaardian individualism gives way to a Hegelian communitarianism (bits of which were there too), where we derive our very selves from our community. This means that people who are socialized into the same culture are fundamentally, even ontologically closer than those from elsewhere. This harmonizes strongly with the Nazi's quasi-mystical emphasis on the special bond Germans share as offspring of the Fatherland. What was jingoistic for them is metaphysical for Heidegger.
>
> One interesting consequence of this interpretation is that Heidegger's views not only don't lead to anti-Semitism, they actually argue against it. A German Aryan is fundamentally similar and related to a German Jew in a way that she can never be to, say, a blue-eyed, blond-haired Californian surfer. Socialization replaces biology on this reading; soil trumps blood. (Lee Braver, *Heidegger: Thinking of Being*. Cambridge: Polity Press, 2014, 149)

14 Indeed Heidegger was to allude to Germans who had been forced to leave their native homeland because of the war in the well-known 'Memorial Address' which we discussed in a previous chapter. This important text, where Heidegger begins to develop the notion of *Gelassenheit*, is not usually seen as controversial and yet he is alluding to these same Germans as part of his invective against rootlessness and the importance of native soil for an historical people.

15  This particular essay adds some considerable weight to Tom Sheehan's claim that Heidegger's lifelong project is a phenomenological one and while Sheehan sometimes argues that Heidegger is not so much concerned with Being (with a capital 'B') as with *das Ereignis*, once one realizes that he is emphasizing Heidegger's enduring obsession with the meaning of being, how beings appear to us meaningfully, then one realizes that the claim is not so controversial as it might appear. And, in that sense, I am inclined to agree that Heidegger's project is a phenomenological one insofar as his continuing effort is to try and shed some light on the way being comes to be meaningful for Dasein at any time in history. In that sense, Heidegger thinks his phenomenology will get us closest to 'the things themselves', that is, the things that appear to us as being in this or that way, as meaningful.

16  Heidegger's claim that this is a painting of a peasant woman's work boots has generated a certain amount of controversy; much has been made in some quarters of the fact that these were not the boots of a peasant labourer but belonged in fact to van Gogh. Van Gogh apparently purchased these secondhand boots at a flea market in Paris in 1886 but found them to be such a poor fit that he opted to use them as a painting prop instead. The commotion over this aspect of Heidegger's essay really seems a little petty insofar as Heidegger is not writing in some capacity as an art critic; regardless of whether the shoes belong to van Gogh, a peasant labourer or someone else, he really is only interested in how such a painting of these quotidian objects can allow a world to emerge.

17  Insofar as they were quotidian or commonplace in that world.

18  Seamus Heaney. *New Selected Poems: 1966 – 1987*. London: Faber & Faber, 1988.

19  Moyola is the name of a river in the North of Ireland.

20  This is how Heaney describes the voice of Joyce as he imagines meeting the ghost of the Irish writer upon reaching dry land following a three-day pilgrimage on Station Island on Lough Derg. It is from the twelfth and final canto in the title sequence of the collection *Station Island*.

21  Patrick Kavanagh. 'Epic'. *Collected Poems*. London: Penguin, 2004, 184.

22  Granted, many of these ideas have proved quite controversial within the field of aesthetics; however, that is not really something with which we need to concern ourselves here. We are interested rather in the political backdrop to these claims. Though it does seem worth mentioning that Heidegger's claims concerning a temple can't be thought to automatically transpose on to every other art form. If one considers a monument, for example, it is very much designed with a view to articulating something which is not simply derivative or debased to future generations that belong to an entirely different world. Museums themselves are sites often used by artists to exhibit their works and represent precisely the context at times that the artist has in mind. Again, the strength or weaknesses of Heidegger's arguments in this regard are not central to our discussion, but it is worth noting at least that Heidegger takes liberties in this essay.

23  'And maybe in this 'struggle' – which struggles over goallessness itself and which hence can be only the caricature of 'struggle' – the greater groundlessness will 'triumph', which is bound to nothing and makes everything serviceable to itself (Jewry). But the authentic triumph, the triumph of history over the historyless, is won only where the groundless excludes itself because it does not venture be-ing, but instead always merely calculates with beings, and posits its *calculations* as what is real' (Martin Heidegger. GA, 95: 97, *Überlegungen* VIII, 4). Translated by Richard Polt).

On the same page he writes: 'One of the most secret forms of the *gigantic*, and perhaps the oldest, is the tenacious skilfulness in calculating, hustling, and intermingling through which the worldlessness of Jewry is gounded.'

24  See 'Only a God can Save Us'. In *The Heidegger Controversy: A Critical Reader*, 112, 113. Heidegger suggests that the only possibility of salvation involves a dialogue between the German people and Hölderlin.

25  Jacques Taminiaux has written an interesting paper on the rectoral address and, the central argument notwithstanding (which is problematic in certain respects – not least as a result of the readings of Plato and Aristotle that it involves) it makes a salient point: if one takes on board Arendt's account of what constitutes ideology, then there is no Nazi ideology in Heidegger's speech. Rather one finds Heidegger's own attempt to map his accounts of authenticity in *Being and Time* onto a political vision in a way which supposedly harks back to Plato's *Republic*:

> There is no trace in the rectoral address of an endorsement by the speaker of what lay at the very foundation of the totalitarian regime then taking shape in Germany: its *ideology*. (Jacques Taminiaux. 'The Platonic Roots of Heidegger's Political Thought'. *European Journal of Political Theory* 6, 11, (2007): 1.)

He goes on to write:

> If we concede that the analysis outlined here provides a fair picture of Nazi ideology, then we must also concede that Heidegger's Rectoral Address does not fit with it at all. On closer scrutiny, with the exception of a celebration of the *Führerprinzip* and a vague allusion to the slogan *Blut und Boden*, in its language and its principal themes the speech can be seen as a kind of repetition of the first major text in the tradition of political philosophy, namely, Plato's *Republic*. (Ibid., 13)

> There is an obvious echo of Plato's *Republic* in Heidegger's picture of a corporatist state wherein each of the estates (*Stände*, a favourite word of Hegel's political philosophy, which was itself inspired by Plato) provides a distinct service to a particular people, the German *Volk*, a service of work, a service of defence and, at the top, a service of knowledge, above all a service of metaphysics, in order to prevent the dispersion of sciences into specialized disciplines. There is no allusion whatsoever to the transformation of classes into masses. Rather, the movement to which Heidegger alludes in the Rectoral Address is a conscious movement towards Being, not a mass mobilization. Likewise the world alluded to is not a universal *Lebensraum* for the race of the Lords but the ontological site of *Dasein*.
> This long introduction is sufficient to suggest that Heidegger's political thought at the time of his most notorious compromise with Nazism was not the thought of an ordinary Nazi. (Ibid., 14)

26  Martin Heidegger. 'The Self Assertion of the German University'. Translated by Karsten Harries. In *The Review of Metaphysics* 38, 3 (March, 1985): 470.
27  Ibid., 470.
28  There is a further element of politicizing at work here which is often left unaddressed by commentators. Heidegger characterizes Freiburg University as the 'highest school of the German Volk'. What can Heidegger mean by this? Does he mean that it is, in his estimation, the best university in Germany? That doesn't

seem to quite capture what he's saying. He seems to be saying that the university is something for the German *Volk* and, as such, we cannot help wondering if there is a kind of exclusionist aspiration at work in this notion alone? Why should the university, the ultimate site for the open exchange of ideas from every corner of the Earth and from every culture and era, past and present, why should such a place be a site for the 'German' people? Why not the highest academy in Germany for people from all over the world? Heidegger notes at the same time that some notion of autonomy or freedom is central to the general conception of the university and he notes that he wants to retain some sense of self-governance. This in turn allows Heidegger to begin to introduce his own version of the willing required.

29  See discussion of Heidegger's 'Memorial Address' in Chapter 3.
30  Ibid., 470.
31  Taminiaux cites Janicaud's observation on this issue:

> As Dominic Janicaud observed, this self-affirmation of the German university is "a call to *self*-affirmation for the self and the people (for oneself in the people)". This appeal explains why, on the one hand, a representative of official Nazi ideology such as the Minister for Education in Baden, Otto Wacker, could criticize the discourse as a document of "private national-socialism" and why, on the other hand, Karl Jaspers, who never compromised with the regime, on receiving a copy of the speech, intended to send a letter of congratulation to the author'. (Jacques Taminiaux. 'The Platonic Roots of Heidegger's Political Thought', 14)

Heidegger makes a similar point in his reflection on his rectorate:

> To be sure, the address and with it my attitude were grasped even less by the party and the relevant agencies, yet it was 'understood' in as much as one sensed immediately the opposition. Minister Wacker gave me his "opinion" of the address he had heard on the very same day ... (1) That this was a kind of 'private National Socialism', which circumvented the perspectives of the party program. (2) Most importantly, that the whole had not been based on the concept of race. (3) That he could not accept the rejection of the idea of 'political science', even if he would be willing to admit that as yet this idea had not been given sufficient foundation. ('The Rectorate 1933/34: Facts and Thoughts', 490)

32  In the same text Heidegger writes:

> I saw in the movement that had gained power the possibility of an inner recollection and renewal of the people and a path that would allow it to discover its historical vocation in the Western world. I believed that, renewing itself, the university might also be called to contribute to this inner self-collection of the people, providing it with a measure. (483)

Following this Heidegger wants to say that he was looking to preserve the university from some of the more corrosive elements of National Socialism and yet he has openly admitted at the outset that he believed that National Socialism was the right way to go for Germany and that the university would need to be brought into line in accordance with National Socialist principles – or at least the National Socialism which he himself embraced which is not at all an unproblematic stance. He then goes on to suggest that in taking up the rectorate he was making 'the attempt to save, purify, and to strengthen what was positive', ibid., 486. He goes on to explain that at the meeting where he tendered his resignation 'it became clear that a rift separated the National Socialist conception of university and science from my own, which could not be bridged', ibid., 497. And yet, Heidegger has argued earlier that he took the position in the first place because he knew that there was such a rift and that he was looking to protect the university for that very reason. Heidegger refuses to acknowledge any culpability at all during the letter and occasionally suggests that he simply lacked the foresight that many of those who criticize him apparently had in terms of the dangers of National Socialism within the university structure. Heidegger's defence is rather petty and unworthy of someone blessed with a unique philosophical mind:

> Those who even then were so endowed with the gift of prophecy that they foresaw all that came, as it came – I was not so wise – why did they wait almost ten years before opposing the threatening disaster? Why did those who in 1933 thought they possessed such wisdom, why did they not they, especially, then arouse themselves to turn everything, from the very bottom, towards the good? (Ibid., 486)

This is a rather disingenuous stance on Heidegger's part since it first conveniently ignores the very animated remonstrations of some of his colleagues and friends (Jaspers for example) which Heidegger stridently dismissed and, second, Heidegger himself was guilty of finding ways to silence and oppress those who wished to resist or challenge the regime's influence in the university when he himself was Nazi rector of the university.
33  Martin Heidegger. 'The Self Assertion of the German University', 471.
34  Ibid., 471.
35  Taminiaux argues convincingly that in this context, 'the Greeks', for Heidegger, was a reference exclusively to Plato and Aristotle.
36  'The Self-Assertion of the German University', 473.
37  Ibid, 473.
38  Ibid., 474–5.
39  Victor Farias. *Heidegger and Nazism*, 210.
40  Ibid., 210.
41  Indeed, it is a testament to his strength of character and generosity of spirit that he actively campaigned to have Heidegger denazified and reinstated to the University; Baumgarten even went so far as to reproach Jaspers for the latter's letter to the denazification committee which ultimately cost Heidegger his teaching privileges since Jaspers took the liberty of using the letter concerning Baumgarten as evidence against Heidegger.
42  Berel Lang. *Heidegger's Silence*. Appendix, 104.
43  Ibid., 104–5.
44  Ibid., 105.
45  Ibid., 107.
46  Ibid., 109.
47  For all of Ott's protestations to the effect that he is merely an historian and chronicler, his biography is a series of character assassinations designed to convince the audience that not only was Heidegger a Nazi but that he was a fairly objectionable human being as well. The problem is that his journalistic tendencies tend to interfere with his historical interpretations and it leads to a certain biased selectivity in terms of what counts as historically significant and what doesn't. Ott

openly admits for example that he deliberately chooses to ignore parts of Heidegger's philosophy which don't easily reconcile with the case he looks to build against him claiming that such philosophical analysis is beyond his philosophical expertise. And, if that were in fact true of his text in general, then it would be a commendable act of restraint. The problem of course is that Ott frequently fails to exercise the same restraint any time he thinks that an analysis of Heidegger's philosophy will yield the kinds of incriminating evidence he so desperately seeks. And, to compound the problem, the disingenuity of Ott's confession to the effect that he has not the requisite expertise to analyse Heidegger's philosophy becomes painfully apparent when he looks to offer critical overviews of Heidegger's philosophy. In any case, leaving to one side the relative merits and demerits of this disappointingly jaundiced study, there is plenty of testimony and evidence which we can yet assess without the journalistic excesses the author encumbers his story with.

48  Hugo Ott. *Martin Heidegger: A Political Life*. Translated by Allan Blunden. Basic Books, 1993, 187.
49  Interestingly, Ott also gives the lie to another rumour that had been circulating for some time to the effect that Heidegger had issued an injunction against his former teacher being allowed access to the university library while he was rector: 'Let us be quite clear about one thing: as a rector and head of department Heidegger did not issue a ban of any kind on the use of the university library or the departmental library. This oft-repeated charge is without foundation', ibid., 174.

# Conclusion

1  Richard Wolin attributes the following dictum to Heidegger in a number of places: 'When they can't attack the philosophy, they attack the philosopher.'
2  Cf. Martin Heidegger. 'Letter on Humanism'. In *Basic Writings*. Edited by David Farrell Krell. London and New York: Routledge, 1993, 223–4.
3  Felix O'Murchadha. *The Time of Revolution*, 175.
4  Marcuse comments on this in his well-known interview with Olafson in 1977:

> He [Heidegger] refused (and I think that somehow I find this rather sympathetic), he refused any attempt to deny it or to declare it an aberration, or I don't know what, because he did not want to be in the same category, as he said, with all of his colleagues who suddenly didn't remember anymore that they taught under the Nazis, that they ever supported the Nazis, and declared that actually they had always been non-Nazi.

See 'Heidegger's Politics: An Interview with Herbert Marcuse'. Frederick Olafson. In *The Essential Marcuse: Selected Writings of Philosopher and Social Critic Herbert Marcuse*. Edited by Andrew Feenberg and William Leiss. Boston: Beacon Press, 2007, 122.

5  Aristotle famously makes this point in the third chapter of Book 1 of his *Ethics*:

> For even if the good of the community coincides with that of the individual, it is clearly a greater and more perfect thing to achieve and preserve that of a community; for while it is desirable to secure what is good in the case of an individual, to do so in the case of a people or a state is something finer and more sublime.

> Such, then, is the aim of our investigation; and it is a kind of political science.
> 
> Our account of this science will be adequate if it achieves such clarity as the subject-matter allows; for the same degree of precision is not to be expected in all discussions, any more than in all the products of handicraft. Instances of morally fine and just conduct – which is what politics investigates – involve so much difference and variety that they are widely believed to be such only by convention and not by nature ... Therefore in discussing subjects, and arguing from evidence, conditioned in this way, we must be satisfied with a broad outline of the truth; that is, in arguing about what is for the most part so from premises which are for the most part true we must be content to draw conclusions that are similarly qualified. The same procedure, then, should be observed in receiving our several types of statement; for it is a mark of the trained mind never to expect more precision in the treatment of any subject than the nature of that subject permits; for demanding logical demonstrations from a teacher of rhetoric is clearly about as reasonable as accepting mere plausibility from a mathematician. (Aristotle. *Ethics*. Translated by J. A .K. Thomson. London: Penguin Books, London, 1976, 64–5)

6 "By the late 1930s, the Notebooks demonstrate the inevitable consequences of such extraordinary hubris and risk-taking on the grand scale: a Heidegger lost to bitter despair. Of his tenure as head of his university and the speech he gave to inaugurate it, he says, 'the great error of this speech consists in this, that it still assumed that there would be a hidden generation of those ready to question in the context of the German university, that it still hoped to bring them to dedicating themselves to the work of inner transformation.' Heidegger had not failed; Germans, the university, the revolution itself had failed to shoulder the task set for them by history. Virtually nothing and no one escapes his withering scorn and critique. The university is incapable of genuine, creative questioning; the German people fails to find the strength for the essential tasks of thinking; National Socialism caves in to its petty-bourgeois careerists; America represents the full-fledged outbreak of gigantism upon the world stage; racial doctrine emerges as just another manifestation of a modern thinking that reduces what it means to be human to some biological feature that can be adapted to metaphysics' programs of machination. The only consistent exception to Heidegger's sweeping condemnations is his beloved German poet, Friedrich Hölderlin, whom he grants the honor of prefiguring the overturning needed by Western history in the confrontation between the Greek inception and what should have been its German rejoinder."

See Gregory Fried. 'The King Is Dead: Heidegger's "Black Notebooks"', https://lareviewofbooks.org/review/king-dead-heideggers-black-notebooks

7 Martin Heidegger. 'Letter to the Rector of Freiburg University'. In *The Heidegger Controversy*, 6–62.
8 Ibid., 63.
9 Heidegger makes a number of references to world or international 'Jewry' in the notebooks. See GA: 96, 133, 243, 261–2 for some examples.
10 In his biography of Heidegger, Rüdiger Safranski alludes to Elfride's antisemitism in the context of Heidegger's fledgling relationship with Hannah Arendt:

> Heidegger was her [Arendt's] senior by seventeen years, the father of two boys, married to an ambitious woman who guarded most carefully the

family's reputation and who was suspiciously watching her husband as he enjoyed the adulation of his female students. Elfride was especially reserved toward Hannah Arendt, not only because Heidegger was obviously treating her preferentially but also because she was Jewish. Elfride's anti-Semitism was notorious even in the 1920s. Günther Stern (Anders), who was subsequently married to Hannah Arendt for a number of years, recalls how, on the occasion of a party at Todtnauberg, Elfride Heidegger asked him if he did not want to join the Nationalist Socialist group in Marburg, and how horrified she was when he informed her that he was a Jew. (*Martin Heidegger: Between Good and Evil*. Translated by Ewald Osers. Cambridge, MA: Harvard University Press, 2002, 139–40.

11  Consider for example entries such as the following: 'one of the most secret forms of the *gigantic*, and perhaps the oldest, is the tenacious skilfulness in calculating, hustling, and intermingling through which the worldlessness of Jewry is grounded', GA: 95; 97 (*Überlegungen* VIII, 5). Translated by Ricahrd Polt.

# Bibliography of Works Cited

Adorno, Theodor. *The Jargon of Authenticity*. Translated by Knut Tarnowski and Frederic Will. London and New York: Routledge Classics, 2003.
Arendt, Hannah. *Eichmann in Jerusalem: A Report on the Banality of Evil*. London: Penguin Books, 1963.
Aristotle. *Ethics*. Translated by J. A. K. Thomson. London: Penguin Books, 1976.
Babich, Babette. 'The Essence of Questioning After Technology: Techne as Constraint and the Saving Power'. *British Journal of Phenomenology*, 30/1 (January 1999): 106–24.
Bambach, Charles. *Heidegger's Roots: Nietzsche, National Socialism, and the Greeks*. Ithaca, NY: Cornell University Press, 2003.
Bourdieu, Pierre. *The Political Ontology of Martin Heidegger*. Cambridge: Polity Press, 1991.
Braver, Lee. *Heidegger: Thinking of Being*. Cambridge: Polity Press, 2014.
Browning, Christopher. *Ordinary Men: Reserve Police Battalion 101 and the Final Solution in Poland*. London: Penguin Books, 2001.
Caputo, John D. 'Heidegger's Revolution: An Introduction to an Introduction to Metaphysics.' In *Heidegger Toward the Turn*. Edited by James Risser. Albany, NY: State University of New York Press, 1999.
Cooke, Alistair. 'Address to the Joint Houses of the United States Congress'. 1974. Available from http://www.pbs.org/wgbh/masterpiece/series/cooke address.html
Dahlstrom, Daniel O. *The Heidegger Dictionary*. London and New York: Bloomsbury, 2013.
Derrida, Jacques. *Of Spirit: Heidegger and the Question*. Translated by Geoffrey Bennington and Rachel Bowlby. Chicago: The University of Chicago Press, 1987.
Farias, Victor. *Heidegger and Nazism*. Edited, with a Foreword by Joseph Margolis and Tom Rockmore. French materials translated by Paul Burrell, with the advice of Dominic Di Bernardi. German materials translated by Gabriel R. Ricci. Philadelphia: Temple University Press, 1989.
Faye, Emmanuel. 'Nazi Foundations in Heidegger's Work'. *South Central Review*, 23 (1), Fascism, Nazism: Cultural Legacies of Reaction (Spring 2006): 55–66.
Faye, Emmanuel. *Heidegger: The Introduction of Nazism into Philosophy in Light of the Unpublished Seminars of 1933-1935*. Translated by Michael B. Smith. New Haven, CT: Yale University Press, 2009.
Feenberg, Andrew and Leiss, William (eds). *The Essential Marcuse: Selected Writings of Philosopher and Social Critic Herbert Marcuse*. Boston: Beacon Press, 2007.
Fried, Gregory. *Heidegger's Polemos: From Being to Politics*. New Haven, CT and London: Yale University Press, 2000.
Fried, Gregory. 'The King Is Dead: Heidegger's "Black Notebooks"'. https://lareviewofbooks.org/review/king-dead-heideggers-black-notebooks. 2014.
Fritsche, Johannes. *Historical Destiny and National Socialism in Heidegger's Being and Time*. Berkeley, Los Angeles and London: University of California Press, 1999.
Gilbert, G. M. *Nuremburg Diary*. Cambridge, MA: Da Capo, 1995.

Goldhagen, Daniel Jonah. *Hitler's Willing Executioners: Ordinary Germans and the Holocaust*. London: Little, Brown and Company, 1996.
Goldhagen, Daniel Jonah. *Hitler's Willing Executioners: Ordinary Germans and the Holocaust*. London: Abacus, 1997.
Habermas, Jürgen. *The Philosophical Discourse of Modernity*. Translated by Frederick Lawrence. Cambridge, MA: MIT Press, 1987.
Heaney, Seamus. *New Selected Poems: 1966–1987*. London: Faber & Faber, 1988.

## Works by Martin Heidegger

*Beiträge zur eine Philosophie (Vom Ereignis)*. Frankfurt-am-Main: Klosterman, 1989. *Contibutions to Philosophy (from Enowning)*. Translated by Parvis Emad and Kenneth Maly. Bloomington and Indianapolis: Indiana University Press, 1999.
*Die Grundbegriffe der Metaphysik: Welt-Endlichkeit-Einsamkeit. Gesamtausgabe 29/30*. Frankfurt: Klostermann, 1983. *The Fundamental Concepts of Metaphysics: World, Finitude, Solitude*. Translated by William McNeill and Nicholas Walker. Bloomington and Indianapolis: Indiana University Press, 1995.
*Einführung in die Metaphysik*. Niemeyer, Tübingen, 1953, 3rd edn 1966. *Introduction to Metaphysics*. Translated by Gregory Fried and Richard Polt. New Haven, CT: Yale University Press, 2000.
*Gelassenheit*. Pfullingen: Gunther Neske Verlag, 1959. *Discourse on Thinking*. Translated by John M. Anderson and E. Hans Freund. Introduction by John M. Anderson. New York: Harper & Row, 1966.
*Gesamtausgabe 79: Bremer und Freiburger Vorträge*, edited by Petra Jaeger. Frankfurt-am-Main: Klostermann, 1994. *Bremen and Freiburg Lectures: Insight Into That Which Is and Basic Principles of Thinking*. Translated by Andrew J. Mitchell. Bloomington: Indiana University Press, 2012.
*Gesamtausgabe 94: IV. Abteilung: Hinweise und Aufzeichnungen, Überlegungen, II–VI* (*Schwarze Hefte 1931–1938*. Herausgegeben von Peter Trawny. Frankfurt-am-Main: Klostermann, 2014.
*Gesamtausgabe 95: IV. Abteilung: Hinweise und Aufzeichnungen, Überlegungen, VII–XI* (*Schwarze Hefte 1938–1939*). Herausgegeben von Peter Trawny. Frankfurt-am-Main: Klostermann, 2014.
*Gesamtausgabe 96: IV. Abteilung: Hinweise und Aufzeichnungen, Überlegungen, XII–XV* (*Schwarze Hefte 1939–1941*). Herausgegeben von Peter Trawny. Frankfurt-am-Main: Klostermann, 2014.
*Holzwege*. Frankfurt-am-Main: Klosterman, 1950. *Off the Beaten Track*. Translated by Julian Young and Kenneth Haynes. Cambridge: Cambridge University Press, 2002.
*Introduction to Metaphysics*. Translated by Gregory Fried and Richard Polt. New Haven, CT: Yale University Press, 2000.
*Off the Beaten Track*. Translated by Julian Young and Kenneth Haynes. Cambridge: Cambridge University Press, 2002.
*Pathmarks*. Edited by William McNeill. Cambridge: Cambridge University Press, 1998.
*Sein und Wahrheit*. Frankfurt am Main: Klostermann, 2001. *Being and Truth*. Translated by Gregory Fried and Richard Polt. Bloomington and Indianapolis: Indiana University Press, 2010.

*Sein und Zeit*. Tübingen: Max Niemeyer Verlag CmbH & Co., 1993. *Being and Time*. Translated by John Macquarrie and Edward Robinson. Oxford: Blackwell, 1962.
*Sein und Zeit*. Tübingen: Max Niemeyer Verlag CmbH & Co., 1993. *Being and Time*. Translated by Joan Stamburgh. Albany, NY: State University of New York Press, 1996.
*Vorträge und Aufsätze*. Gunther Neske, Pfullingen, 1954, 6th edn, 1990. Citations from passages in *Holzwege* and *Vorträge und Aufsätze* were taken from the following translations: *Poetry, Language, Thought*. Translated by Albert Hofstadter. New York: Harper Colophon Books, 1975; *The Question Concerning Technology and Other Essays*. Translated by William Lovitt. New York: Harper & Row, 1977.
*Was Heisst Denken*. Tübingen: Max Niemeyer Verlag, 1954. *What is Called Thinking*. Translated by Fred D. Wieck, J. Glenn Gray. New York: Harper & Row, 1976.
*Wegmarken*. Frankfurt-am-Main: Klosterman, 1967. *Pathmarks*. Edited by William McNeill. Cambridge: Cambridge University Press, 1998.

## Other works by Heidegger in English

*Basic Writings*. Edited by David Farrell Krell. London: Routledge and Kegan Paul, 1977.
*Nature, History, State: 1933-34*. Translated and edited by Gregory Fried and Richard Polt. London and New York: Bloomsbury, 2013.
*Nietzsche Volume One: The Will to Power as Art*. Translated by David Farrell Krell. New York: Harper & Row, 1979.
'Only A God Can Save Us'. Translated by Maria P. Alter and John D. Caputo. *Philosophy Today*, XX (4/4) (1976): 267-85. (This version is available in *The Heidegger Controversy*). There is an alternative translation by David Schendler. *Graduate Faculty Philosophy Journal*, 6 (1) (Winter 1977). These are translations of an interview which Heidegger gave to *Der Spiegel* in 1966 on condition that it not be published until after his death. Heidegger died in 1976 and shortly after his death the interview was published in the Spring edition of *Der Spiegel*.
'The Rectorate 1933/34: Facts and Thoughts'. Translated by Karsten Harries. *The Review of Metaphysics*, 38 (3) (March 1985).
'The Self Assertion of the German University'. Translated by Karsten Harries. *The Review of Metaphysics*, 38 (3) (March 1985).

## Correspondence

Heidegger, Martin. *Letters to his wife 1915-1970*. Selected, edited and annotated by Gertrud Heidegger. Translated by R. D. V. Glasgow. Cambridge: Polity Press, 2008.
Heidegger, Martin and Jünger, Ernst. *Briefwechsel 1949-1975*. Stuttgart: Klett-Cotta Verlag, 2008.

****

Höss, Rudolf. *Death Dealer: The Memoirs of the SS Kommandant at Auschwitz*. Translated by Andrew Pollinger. Edited by Steven Paskuly. New York: Da Capo Press, 1996.
Jünger, Ernst. *The Peace*. Translated by Stuart O. Hood. Hinsdale, IL: Henry Regnery Company, 1948.
Kavanagh, Patrick. 'Epic'. In *Collected Poems*. London: Penguin Books, 2004.

Lacoue-Labarthe, Philippe. *Heidegger, Art and Politics: The Fiction of the Political*. Translated by Chris Turner. Oxford: Blackwell, 1990.
Lacoue-Labarthe, Philippe. Interview in *The Ister* (Documentary). Produced and directed by David Barison and Daniel Ross. New York: First Run/Icarus Films, 2004.
Lang, Beral. *Heidegger's Silence*. New York: Cornell University Press, 1996.
Lyotard, Jean-François. *Heidegger and "the jews"*. Translated by Andreas Michel and Mark Roberts. Minneapolis: University of Minnesota Press, 1990.
McKirahan, Richard D. *Philosophy Before Socrates*. Indianapolis: Hackett Publishing Company, Inc., 1994.
Metcalf, Robert. 'Rethinking "Bodenständigkeit" in the Technological Age'. *Research in Phenomenology*, 42 (1) (2012): 49–66.
Milchman, Alan and Rosenberg, Alan (eds). *Martin Heidegger and the Holocaust*. Atlantic Highlands, NJ: Humanities Press International, Inc., 1996.
O'Brien, Mahon. *Heidegger and Authenticity: From Resoluteness to Releasement*. London and New York: Continuum, 2011.
O'Brien, Mahon. 'Leaping Ahead of Heidegger: Subjectivity and Intersubjectivity in *Being and Time*'. *International Journal of Philosophical Studies*, 22 (4) (October 2014).
Olafson, Frederick. 'Heidegger's Politics: An Interview with Herbert Marcuse'. *Graduate Faculty Philosophy Journal*, 6 (1) (1977).
O'Murchadha, Felix. *The Time of Revolution: Kairos and Chronos in Heidegger*. London and New York: Bloomsbury, 2013.
Ott, Hugo. *Martin Heidegger: A Political Life*. Translated by Allan Blunden. New York: Basic Books, 1993.
Petzet, Heinrich Wiegand. *Encounters and Dialogues with Martin Heidegger, 1929–1976*. Translated by Parvis Emad and Kenneth Maly. Chicago: University of Chicago Press, 1993.
Pressac, Jean-Claude. *AUSCHWITZ: Technique and Operation of the gas chambers*. Jean-Claude Pressac © The Beate Klarsfeld Foundation, 1989.
Safranski, Rudiger. *Martin Heidegger: Between Good and Evil*. Translated by Ewald Osers. Cambridge, MA: Harvard University Press, 1998.
Santayana, George. *The Life of Reason*. Vol. 1. New York: Scribners, 1905.
Sheehan, Thomas (ed.). *Heidegger: The Man and the Thinker*. Chicago: Precedent Publishing, 1981.
Sluga, Hans. *Heidegger's Crisis*. Cambridge, MA: Harvard University Press, 1993.
Spengler, Oswald. *Man and Technics: A Contribution to a Philosophy of Life*. Translated by Charles Francis Atkinson. Westport, CT: Greenwood Press, 1976.
Spengler, Oswald. *The Decline of the West* (an abridged edition by Helmut Werner,- English abridged edition prepared by Arthur Helps, from the translation by Charles Francis Atkinson). Oxford and New York: Oxford University Press, 1991.
Steiner, George. *Martin Heidegger*. Chicago: University of Chicago Press, 1991.
Taminiaux, Jacques. 'The Platonic Roots of Heidegger's Political Thought'. *European Journal of Political Theory*, 6 (2007): 11.
'The Wannsee Protocol'. Available from http://www.writing.upenn.edu/~afilreis/Holocaust/wansee-transcript.html
Wisser, Richard. 'Das Fernseh-Interview'. In *Erinnerung an Martin Heidegger*. Edited by Günther Neske. Pfullingen: Verlag Günther Neske, 1977.
Wolin, Richard. *The Politics of Being*. New York: Columbia University Press, 1990.
Wolin, Richard (ed.). *The Heidegger Controversy*. New York: Columbia University Press, 1991.

Wolin, Richard. 'Socratic Apology: A Wonderful Horrible Life of Hans-Georg Gadamer'. Available from http://www.bookforum.com/archive/sum/ 03/wolin.html.
Young, Julian. *Heidegger, Philosophy, Nazism*. Cambridge: Cambridge University Press, 1998.
Zimmerman, Michael E. *Eclipse of the Self*. Athens: Ohio University Press, 1986.
Zimmerman, Michael E. *Heidegger's Confrontation with Modernity: Technology, Politics, Art*. Bloomington and Indianapolis: Indiana University Press, 1990.
Zimmerman, Michael E. 'The Death of God at Auschwitz'. In *Heidegger and the Holocaust*. Edited by A. Milchman and A. Rosenberg. Atlantic Highlands, NJ: Humanities Press, 1994.

# Index

Adorno, Theodor 8, 44, 46–8, 50, 144 n.6, 144 n.8, 145 n.11, 145 n.12
anti-modernism 7, 13, 43, 45, 48, 51, 65, 70, 130
antisemitism 1, 6, 9, 10, 11, 30, 39, 78, 95, 96, 104, 112, 119–24, 126, 131, 132, 155 n.13, 161 n.10
Arendt, Hannah 9, 17, 98, 121, 132, 139 n.22, 157 n.25, 161 n.10
Aristotle 25, 28, 43, 65, 78, 95, 102, 125, 127, 128, 157 n.25, 159 n.35, 160 n.5
Auschwitz 6, 11, 17, 18, 24, 33, 34–8, 41, 91, 143 n.29
authenticity 3, 46, 49, 56, 70, 77, 79, 81, 82, 83, 85, 88, 89, 90, 93, 94, 100, 101, 104, 105, 114, 123, 127, 157 n.25
autochthony 72, 74, 115

Babich, Babette 140 n.32
Bambach, Charles 44
Baumgarten, Eduard 118–22, 128, 151 n.1, 159 n.41
being-towards-death 82–4, 124, 150 n.8
being-with 80–5, 93, 99, 100, 150 n.9
Blubo 48, 70, 74, 88
*Blut und Boden* 7, 76, 115, 117, 127, 157 n.25
*Bodenständigkeit* 45, 71, 74, 76, 77, 115
Bourdieu, Pierre 8, 9, 10, 44, 46, 48–51, 57, 131, 145 n.13
Braver, Lee 155 n.13
bringing-forth 26–8, 141 n.9
Browning, Christopher 6, 62, 96

Caputo, John D. 13, 136 n.5
Char, René 29
communism 86, 93, 123, 127
Cooke, Alastair 13

cultural pessimism 45, 47, 49, 55, 63, 67, 70, 86

Dahlstrom, Daniel O. 140 n.4
*das Man* 49, 83, 85, 88, 144 n.4
Derrida, Jacques 15, 16, 134

Enframing 24, 29, 31, 36, 38, 40, 55, 64, 140 n.4, 141 n.15
ethnic chauvinism 5, 7, 9, 70, 71, 73, 94, 95, 97, 98, 117, 122, 123, 124, 131, 149 n.1, 154 n.12
everydayness 59, 83, 85, 89, 99, 150 n.10

Farias, Victor 4, 8, 12, 15, 16, 46, 117, 118, 130, 131, 134 n.13, 137 n.8, 143 n.2
Faye, Emmanuel 1, 3, 4, 8, 12, 46, 114, 117, 128, 131, 134 n.14, 139 n.27, 143 n.2, 147 n.40, 151 n.1, 152 n.9
Fichte, Johann Gottlieb 150 n.12
Final Solution 17, 30–41, 132, 139 n.26, 142 n.16, 143 n.24
Fränkel, Eduard 118, 120
Frege, Friedrich 43, 125, 133 n.4
Fried, Gregory 15, 128, 135 n.14
Fritsche, Johannes 152 n.9
*Fürsorge* 79, 81, 149 n.4

Gadamer, Hans Georg 137 n.8
Gelassenheit 56, 71–7, 115, 155 n.14
Gestell 6, 18, 19, 20, 24, 27, 29, 39, 41, 57, 60, 63, 67–75, 123, 126, 140 n.4, 141 n.15, 142 n.22, 151 n.2
*Gleichschaltung* 114
Goldhagen, Daniel Jonah 5, 13, 39, 141 n.14, 152 n.3
Gordon, Peter E. 97

Habermas, Jürgen 44–6, 49, 50, 57, 144 n.4, 144 n.5
Harries, Karsten 148 n.53, 152 n.5

# Index

Heaney, Seamus 107–9, 156 n.20
Heidegger, Elfride 78, 85, 135 n.15, 161 n.10
hermeneutic(s) 3, 4, 8, 44, 50, 90, 125, 141 n.7
historicity 1, 3, 5, 70, 77, 79, 90–4, 95, 98, 102, 105, 112, 114, 123, 124, 127, 128, 133 n.4
Hitler, Adolf 1, 31, 32, 33, 34, 35, 89, 102, 121, 133 n.7, 135 n.14, 142 n.17, 143 n.24, 147 n.39
Hölderlin, Friedrich 49, 113, 156 n.24, 161 n.6
Holocaust 6, 7, 12, 13, 15, 17, 18, 19, 20, 21, 23, 24, 25, 27, 31, 32, 38, 39, 40, 41, 70, 78, 90, 91, 96, 119, 133 n.8, 134 n.12, 138 n.20, 139 n.26, 140 n.31, 140 n.1, 143 n.31
Höss, Rudolf 33–7, 142 n.23, 143 n.24
humanism 4, 15, 16
Husserl, Edmund 9, 49, 65, 78, 120–2, 135 n.15, 135 n.16

intersubjectivity 82, 89, 93, 123, 149 n.4

Jaspers, Karl 5, 8, 9, 122, 123, 132, 134 n.13, 158 n.31, 159 n.32, 159 n.41
Jünger, Ernst 8, 12, 45, 49, 54, 65–71, 136 n.4, 143 n.3, 146 n.26, 148 n.53, 148 n.57

Kant, Immanuel 65, 91, 95
Kavanagh, Patrick 108, 109
Kierkegaard, Søren 65, 130, 155 n.13

Lacoue-Labarthe, Philippe 15–17, 40, 44, 138 n.9, 143 n.31
Lang, Berel 119, 128, 139 n.24, 150 n.14
leaping-ahead 81, 84, 85, 92
leaping-in 79, 81
Levinas, Emmanuel 150 n.8
Löwith, Karl 8, 57, 79, 102, 133 n.6
Lyotard, Jean-Francois 1, 2, 14, 51, 138 n.9

Marcuse, Herbert 17, 134 n.10, 138 n.14, 139 n.30, 146 n.35, 160 n.4
Marx, Karl 121
metaphysical humanism 15, 16

Metcalf, Robert 76
*mitsein* (being-with) 82, 83, 88, 92, 93, 101, 150 n.8
modernity 4, 5, 7, 10, 13, 44, 45, 48, 71, 85, 88, 93, 94, 110, 126, 127, 128, 130

National Socialism 3, 6, 8, 9, 10, 12, 16, 17, 21, 43, 45, 60, 65, 70, 73, 74, 76, 77, 79, 98, 114, 115, 116, 117, 118, 125, 126, 130, 131, 134 n.13, 137 n.5, 137 n.8, 140 n.31, 152 n.9, 154 n.12, 158 n.31, 158 n.32, 161 n.6
Nietzsche, Friedrich 16, 52–4, 56, 57, 65, 66, 148 n.57
nihilism 65, 66

Olafson, Frederick 146 n.35, 160 n.4,
O'Murchadha, Felix 125, 137 n.5, 153 n.12, 155 n.13
ordinance of revealing 29, 30, 68, 69, 73
Ott, Hugo 8, 117, 120, 121, 122, 159 n.47, 160 n.49

Petzet, Heinrich 104, 139 n.28, 155 n.13
phenomenology 4, 135 n.15, 156 n.15
  phenomenological 76, 82, 85, 155 n.15, 156 n.15
*physis* 26, 27
*poiesis* 26, 28
*polis* 62
Polt, Richard 151 n.2
Prüfer, Kurt 36–8
publicness 49, 59

rootedness (*Bodenständigkeit*) 44, 45, 48, 70–8, 87, 97, 104, 108, 114, 115, 123, 131, 145 n.12

Safranski, Rudiger 139 n.30, 161 n.10
Santayana, George 6, 16
Sartre, Jean-Paul 150 n.8
Sheehan, Thomas 125, 134 n.13, 135 n.17, 144 n.8, 145 n.9, 155 n.15
Sluga, Hans 44
solicitude (*Fürsorge*) 79, 81, 84, 91, 93, 149 n.4
Spengler, Oswald 8, 45, 49, 51–66, 68, 70, 71, 146 n.26, 146 n.28, 146 n.36, 147 n.45, 147 n.49, 148 n.53

standing-reserve 20, 28, 29, 90
Steiner, George 46, 47, 50
Streicher, Julius 152 n.7
subjectivity 29, 137 n.8

Taminiaux, Jacques 157 n.25, 158 n.31, 159 n.35
technocracy 144 n.4
thrown/thrownness 14, 27, 28, 29, 30, 35, 55, 57, 58, 73, 75, 79, 82, 84, 89, 93, 98–102, 110, 124
Topf & Sons 36–8, 139 n.26
total mobilization 45, 65–70, 148 n.57
the they (*das Man*) 85
   the they-self 83, 84, 150 n.10

voluntarism 16, 56, 59

Wannsee Conference Protocol 32
Wisser, Richard 144 n.6
Wolin, Richard 1, 4, 12, 13, 44, 46, 50, 65, 66, 134 n.13, 137 n.6, 137 n.8, 160 n.1

Young, Julian 134 n.13, 139 n.26, 153 n.12

Zimmerman, Michael E. 8, 10, 17, 18, 44, 47, 51–3, 140 n.31, 143 n.2, 145 n.18, 147 n.49, 148 n.53

www.ingramcontent.com/pod-product-compliance
Lightning Source LLC
Chambersburg PA
CBHW050140240426
43673CB00043B/1739